SCOPENA

D1113864

SCOPENA

A Memoir of Home

CHARLES E. "BUDDY" ROEMER III

2017
University of Louisiana at Lafayette Press

ISBN 13 (paper): 978-1-946160-02-7

http://ulpress.org
University of Louisiana at Lafayette Press
P.O. Box 43558
Lafayette, LA 70504-3558

Printed on acid-free paper in Canada

Library of Congress Cataloging-in-Publication Data

Names: Roemer, Charles E., III, author.
Title: Scopena : a memoir of home / Charles E. (Buddy) Roemer III.
Description: Lafayette, LA : University of Louisiana at Lafayette Press, 2017.
Identifiers: LCCN 2017004485 | ISBN 9781946160027 (alk. paper)
Subjects: LCSH: Roemer, Charles E., III. | Governors--Louisiana--Biography. |
Politicians--Louisiana--Biography.
Classification: LCC F376.3.R64 A3 2017 | DDC 976.3063092 [B] --dc23
LC record available at https://lccn.loc.gov/2017004485

For Dad and Mom,
Budgie and Adeline Roemer

TABLE OF CONTENTS

ACKNOWLEDGMENTS

This is to say "thank you" to a few people without whom I could not have written these thoughts.

First, I want to thank a young man who stuck with me from the beginning, Taunton Melville, my youngest nephew, a lawyer in Shreveport. He helped me with things that should be deleted; things that should be included; and things that should be reviewed and thought about. He did it without pay and with little "thank you." None at all, save mine.

I want to thank Tyler Bridges, a professional writer and journalist, who was so crucial to my first effort. Sometime he made his effort between Bolivia and New Orleans, sometime between Baton Rouge and God knows where else. He always kept me focused.

Thanks also to a friend of Tyler's, who proofread and edited the book from Mississippi, Jed Horne.

I want to thank the whole UL Press team who were extra-ordinary, especially Mary Duhé and Michael Martin. A job well done on behalf of a tenderfoot.

I thank my immediate sisters and brother (Margaret, Danny, Melinda, and Melanie) for answering a million and one questions—amazing what you can forget that you never thought you would—and for proofreading the manuscript. Special thanks to Melinda for the photo selections.

Thanks to Len Sanderson for his early and often feedback. I didn't make some people happy on my Budgie Roemer profile, but what you see is a young boy who can only see Dad as a son.

Thanks to Cookie Roemer and Patti Crocker for approving and encouraging. They knew Mom, and Dad, and me well.

Many thanks to my children, Caroline, Chas, and Dakota. They make me proud and they carry on, each in their own way, the legacy of their grandparents.

And finally, thank you to Scarlett, my lovely wife. She provided critical support during these past two years of writing. This book is about an earlier season of my life and the people who made that season special. Scarlett is with me in a different season, and she is making this season special, as well. I'm a lucky man.

FOREWORD

Welcome to a love letter to one's parents, and to one's home, and to one's early times. Governor Buddy Roemer—of all the reflections he could have selected from a long and successful political and business career—has chosen to pay homage to his early home and home life for whatever success he has enjoyed. And the reflections read like the narrative only a Louisiana governor can weave. You see, Louisiana governors are special individuals, who have special formative years. But few, if any, governors have written so lovingly of their formative years as this one.

As Buddy was entering elective politics for the first time, when he was elected as a delegate in 1973 to the Louisiana Constitutional Convention, I was entering his family by marrying his sister, Melanie. I didn't have far to travel, because my family and the Roemers lived on adjacent farms. Although I had been "in the family" for a long time, growing up with the five Roemer siblings and watching our parents work the land together, it wasn't until I literally moved in that I began to sense the special place and family that had been next door all along.

The love for his state, whatever virtues voters saw in him as they elected him to the Constitutional Convention, Congress, and then the Governor's Mansion, whatever risky, bold and courageous actions he took (sometimes to his political detriment) . . . in this memoir Buddy shows how each was planted, nourished, and culti-vated in very special land of Northwest Louisiana: Scopena.

Quite frankly, I did not appreciate how close Buddy was to Sco-pena, to his parents, and to his siblings even when he was at Har-vard, or in Washington, D.C., or Baton Rouge—or the snow of New Hampshire when he presented himself to the primary voters there as a candidate for president. But in his mind and in his actions he was never far away, and I am grateful he presents within these pag-es the reasons why.

As you read these pages, every once in a while remember your own roots, and thank someone for them, while you have the chance. The people Buddy has chosen to highlight are as colorful, as solid, and as influential on him as he portrays. I bet you have similar people in your life. Acknowledge them and thank them, as Buddy has so thoughtfully done.

–Reverend David Melville

PROLOGUE

I am seventy-four, and I had a stroke July 2014. The stroke affected my fine motor skills and weakened my right side, but with physical therapy I've managed to regain my physical abilities enough to return to work in an investment bank that my son, Chas, started seven years ago. And although the stroke causes me to slur my words occasionally, the biggest enemy to my good health is diabetic-neuropathy.

Neuropathy is an affliction of your nerves causing you to lose feelings in your legs and other nervous connections. It is the result of Type 1 diabetes—in my case, a disease that I've had since I was twenty-nine. As a result of my neuropathy, I walk with a cane.

My stroke occurred when, as my wife Scarlett and I were leaving Sunday School one July morning, I slurred three words in talking about going to eat lunch.

Scarlett, a registered nurse, and I decided to go quickly to India's Restaurant to eat and avoid the onset of a diabetic attack (due to low blood sugar). We didn't have the testing meter for blood sugar with us, and Scarlett thought that if we ate I would be alright. So we did, and things were fine at the restaurant, but while we stopped at a gas station on the way home, I slurred several words, and Scarlett decided to rush me straight to the emergency room at the local hospital.

She called ahead, and they were ready for me. I was former governor of Louisiana and was well-known by most people, so I waved at a couple of folks on my way into the hospital. As a nurse, Scarlett was trained to let the doctors know what was happening with me.

I was feeling no pain but I noticed that my face was drooping and that the hand motions that they wanted me to do were not going well. I couldn't touch the end of my nose with my right finger-tips, for example. They decided to do an MRI and, as they suspected, discovered I had suffered a stroke that affected me in my small motor skills and right side of my body. They kept me for several days, and finally released me to go home with a cane, recommending physical therapy on a daily basis.

About nine months after the stroke, I was struck with the onset of neuropathy, a nerve disorder common to many people as they age, but particularly pronounced among people with Type 1 diabetes. People with neuropathy lose feelings particularly in their feet, but all nerves are affected. As a result, people affected often walk haltingly—like a person older than their age. While my speaking and walking had improved in strength for a year after the stroke, my neuropathy has decreased my walking abilities to about 50 percent of my former self.

So I have had a challenging two years with a stroke and operations on my right and left carotid arteries as a result, surgery on my prostate unrelated to the stroke, two cataract surgeries, and neuropathy. I have survived, and I have started thinking about my childhood and growing up on a cotton farm in north Louisiana—Scopena. My parents had both died recently, so I started remembering my childhood, how different it was from most people's, how I was the oldest child and the natural one to tell about the events at Scopena, and how it might be of interest to new family members.

For years I have resisted writing about my growing up on Scopena in south Bossier Parish in the far northwest corner of Louisiana. I'm not a writer. Never wrote a book in my life. But Dad died on July 7, 2012, after a twelve-year bout with Alzheimer's at the age of eighty-nine, and Mom died at ninety-two in bed at home in February 2016,

Charles E. Roemer II, "Dad"   Adeline Roemer, "Mom"

and, in effect, I was free for the first time to write my own personal account of the events on Scopena in the 1950s, when I was growing up. Plus I felt a need to tell about events of which only I knew.

Despite my stroke, I count myself lucky not to be handicapped in my thinking and writing skills. I wish I could speak better—clearer and stronger and in my old rhythm, but it is a miracle that I speak at all. In the past my ability to speak well has always played a role in my success. Now, the premium is on listening. Dad always told me it would be that way—"Listen, Butch. Listen," he would say, when I hadn't paid attention to some important instruction. He was right, as usual.

So, unable to be as physically active as before, and with more time on my hands, my thoughts began to turn to writing about my Dad, my Mom, and our life at Scopena. It's something that others have asked me to do over the years. Why have I resisted? Writing seemed something that somebody else did. Besides, to write about one's father and mother is something that I hesitated to do. The damage to the perceptions of the living is always a danger. People might have different memories of events or they might have been told a skewed version of the truth that they have come to believe. Plus, it seemed almost arrogant to me for a man to write about himself, although when friends would write a book of memories or of some event, I would read it with pleasure. It was not something that I would do myself, I thought. But I was wrong, and worked for more than two years on this memoir of my early life and growing up on Scopena.

Dad and Mom were wonderful parents: careful, loving, protective, so I don't write to expose a flaw I found in them. Any flaw is in me. What can I add to their legacy? Mom was a wonderful mother of five, smart as a whip, and beautiful as a spring morning. Dad was a leader in everything he did: Bossier Rural Electrification Cooperation, Bossier Farm Bureau, Louisiana Generation and Power Cooperation, National Democratic Party, and Louisiana State Commissioner of Administration, not to mention the father of five children who spent countless hours with each child when they needed it most.

Any flaw or fault that someone finds in these pages is a result of my experience. These are my perceptions and no one else's.

So too, it's hard for a son as close to his father as I was, to write about his father—particularly a father who is well-known in political circles, but not well understood; a father who never ran for political office himself, yet raised a son who ran eleven times and won seven, including races for congressman and governor, and lost for president. Dad never ran for political office so he never had to disclose his inner-self or his private records. He could appear to be one thing, but in reality he was something completely different.

He appeared to be in command of whatever situation he was thrust in, but that wasn't always the case. He was good at appearing in control, but, in truth, he was often ill at ease and asked for guidance from my mother, and from his own mother. The things that confused him at times, that made him seek guidance from someone he trusted, were "people" problems. The people problems weren't a phobia for him. He wasn't a head case. He just wasn't as comfortable with people as he was with the "problems" they caused. He wasn't a glad-hander, a slap-on-the-back kind of guy. He was quiet, and many considered him a "loner." He wasn't a mixer, to put it in a collegiate or political way. He was an "intimidator" in his approach to people. His tone; his attitude; his bluster were all designed to keep people away; to keep people ill at ease; to intimidate them. He would take the position that it had to be done his way or nothing would get done.

Maggie Crocker Mayer, "Mine"

"People" problems were something that Dad at times needed help with. His mother, "Mine," often would advise him about reaching out to people to solve a problem, but Mom was the real champion in quietly talking him into seeing the other person's point of view. Many a time on the farm I can remember waiting for Dad to listen to Mine or Mom to decide how to implement a strategy that affected people. He was so sure on hedging or planting strategies, yet so uncertain in trusting a foreman to supervise an operation out of his sight.

This flaw was to bedevil him when he found himself, years later, in the turmoil of Louisiana politics—a politics that were "people," not "performance," oriented. He didn't suffer fools well, and he had no patience with people. This was a thicket that Dad wanted to tame—he wanted the challenge—but he tried to do it by himself and without the help he needed from Scopena, including Mom or Mine. In fact, he left Scopena behind for this new challenge. It was a mistake, because he wasn't prepared to handle the world by himself.

✳ ✳ ✳

It has been relatively easy for me to avoid writing about when I was governor. A professional writer called me up after my term ended and made the case for me to write a book under his tutelage that would set the record straight on what I had done and why. I could care less what people think, although there is a story or two to tell about how we had pulled Louisiana back from the brink of bankruptcy and put the state's finances on a stable path; how we had battled the teacher unions over my efforts to bring greater accountability to Louisiana's schools; how we had attempted to create a single board to oversee the state's colleges and universities to bring coherence and coordination to their budgets and planning; how we had gone to the mat with state legislators over my view that they had passed unconstitutional acts to restrict the right of women to abortion; how we had passed the first tough campaign finance disclosure bill in Louisiana history; how we had been the first administration to insist on tough standards to protect Louisiana's air and water. The writer thought these issues would be most interesting if written from my point of view. Boring, it seemed to me. Too self-serving, I thought.

My problem as governor, looking back after twenty-five years, was often just the opposite of my father's. He wouldn't waste (his word, "waste") any time with people working out a problem. Just do it his way, and everything would be fine. I wanted to hear opinions opposite mine from the people who were most involved. Maybe that's what made me a "politician," unlike Dad, who never was described as "political" in any of his dealings with people.

✳ ✳ ✳

One thing that I took the lead from Dad on was the suspicion of money and politics. Dad always had a deeply felt belief that Washington, D.C., was too heavily influenced by people with money. He thought that money interests controlled Washington and kept it from representing Americans in general and the average man in particular.

When I ran for president in 2012, I expressed my concern

about political action committee (PAC) money and influence-peddling in the presidential campaign of that year. That is what Dad believed, and that is what he taught me. He just couldn't turn a political phrase with it. He couldn't run a political campaign with it, because for a man deeply mired in politics—eight years as commissioner of administration of Louisiana—and never elected to a political office, he was the most anti-political animal on the planet. In fact, "politics" was a thing of derision to him. It was a game that he didn't take seriously.

From Dad I got my cynicism of politics. From Mom, I got my idealism. Both can be valuable traits to have. Mom's political idealism shone in 1978 when I lost my first race for Congress by two thousand votes in the midst of 100,000 cast ballots because I said a local project was a "boondoggle" with a couple weeks before the election; saying that we should balance the budget before building a "boondoogle." After dropping to fifth place in a sixteen person field, I struggled to finish a close third in a losing election. Mom said she was proud of me for taking a stand, and the people would come to understand. (I won the next election for Congress two years later in 1980.) Dad said I ought to learn to keep my mouth shut during the two weeks before the election, although I could tell he was proud of me too.

In 2012, a New York publishing company tried to interest me in writing a book about my campaign for president that year under my signature issues: limiting contributions to no more than $100 per individual, not taking PAC or super PAC money, and reporting every penny contributed to the campaign. Let's shine a light on money in politics, I thought. People now are clueless on where political money comes from and the influence over the politician and the politics that comes with it.

My ideas didn't get much of a hearing, however. I got a good reception when I appeared on cable TV shows like *Morning Joe*, but the Republican Party established rules that shut me out of the debates. They set a minimum percentage in the latest poll for a candidate to qualify for the debate. I never qualified. I was always a point too low.

If four percentage points were needed to qualify in South Carolina, I had three. If five were needed in New Hampshire, I had four. The highest I got was Florida at nine percentage points. They set the bar for entry at 10 percent, of course.

It was very difficult to gain in the polls if you didn't participate in the debates because that was the way that you gained name recognition with the masses. And if you didn't gain name recognition with the masses, you didn't climb in the polls and earn a right to be in in the next debate. As Dad would have expected, since I had no money of my own, I ended my campaign for president after getting only a handful of votes in New Hampshire. Donald Trump four years later was to prove the power of my campaign stance. He didn't know anything about politics except one important fact: money controls everything in Washington, D.C. I just couldn't get the publicity he could, and he had wealth of his own and cut right to the chase: he didn't care what the insiders felt, because they were the problem.

The idea of writing a book about running for president was a good one, but I was too frustrated with the result of the campaign. I was fed up with the sham the general election campaign had turned out to be. It was too painful, too recent for me to want to do it, given the difficulties of the effort. What seems so obvious to me—important elections are too often bought by the special interests—wasn't so obvious to everyone else, or, if it was obvious, they didn't want to acknowledge it. I was too close to the race, and too upset to write unemotionally about my race for president.

❋ ❋ ❋

My thinking has changed about a book about my childhood and my Mom and Dad now that they are gone, and now that I'm over seventy and realize that I probably won't be so lucky on my next stroke. I warmed to an idea I had been thinking about for a long time: writing an account of what it was like to grow up on Scopena—our farm where I lived as a boy from 1950 until 1960, when I went away to college at age sixteen—and what lessons my Dad taught me about family, hard work, race, and life; and Mom, about love and people. Dad was a wonderful father. He raised me to be independent in all my interactions with people and with groups. And Mom—she was the best.

From the very beginning, I was an unusual politician, an independent-minded congressman in a highly charged partisan atmosphere who refused to take PAC money. Because of my independence, I stood out from other Democratic congressmen in joining Republicans to work for what I thought was the good of the country. For example, I joined some forty members of Congress—all Democrats and out of 535 house members—to form the "boll weevils" caucus to support the initiatives of President Reagan, a Republican. But no colleagues joined with me to prevent the purchase of Congress by PACs by not taking their money. Many were good, decent members of Congress, but they were compromised by taking the PAC money. I see it now; I didn't see it then.

I decided it would be important for me to go back to my roots at Scopena and try to gain an understanding of why my views were so different than those of the typical politician. Was it an accident of time and place, or did it have to do with my upbringing?

I grew up during a time when "family" meant security and sharing more than it does now. There are many examples of lessons learned that can still be relevant in twenty-first-century America, but they are seldom taught these days. My Mom and Dad were extraordinarily devoted parents who had unusual ideas about childrearing that led them to raise five gifted children. This book is about my mother and father, mostly my father, because of the tragedy that befell him when he dared stick his head into Louisiana politics. But most of all, it is about the farm that we grew up on in the 1950s. It is about Scopena.

In those ten years that I lived at Scopena, I formed my views of the world based on the value of individuals rather than on the color of someone's skin, and I learned the keys of success that I carried into the world far from there, keys like hard work, team effort, honesty in reporting what you saw. The truth is that the highest hurdle I had to jump in life and the thing that prepared me the most for politics, Louisiana-style, were the demanding standards set by my father years ago—at Scopena.

Scopena is a place. You can see it from Highway 71 South, and see its cotton gin, tennis courts, swimming pool, shop, its big front yard, and its tall pecan trees. But the heart of Scopena—the life of Scopena, the magic of Scopena, the uniqueness of Scopena—was Mom and Dad, raising five kids under a philosophy that ignored what the rest of the world thought and that emphasized individual effort. With Dad and Mom gone, I want to tell the story of Scopena before it too is gone or unrecognizable.

Race relations in the 1950s were relatively progressive at Scopena, unlike what was happening in the rest of the South. This is not to say that black people had no problems at Scopena, many of their rights as people were not protected, but Mom and Dad ensured that on Scopena they counted as much as white families—in pay, in housing, in opportunity for advancement, even in voting. Regardless, to be black, even on Scopena, was to be a second-class citizen.

⁘ ⁘ ⁘

In the 1950s, when the bulk of this tale takes place, Scopena was a big, and getting bigger, farm, far away from the city and what was happening in Louisiana and in the nation. It was far from Louisiana politics. It was a scene of political discussions to be sure, but it was the type of place to which politicians came to seek support and money, not a place that grew politicians. For a long time when I was growing up, Scopena meant farming, not politics. For me, Scopena was the most important place in the world, but to most people in the city, it was where we country-people lived.

We were twelve miles from Bossier City. Dad was the boss man. And there was nothing to challenge his dominance. He didn't have to put up with backtalk from anyone, because we lived in a special world, in which he was in charge.

RUNNING AWAY FROM SCHOOL

I thought about this particular day when I was waiting to see my father in the visiting room of the federal penitentiary in Fort Worth, Texas, in 1983. I was a congressman from north Louisiana in Washington, D.C. I had been elected in November of 1980 (4th Dist. of La.–D), and I had agreed to fly over to Fort Worth from Shreveport in a private plane with former governor Edwin Edwards to visit Dad (I made many visits over the months), who was serving a three-year sentence for bribery in dealings with alleged gangster Carlos Marcello for a state contract according to the federal prosecutor.

Dad protested his innocence and was later released and had his record expunged by a U.S. Fifth Circuit Court decision that followed a U.S. Supreme Court decision ruling penalties under the Rico (federal racketeering) statutes as unconstitutional. But there he was on this day, in a federal penitentiary, ruined in his own mind—he was a very proud man and felt that he should not have to depend on the Supreme Court to prove his innocence—and he was my father, and I remembered the many times that he meant the most to me. I thought of this story, as an example about one of those times that Dad had taken my life to a different and more positive level.

You were supposed to be six when you started first grade, but I had an awkward birthday for the regulations: October 4. School started around August 15, but rather than start the following year,

This is how we started. Adeline, Budgie, and Butch Roemer

when I was supposed to, my parents started me early at five. I could already read and write, taught by my mother in afternoon sessions at Scopena. So I would be one of the youngest boys in the first grade, if not the youngest. And I looked it. I was small, and my face was young looking.

In the first five years of my life I had been to Bossier City only a few times with my parents; I had never been to the school; I had never seen the school; and I had never noticed the school bus. The first day of school was all new to me: new ride, new school, new friends, and new experience.

So on the first day, I stood with the other students to go to school like everyone else. No parents were around. It was just us kids—about eight of us, with me the only first-grader. I didn't have the faintest idea what I was in for. I had never been with a group of strange kids before, never. I was nervous.

The school bus picked us up at 6:45 a.m. on Highway 71 South, right in front of Scopena. Bossier Elementary School was fifteen miles away, in an old part of town. Later, when I began my second year of school, the bus only went to Marsigolia Grocery on Highway 71 to pick us up. Marsigolia's grocery was nearer Bossier City by five miles than Scopena. The school district had the route changed because they didn't appreciate the integrated crowd of kids at Scopena waiting on the "white" bus and the "black" bus at the same spot at the same time. Several years later when school district policy changed, the bus went back to Scopena to pick us up. It was still segregated.

When the bus winded its way there for a 6:45 a.m. start bright and early that first morning, I was a little lost and disoriented. It was my first time ever to see the school bus and to see Bossier Elementary School—so many firsts. It was overwhelming to me. I didn't talk on the bus on the way to school.

The older kids said a couple of words to the younger kids ("I hope you don't get Miss Fisher for a teacher, because she will flunk you if you're not careful," was an example of the kind of "positive" thoughts that the older kids shared with us younger ones), but by and large we were on our own on that long journey to deep into the heart of Bossier City.

We had plenty of time to think about things, and when I got to school I had an idea worked out in my head: I decided to run away from school the first chance I got. I would go home, back to Scopena. I didn't know any other student; the other students picked up in front of Scopena were all older than me, so they were in different classes. My sister Margaret and my brother Danny hadn't started the first grade yet. I was alone. My teacher treated me like a normal student, which I didn't consider myself to be—who does at age five? So I made up my mind that I was out of there, Lord willing and if the opportunity arose.

I told no one. Between third period class and lunch, I noticed there was no supervisor in the confusion as we prepared for the lunch room. I slipped outside and started down the street in the general direction toward Scopena. I don't remember that I sneaked past everybody, but surely I did. I was headed toward Scopena, or at least I thought I was headed there. It was a long way away, and I had to navigate across town first. Unbeknownst to anyone, I had paid close attention to the route as we rode the bus to school that morning, but I couldn't be sure about the way to Scopena. I was alone for the first time in what for me was a very big city.

I made my way along the Red River east and south along the edge of town. Finally, I came to a large, two-lane street in the center of town that was labeled "Barksdale Boulevard." It was a street I knew because I had ridden down it before. I knew that if I followed the street through downtown it would lead me to Barksdale Air Force Base. And from there I could make the ten miles to Scopena via Highway 71 South, the exact route I had ridden on the school bus that morning. Alone in the center of downtown Bossier, I walked past city hall, past the two big banks, headed toward Barksdale Air Force Base, and then, south toward Scopena. It seemed far away, but Scopena was calling.

After walking a few more blocks, I saw to my right the A & P grocery where Mom shopped for groceries every Saturday. That was the only building I recognized. I was about to turn south on Barksdale Boulevard extension to go past Barksdale Air Force Base and home, when it happened: a man stopped me.

He was standing outside Peters' grocery, a small independent store, at the end of the main drag in Bossier City.

"Hey, boy. What cha' doing?" he asked.

"I'm walking home to Scopena," I replied.

"Scopena, huh?" he said. "Do you live there? Could I call somebody?"

"Yes, sir," I said. "I live there and I would like to see my Daddy. His name is Mr. Roemer, and my name is Butch." I gave my phone number to the man, and he called Dad at the office. After he got off the phone, he told me his name, Sam Peters, owner of Peters' grocery. He gave me an ice-cold bottled Coke, and invited me into the store to wait on Dad, because, he said, "Scopena is a long way away. But your Dad is coming."

And we waited. It seemed like the longest wait of my life. Hot, noon, cold Coke, looking for my Daddy, a runaway.

After about thirty minutes, I saw Dad's red International Harvester pick-up rolling up Barksdale Boulevard. I was excited because he was coming to take me home. But I also thought for the first time, "I wonder what Dad will think about me running away from school." I peed in my britches a little bit at the thought.

Dad could be tough when I had done something that I knew was wrong. Several times in my young life, he had paddled me with his hand when I had disobeyed him or when I had ignored danger. Spanking was rare, but it had happened. This circumstance, I was thinking for the first time, had the similar markings of a stupid decision and might end up badly for me. I was a candidate for a spanking, I thought.

He pulled up to Peters' grocery with his truck window down. Before he could say a word, I yelled, "hey Dad, sorry I made you come all the way to town to get me." I was trying to defend myself by apologizing before he could stop the pickup truck.

Dad just smiled. He tousled my hair and hugged me after getting out of the truck. He took a minute to thank Mr. Peters for stopping me, for giving me a Coke, and for making me feel welcome.

He didn't fuss at me or lecture me. All he said was, "Let's go home."

He didn't spank me. He didn't chastise me. He didn't say that my running away from school was a stupid thing to do. He didn't say we were going back to school. He just said, "Let's go home. We've got to tell Mom so she can call your school and then we've got some work to do."

We climbed into his truck. It would be the greatest drive of my life. Along the way, Dad talked about everything but school. He talked about the cotton harvest. He talked about the gins. He talked about the mechanical cotton harvesters. We stopped at a couple of cotton fields so he could issue instructions to the supervisors. From there, we drove straight home. The lesson was clear: If the world becomes overwhelming or scary, you can come home, no questions asked. So it was to be. Scopena represented, among other things, safety. Scopena was a place where none of the dangers of the world could intrude. At Scopena, you could always hide, rest, take time out, or gather your strength for a hard fight. There was no place like it.

That was a lesson that had value to me when I was a small boy, scared and alone in public school for the first time, but it was one that I used over and over again growing up. Scopena was a place of safety and security—always, whether I was five or fifty-five. And Dad would treat me as someone of value. That would be important to me, wherever I would go and whatever I may be. Someone of value; that's what I was.

I thought all these things while I was waiting to see Dad in prison. I had nothing to offer to him but to tell him that I loved him, and that he was something of value to me. And so I did.

2

SCOPENA

We called it Scopena plantation. It was really a family farm. But in 1955 it was a big place, with thousands of acres dedicated to growing cotton, soybeans, sunflowers, and hybrid seed corn. We also raised cattle. My Dad, Charles Elson Roemer II, was the owner-operator. Everybody called him Budgie. I was my Dad's oldest child, born on October 4, 1943. My parents were nineteen and twenty at the time. My formal name is Charles Elson Roemer III. Everybody called me Butch. Mom was Juliet Adeline McDade Roemer. Everyone called her "Miss Adeline," that is, everyone but the kids. We called her Mommy. My oldest sister is named Margaret. She is a year younger than me. Her nickname is "Punkin." Next came Danny, my only brother. He is a year younger than Margaret. Melinda and Melanie are my two youngest sisters, three and five years younger than Danny.

Scopena was not the only "plantation" on the banks of the Red River or on delta lands of the Mississippi River, 120 miles to the east. Every twenty or thirty miles along the winding Red River in western and northern Louisiana or along the banks of the Mississippi in northeastern Louisiana there could be found farms that occasionally reached 2,500-5,000 acres in size or larger and were called "plantations." There were maybe twenty such places on the Red River. Scopena had become one of those plantations thanks to the

The Roemer family, from left: Margaret, Melinda,
Budgie, Adeline, Melanie, Butch, and Danny

hard work of Vernon Mayer, Dad's step-father, and Budgie Roemer. Its 2,000 acres in 1953 had reached over 10,000 acres of woodland, pastureland, and cropland by the end of the decade. Some say in 1960 it was the largest plantation in all of north Louisiana. Scopena was a working plantation. Nobody would mistake it for Tara in *Gone with the Wind*. It wasn't a showcase. It wasn't "moss covered." That's Hollywood stuff. That's the kind of place you read about in somebody's novel. Nobody wrote about Scopena. They should have. It was a magical place for a young kid to become a man.

The name "Scopena" came from the name of a truck farmer, who farmed south of Bossier City. Many people went to his place to get their vegetables. "Scopini" was the truck farmer's name, but, said with a southern accent, it sounded like "Scopena." That's the name that stuck.

Scopena started relatively small in the early 1930s, with the purchase of about 250 acres of the Scopini place and neighboring crop land by Vernon Mayer, who would become my step-grandfather. A member of a Shreveport farm family, "Gran" Vernon married a divorced woman named Maggie Crocker Roemer in 1935. She already had two young children in her first marriage: my aunt Peggy, the oldest by a couple of years, and Dad.

Gran Vernon began to expand Scopena in the early 1940s, and this process accelerated after Dad became a full partner in 1948-49. Dad believed that Scopena needed to be a much bigger operation to make economic sense. He and Gran Vernon steadily bought 100 to 1,500 acres at a time from neighboring farmers who had met hard times or decided to retire.

The incremental land deals added up to 10,000 acres for Scopena by the late 1950s. Of that, more than 4,000-5,000 acres were of cultivated row crops, 3,000 were pastureland, and the final 2,500 were loblolly pine timberland.

If you measured Scopena from its top (Vanceville) to its bottom (Coushatta), north to south, it would extend for about fifty-five miles. I should note that Scopena didn't occupy all the property in that fifty-five-mile strip, just major portions.

The southern-most extent of Scopena's reach was Coushatta, Louisiana, about forty-five miles south of Shreveport and Bossier City. In 1949 Dad and Gran Vernon, and a friend, Dick Gibson, bought an International Harvester dealership located in Coushatta (Coushatta Farm Implement, Inc.). Dad had the idea that owning their own dealership would save Scopena millions every four or five years when buying their farm tractors and other necessary equipment. The only thing that Dad and Gran Vernon would lose would be the flexibility of buying machinery on the various farms surrounding Scopena. From that moment on, Scopena was the color red—the color of International Harvester as opposed to the green color of its big competitor, John Deere. The move worked to their financial advantage just as Dad had figured. Gran Vernon and Dad profited handsomely from Dad's idea of dealer ownership when they received their 50 percent price discount on tractors, harvesters, combines, and other equipment worth millions of dollars that they purchased over the years. They also profited from the equipment they sold to other farmers in the region.

✳ ✳ ✳

When the Coushatta dealership was first put up for new ownership by International Harvester in 1948, a large Shreveport and Monroe International Harvester dealer, the largest in the state, was favored to win the bid from the parent company in Illinois. Scopena shocked the whole farming community by outbidding the Shreveport favorite, winning the dealership for that part of the state.

I can remember the day the huge, shiny new red combines and tractors came from Coushatta to be field tested at Scopena. The technology always astounded me, and, in my eyes, helped make Scopena an extra special place.

In the early 1980s Dad sold Coushatta Farm Implement in a fire sale, along with other assets he owned, when he was under pressure of legal debt from his personal political tragedy. He didn't want to sell it, but he had to pay his debts and there were no other options.

Running from west to east, Scopena ran five to seven miles from the Red River if you went in a straight line, although at times the land bunched into large tracts east of Highway 71 that could exceed twelve miles. Any way you looked at Scopena, from top to bottom or side to side, it was a very large holding of land.

Scopena's office and headquarters was about twenty-five miles east of the Texas border, thirty-five miles south of Arkansas's, ten miles south of Shreveport, and eight miles south of Bossier City. We were in Bossier Parish in the northwest corner of Louisiana. Scopena was not as big as the large holdings of the big timber corporations in parts of Louisiana, but for a privately owned holding, it was plenty big.

✗ ✗ ✗

Scopena grew multiple crops, cotton being the largest, as well as cattle and timber holdings. It generated revenue of several million dollars a year as early as 1952, which, measured in 1950s currency, was a substantial income.

Cotton represented almost five million dollars of this revenue alone in 1956, the year that I first ran Scopena. Scopena was a family farm, so we had all had a hand in running it. But in 1956 Dad was hurt in a plane crash, so Mom and I ran the plantation—mostly Mom, since I was only twelve.

Cotton and cottonseed were a dollar per pound in revenue, or $500 per bale, and in 1956 we produced ten thousand bales or $5,000,000 in revenue to Scopena. Soybeans, wheat, and sunflowers made up about $250,000 a year in revenue in different individual amounts. Hybrid seed corn made a $250,000 contribution by 1956, while cattle and timber had about a $350,000 a year income. For 1956, the revenue was more than $6,000,000, without counting the more than $100,000 made from Coushatta farm implements in profit. It was quite a big business for 1956. In fact, if the inflation factor is worth 8.4 to 1 (according to Economics 101) from then, the value of 1956 money would mean Scopena would be making $50.5 million a year today in equivalent gross revenue.

✗ ✗ ✗

Scopena was such a big place that Dad authorized two men as wardens to control the hunting privileges, including allowing strangers to join the hunt. They shot quail, ducks, geese, doves, crows, squirrels, and deer, depending on the season. All the hunting followed state and federal regulations. There was never a charge for hunting on Scopena, as long as you had permission.

The two wardens when I was growing up were Johnny Horton and Claude King, who would become two well-known country music singers. Horton was the more famous of the two and had a number one hit, "The Battle of New Orleans," for an extended period in the late 1950s.

They loved to hunt, and they were paid a handsome fee by Dad to manage the plentiful game on Scopena. Dad just didn't want to be bothered with it. Johnny Horton was bald in real life, but he always wore a toupee in public. Some mornings he would come to work at Scopena without having gotten the toupee "right," as he would say, and the men around the shop fire early in the morning would razz him. He would get angry and go off into the woods to pout. He was mighty sensitive about the lack of hair.

Johnny was killed in a car wreck in east Texas while going to sing at a show in Kilgore when I was a freshman in college. I didn't get to go to the funeral, but Dad did.

Claude retired from his game warden duties while I was away in college. I didn't see him again before he died in 2013. His most famous song was "Wolverton Mountain."

The primary activity at Scopena was farming cotton. But there was a sizeable investment also in cattle, thanks to my grandmother, Maggie Mayer or "Mine," as we used to call her. Mine was a mid-sized tomboy who dressed in khakis and work boots and thought of the cows as house pets. She specialized in buying and keeping cattle, not selling them. She went so far as naming them. She would talk with them, commiserating with them when they were hurt and celebrating with them when they were peaceful. There were 750 head of cattle at Scopena, all known by Mine.

For some reason, Dad was never totally comfortable with the cattle operation. Maybe it was because it didn't generate the income of cotton. But cattle stayed a part of Scopena, as long as Mine was around. She loved those cows and, whatever Dad's objections, the cows stayed on Scopena—and the cowboys, the horses, the corrals, and all the rest.

Scopena was unusual because of its size and because it did things differently than other farms. It was known by the city-folk in the 1950s because it always had some operation going on that was massive in scale: irrigation, corn detasseling, cotton chopping, cotton ginning, and insecticide spraying by airplane, to name a few. Under Dad, Scopena also employed progressive management policies: communicating via short wave radio, aerial application of fertilizer and seed, irrigation based on moisture testing of fields, and cattle impregnation by artificial insemination, for example. In 1950, these practices were new in the Deep South and relatively new on commercial farms in America. Dad read every crop trade journal faithfully and kept Scopena up to date with the latest trends in agronomy and management.

Back in the 1950s Scopena was known to be big and unusual, but it was relatively isolated in the local community. There were not many guests except other farmers, who were customers for one or more of Scopena's services: crop dusting, ginning, aerial application of fertilizer, defoliation, or harvesting cotton or grain. Dad liked Scopena to be mysterious to people who lived in the area. That mystery fitted his personally perfectly. He seldom talked about Scopena to others.

When Danny, Margaret, and I attended Bossier High School, we didn't talk much about Scopena when there. We talked about the horses or the airplanes in general terms, but everything else—how we lived and how we treated employees—was off-limits. When it came to school, what happened on Scopena, stayed on Scopena.

Dad said it had to be that way, because people wouldn't understand. And, when people didn't understand something, they would tear it down and laugh at it. We would do best just to keep quiet. So we did.

We did more talking on the school bus riding to school than we did in actual school, but on the school bus we rode with other country kids, and it was more like family than school ever was.

Dad thought the biggest secrets of Scopena were what kinds and how much of each crop was planted (sunflowers, for instance, or cotton). I never heard Dad lie, except when it came to cotton planting. He might say five thousand acres, when I knew the actual planting was 8,500 acres. No reason to lie; he just didn't want people to know what was actually happening, what we were actually doing at Scopena.

As Jerry Dougherty, an old friend, used to recount, we lived in a region characterized by the three p's: pine trees, poor people, and Protestants. In fact, north Louisiana had more similarities to east Texas, Mississippi, Alabama, Georgia, and South Carolina than to south Louisiana. It was Protestant country and proud of it. The things that made Louisiana different from other southern states— French culture, the large number of Catholics, and a buccaneer spirit—didn't exist in north Louisiana. For example, Mardi Gras—celebrated passionately in south Louisiana—was relatively unnoticed in north Louisiana.

Pine trees grew sporadically in south Louisiana along high ridges and homesteads, but north Louisiana was covered in pine timber—some of the most beautiful and extensive in the world as a forest. The poor people that lived among these pine trees were scrappy descendants from the Irish, Scots, and Englishmen who came to America to escape their servitude to a master family or a barren land. They were fiercely independent and universally impoverished. They worked factory lines when available, small farms and businesses when not. They did not think of themselves as poor and resented being described that way. They were proud and independent, not poor. People in north Louisiana tended to distrust government, support military preparedness, and view foreigners warily.

They were also church-going. The largest bloc of Christians was Baptist. The second biggest bloc was Methodist. We Roemers were Methodist. Each of my parents had been raised Methodist. They were married in the First Methodist Church of Shreveport and worshipped there every Sunday and Wednesday night with their children in tow. That meant we made the thirty-mile round trip drive to Shreveport twice a week.

The Shreveport/Bossier City area is about as far from New Orleans—some 350 miles—as you can get without leaving Louisiana. I always said that Shreveport had a real "Texas" attitude.

In fact, Shreveport, although the second largest city in Louisiana, didn't consider itself part of Louisiana in most aspects. It looked westward, not southward. The Dallas Cowboys were the favorite football team. Dallas was closer to Shreveport (at 180 miles) than was Baton Rouge (at 245 miles) or New Orleans (at 325 miles).

A friend from Dallas called the other day to make sure I was feeling okay, and out of the blue, he mentioned Scopena. He said he sure missed Christine's (the family cook) fried chicken for lunch. He said that the discussions around the lunch table were as memorable as the fried chicken—debates on civil rights, on the place of the farm program in national politics, on the role of American agriculture in feeding the starving in the world, and on a dozen other topics. He said he used to shake his head in wonder that everyone was encouraged to state and defend their opinion—everyone—even me, when I was as young as six or seven years old. Dad allowed only an hour at lunch to discuss whatever was happening in the news or whatever was happening on Scopena or whatever Dad chose to be the topic for lunch that day.

Another friend stopped by recently to see me at my office in Baton Rouge. He is black and said he missed the debate around the lunch table at Scopena. He said it was the only place in the 1950s where he could go to a white man's table and join in integrated conversations about local and world events. It may sound like a small thing today, but in the 1950s at Scopena, it was remarkable that integrated conversations took place as a normal course of business at the lunch table every day.

One of the first lessons that I remember on Scopena from Dad and Mom had to do with colors—the color of one's skin. About 95 percent of our two hundred workers were black. Dad paid them the same as whites. He believed in paying people according to their skills. That was not true on other farms in the area. Race determined pay and benefits in other farm operations, not skill. We weren't paid much, but everybody was paid the same thing, according to their contribution.

Race also affected our friendships beyond school. For example,

Junior Duncantell and I used to ride horses together at Scopena and do other things that young boys do growing up, like playing hide and seek in the seed house where we crawled through tunnels that we hand-dug in the cotton seed. Although we would remain friendly throughout our teenage years, the friendship was handicapped by Junior not going to school with us. He attended the all-black public school in Bossier, while we attended the all-white Bossier schools. We would await the school bus in a mass of youngsters, white and black, but our bus would carry us off to one school, and a separate bus would take them to a different school. Scopena was in the seg-regated land of the Deep South. The few blacks that went to college went to Grambling, a historically black institutuion located about fifty miles away, or traveled the 250 miles down to Southern University in Baton Rouge.

The world was much slower in those days. All the roads were two lanes, so you couldn't get from one place to another very quickly. The phone was still an instrument in the house. A telephone call at Scopena meant somebody running 150 yards to the shop, announc-ing a phone call for Mr. Budgie. You called Memphis once a day to get the raw price of cotton. You couldn't Google it, and there was no real-time "price of cotton" window.

Because of Scopena's awesome size, we were separated from oth-er parts of the community. We were far away from everybody. Neigh-bors—non-employees—were at least three miles away. Distant plac-es were just imagined as being real. Radio was popular. Television was nonexistent, as far as we were concerned. One's imagination counted for a lot more than it does now. When I was a six or sev-en-year-old kid, I used to imagine what all the people I couldn't see were doing. I used to wonder what Texas—just twenty miles to the west—was like. Or I would watch a passing car that I had never seen before and wonder where it had come from and where it was going.

Dad used to say something interesting back in those days, when asked what people that you could not see were doing? "Waiting," he would say, "waiting on some body or something to stir 'em up. They are waiting on leadership or an issue. And when they get it, they will be hard to slow down." He was right. In Louisiana we've seen that a few times.

Life on Scopena was so different compared to what it must have been for people in the city. The country life and the city life had begun to be pulled apart. At my fifty-fifth high school reunion in Bossier City (Bossier High School class of 1960), the men reminisced about Scopena because almost all of them had worked there in the summer. It was a job unlike any they would ever have, and it gave them their only taste of country life. For example, they actually worked with black people in the hay field and in the gin and in the corn fields and in the shop. They were taught and shown that black people made a difference on whether you got a bonus for a job well-done.

A Baton Rouge businessman who is on the board of a bank I started some years ago told me recently that he was one of the many kids who baled hay at Scopena in the summer when he was in high school and college. He had never told me that before. He said he worked with ten men or so in the hay fields. The men were black, and they were paid and treated like the three white guys on the crew. He said that it was an unforgettable experience where he learned the value of hard work and of teamwork regardless of color, lessons that he said he carried with him for the rest of his life. I carry those same lessons with me—that the character of men and women have nothing to do with the color of their skin.

3

THE TREEHOUSE

M y story at Scopena begins on January 1, 1950. My family had moved there three months earlier on my sixth birthday, October 4, 1949. We had been living for a year in McDade, a town a few miles south on Highway 71. In those days, everybody called me "Butch." When I came to Scopena from McDade, my brother Danny, my boyhood friend Emmett England, and I built a treehouse in the last days of the year—although I had no idea it was December 1949, as dates had no meaning for me then. On January 1, 1950, we three kids were in the tree house looking out over Scopena.

The memory stands out. It was a cold, bright, clear day up in that treehouse, and the ground was blanketed from a rare snow. I can remember feeling like we were on top of the world from our perch. It was about thirty-five feet above the ground, higher than anything on Scopena except the trees themselves. We could see the grain elevators, the gin, the delinter, the railroad terminal, the shop, the house, the runway, the airplanes, and the cotton fields that seemed to stretch forever.

Emmett's daddy, Arthur England, was chief cotton ginner at Scopena and in the off season (February to August) was a field supervisor. Emmett, our close friend through many ventures, was ten and big and strong compared to Danny and me. Danny was four, and I was six, but Danny was bigger than me. I was the runt of the

The three men in a house of ladies, from left: Danny, Budgie, and Butch

operation, Emmett was clearly the muscle, and Danny had the ideas. Danny had wanted a treehouse and had planned the construction. Emmett did the heavy lifting.

We all picked the site: a tall, large cypress tree fairly close to the shop and behind the house/office. An old bus that had been abandoned years ago leaned against the tall cypress. We were not far from where Emmett lived with his brother, Raymond, and his Dad and Mom and sister in a white shingled, four-bedroom house.

We climbed onto the top of the bus and nailed planks to the tree to reach a spot where a couple of big branches met the trunk to create a cradle. We tied a rope there and began lifting scrap plywood and linoleum that we gathered. We cut windows in the plywood and covered the floor with linoleum. We made the roof high enough for Emmett to stand since he was half again taller than we were. It was a single-room structure with space for the three of us. That's it. We happened to finish constructing the treehouse right at dark on New Year's Eve, but we didn't officially open it until the next morning— New Year's Day, 1950.

I remember listening to the news on the radio the next morning, as I was eating breakfast. Dad always listened to the 5:30 a.m. farm and commodity pricing report at the breakfast table in the mornings. We listened to the reports, particularly cattle prices, every morning together. This morning, the program was special, because it was a new year and a new decade. "The start of a new decade," the broadcaster was shouting. "The century is half-over. If you can hear this broadcast, you won't live to see 2050."

I've often thought about the treehouse and why it meant so much to me. It sat up high above everything else on Scopena. That kind of height gave me a unique view of the farm. Everything looked different from way up high in the treehouse. I think the self-contained vantage point from the treehouse lent itself to dreaming big and letting your imagination run wild. All of that somehow gave meaning to me, at a time when the world seemed so uncertain—1950.

Questions of life and death were becoming relevant for the first time. I can still hear that radio announcer saying that we wouldn't be alive to see 2050. This possibility of death seemed real, and very scary, for a six year old like me. And then to climb into the new tree house and to know that this was the first day of the rest of my life and there was an end to it seemed like a very real threat to me. I wouldn't live until 2050. I had such a small window. I had never thought of that fact.

I remember sitting in the treehouse and thinking, "Do the other guys know? Should I tell them?"

And so I did. Danny couldn't connect the thoughts or didn't want to, except he was sure that he would live until 2050. He had no sense of urgency. Death was not a factor in any decision. If it came, so be it. Danny has been that way his whole life. He is brilliant, but laid back. I think that helps in all those tennis matches he competed in. It also helped him get into Harvard and the Harvard Business School.

Emmett had thought about it. This was not a new concept for him. I asked, "When do you think you will die?" He said not any time soon. He said that maybe it would happen in ten years, perhaps while he was a soldier in Asia. Places like China and Korea seemed to have a fascination for him.

✳ ✳ ✳

Emmett never made it to China or Korea, although I did years later. He died twenty years after that time in the treehouse in a tragic accident working for the Bossier Rural Electrification Corporation while doing maintenance on power lines far away from the home office and the treehouse on Scopena. There had been an ice storm in north Louisiana, and it was bitterly cold. Emmett was electrocuted while trying to turn the power on when the lines became entangled with the icy limbs and wrapped around him.

Emmett had asked Dad, who was president of the Bossier REA, if he could have a job as a lineman. Emmett went on to have an outstanding record of service and loved the job.

Emmett remained my friend over the years, and I would see him time and again as he traveled the back roads around and through Scopena, fixing the power lines that were often undone by wind and ice storms. The pine forests were high maintenance in that regard. Upkeep of the power lines was not as easy in rural areas as it was in the cities.

When he was buried three days after the accident, Emmett's family asked me to give the eulogy. I spoke of Emmett "the fixer," always repairing things and getting them back to running. I spoke of how I had admired that in him and what a gift it was. It was a gift that I did not have. And I talked about how ironic and fitting it was that Emmett died in the trees, because he loved the trees and their blowing on a windy day and their icing in a winter storm. I then told the story of how Emmett had helped build the treehouse twenty years before and how he stood up there and looked over Scopena. How we talked of living to the year 2050. I would be 106, and he would be 112. Standing there in the tree house, he was king of the world and all things were possible, even living more than a century.

Me? I told Emmett and Danny that day in the treehouse that I would die in some foreign land, saving government secrets, protecting America. I always saw myself living to a ripe old age, and having a funeral with a lot of speakers and a lot of honors, when I was forty or fifty. Dying didn't seem to scare me so much. Dying without recognition, however—now, that I couldn't imagine.

That day on top of the treehouse—with my best friends Danny and Emmett—I felt like I was beginning a new decade and indeed the rest of my life. I had a feeling of optimism and preparedness unlike anything I've ever felt before or since. The world was going to turn out right, and it all began with Scopena.

4

BOUNCING MY LIFE AWAY

In my early days at Scopena I would daydream about honors, triumph, and my glorious funeral. I don't know why I lived this fantasy life in my head, because I had no outstanding physical attributes to justify such a whirlwind of daydreaming. I wasn't big, nor fast, nor outstanding in any physical way, but my mind raced far ahead with possibilities for fame with me as the hero. As I did, I would rock back and forth in the family car, parked in back of the house. I was six or seven years old. It was just me alone on the back seat of a car dreaming often about dying with honor while I bounced. (By bouncing I mean rocking backward and forward-on the seat.) I daydreamed about many things while I bounced—recognition at school, some heroic deed—but always I was some recognized hero.

People noticed when I bounced. The car rocked. The car was steaming hot in the Louisiana summer, and I sweated like a horse ridden too far, because I never put the windows down. In the house I rocked in the big chair right in the midst of everyone. It didn't matter to me. I would rather have privacy when I bounced, but rocking was the thing—not privacy. I bounced in the car with other people in it.

Why I did it, I don't know. I never saw anyone else do it. I didn't rock to music, although at times I had the record player on to some inspiring tune like "Bolero." No one told me to do it because it was good for my health or good for my image. I didn't do it with anyone.

My parents tried to get me to stop. They had no effect on me. My brother and sisters laughed at me or said that I was weird, but they had no effect on me either. My parents talked to doctors about it to see if my health was affected by bouncing. There were no health issues, and no doctor stopped me. I did it on my own, sometime after my eighth birthday; I don't know why, but I finally decided I didn't want to bounce anymore. Simple as that: I quit.

Maybe tennis was the reason I quit bouncing. Dad might have figured it out. In the middle of my bouncing period, when I was seven, Dad built the first tennis court in our front yard—a beautiful concrete court. It was designed for singles play and could expand for doubles play as well. It had a large apron of concrete behind the ends of the court so that you never had to hit a ball from the grass. (I had to hit from the grass surrounding the tennis court at the governor's mansion years later, and I stumbled and hit the ground and broke my collar-bone, a danger that Dad had avoided by laying out the court at Scopena with plenty of extra concrete around it.) It was a smooth, fast court with true bounces. It was certainly an anomaly in our world. The nearest tennis courts to Scopena were an old concrete court five miles away at the Caplis plantation, and twelve miles away in Bossier City at the rec center.

Dad and Mom had played tennis while in college and were big fans. Dad taught me, my sister Margaret, and Danny how to play. We all picked it up quickly as we all had natural athletic ability. I began to play for hours each day, singles against Dad or Danny or doubles against Margaret and Dad. Dad hired a professional to give us lessons while we were in high school, after 7:00 on school nights, under the lights.

I went on to play #1 on Bossier High's tennis team and won many local tournaments, but I didn't have the success that Margaret and Danny did. They were awesome. Margaret ranked as the #1 girl at Bossier High. She also won the mixed doubles state championship with Danny and the state girls double with her partner at Bossier. She ended up being ranked as the #1 girl in Louisiana and went on to play at Simmons University in Boston.

Danny went on to be #1 in the state, too. He won many championships and went on to play on the Harvard tennis team. Tennis has been fun and worthwhile for my family. Margaret doesn't play much anymore, and my stroke and neuropathy have put an end to my game. But Danny persists and was national champion in the over-fifty group several years ago.

Who would have known where tennis would take us? I, for example, played on the White House court with Vice President George H.W. Bush, in the Ronald Reagan era. I played a practice session with the great Brazilian Davis Club team when I was a guest of the Brazilian president one week, and he and I talked trade between the two countries.

It was from my training as a tennis player that I became one of the most active players on the racquet ball courts at the house gymnasium in Washington, D.C., playing daily with such men as Sonny Montgomery (D-Mississippi), Lee Hamilton (D-Indiana), and George H.W. Bush, when he was vice president and president. All from Dad's interest, a court built at Scopena some sixty-five years ago, and a desire to give me something to do to break a bouncing addiction.

Looking back, Dad was one of the most competitive men I ever met. His main competition was his two boys: me and Danny. As our physical skills first equaled and then exceeded his, he developed a tennis game of slices and tricky, unusual shots to keep us at bay. He wouldn't be beaten by Danny or me if he could figure out a way by using a slice or trick shot on the court. He never gave up or resigned himself to defeat against his boys. The doubles matches of Dad and any partner against Danny and me remained competitive for decades, long after Danny and I were champions in outside tournaments, and long after Dad crashed an airplane at Scopena that resulted in his ankles being surgically fused in-place for the rest of his life.

5

Mr. Budgie

Dad grew up at Scopena when it was a relatively small farm owned by Gran Vernon, who had married Dad's mother, "Mine," when Dad was eight. Dad loved the farm life and spent hours walking among the rows of the cotton fields.

Dad and Mom met at Elm Grove School beginning in seventh grade and became inseparable from then on. They were married in a civil ceremony in the late fall of 1942, before Dad enlisted in the Army Air Corps. During his Army Air Corps stint in World War II, he was stationed domestically, and Mom traveled with him around the United States, including Ohio and Biloxi, Mississippi.

After the war ended, we moved to Baton Rouge so Dad could study mechanical engineering at LSU. He helped pay for his studies by working as a welder during the construction of the original Exxon refinery in Baton Rouge. After Dad graduated Phi Beta Kappa in 1947, we moved to the village of McDade. There, Dad leased a house big enough for his growing family—by now there were three children (soon four)—and only seven miles south of Scopena. McDade was the home of my mother, who grew up on the farm of my grandfather, Ross McDade. McDade was named after "Tin" McDade, Granddaddy's brother who was postmaster.

Gran Vernon agreed to take on Dad as a full partner when he was only twenty-three years old. Moving from Baton Rouge to Mc-

Budgie Roemer in a field of cotton at Scopena

Dade allowed Dad to oversee the building of a new house and office headquarters at Scopena. When they were completed in 1949, we moved from McDade to Scopena.

Dad grew to be stocky, 5'10" and 200 pounds, with a powerful chest and heavily muscled arms. From an early age, he was his own man, whether it was while playing quarterback for his high school football team, earning a Phi Beta Kappa at LSU, managing a campaign for governor, or running state government as commissioner of administration. He was neither big nor tall, but he definitely had a presence in a room. His voice commanded attention when he spoke, which was rare. His most noticeable feature was his full head of brown, wavy hair, which emphasized a head that was larger than a normal man of his size. His hands were still and very strong. He didn't wear glasses at the time.

Dad was called "Budgie." I don't know how or when he got the nickname, but by Elm Grove High School he was known as Budgie, which is an informal name for a male parakeet. At Scopena, he was called "Mr. Budgie" by whites and blacks alike. It was a misnomer because Dad was anything but a talkative parakeet. Quiet and intense, he avoided most social contact that didn't have to do with his business.

Dad was almost shy. His preference was that he work alone or with one or two people he knew and trusted. He was not a political person in that he liked a lot of people around him or to be the center of attention. He was just the opposite in that he liked working by himself or with family members. But he cared about people. He just didn't get involved with them, unless they were family; even then, it was often competitive, not familial. All of his life he worked with people and led them, but he didn't normally socialize or chit chat with them. He was focused on his business—always. This was not a weakness of his; it was a fact, with powerful effects. He worked best alone and wouldn't let himself trust others.

He was polite, but he gave the impression of being too busy for idle conversation. Idle chatter and social gossip was a waste of human talent, and he wouldn't tolerate it. He was by temperament the opposite of his business partner and stepfather, Vernon Mayer, who was outgoing and a natural salesman.

Visiting over a cup of coffee was something that neighboring farmers did at the Scopena office every day, but not Dad. He never saw having a cup of coffee as a positive thing. If he was trapped with a farmer who wanted to chit chat, he ordered a cup of hot tea from the kitchen. No coffee for him. It was too much a "social" drink for him.

Don't misunderstand me, Dad didn't dislike people. He just didn't like them to be up close or to be in his business or to be dependent on them.

In fact, Dad was so taciturn that the nickname "Budgie" might be like calling a seven-footer "shorty" just to make the point. Dad excelled in leadership qualities, but he was not a talkative male parakeet.

He did enjoy a good cigar and often kept an unlit one, which he would occasionally light, in his mouth. But I never saw him smoke a cigarette. Cigarette smokers made him uncomfortable.

I started smoking cigarettes on a regular basis in college. When I came home during a break, I would avoid lighting up at Scopena. Later, when I did feel grown up enough to smoke in front of Dad, he wouldn't say anything. He would observe that it would be nice to have an ashtray for that thing and wait for me to use a cup or a saucer before we would continue our conversation.

I was always engaged in some attempt or remedy to stop smoking (the patch, abstinence, etc.). When I announced my latest scheme for stopping smoking, he would mumble that it was about time or would simply congratulate me for stopping. None of my four siblings ever smoked around Dad, and in fact, never smoked at all as far as I knew. Danny occasionally smoked corn silk when we were kids, but as a tennis player at Harvard, he avoided tobacco.

I think I enjoyed smoking in part because Dad didn't smoke. It set me apart from him at a college age. I mean there were a lot of reasons why I became a smoker—trying to be like the men around the shop fire early in the morning or because of the addictiveness of the nicotine—but one of the reasons was because it caused me to be set apart as my own man, separate from Dad.

Dad's anti-social behavior extended to activities on the farm that included other people, like hunting and fishing. Although I saw him dove hunt five or six times, he avoided the hunt, and I can count on the fingers of a single hand the times that I saw him fish. He was an excellent shot, however. He allowed others to hunt at Scopena, but he himself almost never participated. We went duck hunting on small lakes in the back of Scopena once or twice when I was in high school. But Dad usually let us boys go alone or with friends.

Dad dressed the same every day when I was growing up: khaki pants with a khaki shirt and work, not cowboy, boots. When the day was done, his khaki shirt and pants were streaked with grease and dirt.

He loved to work in the shop on farm equipment that needed to be repaired or modified so that it would work better or easier: a hay baler that needed to bale more hay, a corn detasseler that wasn't functioning properly, a tractor that wouldn't shift gears, a mechanical cotton harvester that wasn't picking the cotton row cleanly—all were targets of his attention in the shop. He wasn't the shop foreman, but that didn't stop him from pitching in and getting the repair done. He prided himself on his mechanical repair abilities, regardless of the machinery involved.

When he took over the operation of Scopena in 1947, it was a relatively small farm with about four hundred acres of cultivatable land. In 1948, a neighboring farmer came to Dad wanting to sell his farm and move west to Texas. Dad and Gran Vernon bought the farm and in the years ahead began to buy most nearby land that came available.

The local bank or land bank would help them finance the purchases, using the land purchased as collateral against the loan. It worked fine because they typically bought the land at a low price in a distress sale, and it rose in value most every year thereafter. So they always had credit available at the bank for the purchase of more land.

Scopena would grow in size over the next ten years to become one of the largest plantations along the Red River. Small farmers were having a tough time economically because of the high investment cost of new technology (especially with mechanical cotton harvesters and giant tractors that could till more than five times more acres in a day than old tractors). They couldn't afford to modernize, and they couldn't afford not to. As a result, they were often forced to sell and try another line of work.

Scopena, because of the focused energy of Dad, became a buyer in this industry transformation and rapidly increased its acreage to more than 10,000 acres, with more than 4,000 acres of row-crop cultivatable land. The expansion stemmed from Dad's belief that to succeed you needed size to achieve economies of scale.

His military training contributed to his sense of organization and his willingness to utilize new technology. He drove a Jeep around the plantation that he bought from Army surplus, and, at his insistence, Scopena was equipped in the early 1950s with a Motorola two-way shortwave radio in all farm vehicles. With it, Dad would know what his men were doing no matter where they were. "KKX-465" were the call letters, and it was unique among the farms of northwest Louisiana. Supervisors at other farms passed along orders or got information from the fields via horseback or a vehicle. Scopena was so big that the radio link allowed Dad to communicate throughout the farm much faster. It had a revolutionary effect.

Close-lipped with others, Dad was a different person with his family. He devoted himself to my mother and their five children. Family vacations each summer were sacrosanct. On those vacations Dad would be full of facts and figures about the national park or state we would be visiting. I loved those facts and figures. At night, we would play canasta, poker, Monopoly, or Yahtzee, and he was always available for a long talk if you needed help overcoming a crisis. While each of us was away at college—we all went outside of the state, far from home—he wrote us substantive letters every week. I wish I had kept them, because the letters from Dad were like a lifeline to the world we knew and loved so much.

The letters were written on many pages of long yellow tablets that you might find around the office on Mom's desk. They were written in longhand, front and back. They were written once or twice a week, and were eight to twelve pages long. They were a book and were a detailed look at some problem or problems facing Scopena: water, insects, cattle, cotton, corn, sunflowers, wheat, irrigation, gin, shop, dog, horses, kids, Mom, workers, family of workers, storage sheds, pecan trees, McDade, Oklahoma, Hopewell, Red River, the weather, the Methodist Church. He couldn't and didn't talk much, but he was a writer extraordinaire. The letters helped hold off homesickness from me and were an awaited treat for a boy long away from Scopena.

I talked to my sister Margaret and my brother, Danny, when they were students at Harvard and Simmons, and they used to get these same long epistles every few days, and they weren't copies. He'd often talk about the same topics in each, but the letters were different for the different people. Imagine the time that it took to write those letters. The hours and hours of time to write to five kids two thousand miles from home (Melinda and Melanie would enter Pine Manor in Boston when Danny attended Harvard); kids with different dreams and different interests and different personalities; kids that had different needs. Imagine?

✗ ✗ ✗

Dad's real father, Charles E. Roemer, known as "Pete," had divorced "Mine" early in Dad's life. Granddaddy Pete lived in New Orleans where he owned and ran a successful independent dairy, Roemer's Milk. Granddaddy Pete was a character. He drove a Mercedes sports car, had only one eye, having lost the other one to a botched operation years before.

He wore a black patch over his bad eye and a hat almost all the time late in life. I never knew why Granddaddy Pete divorced my grandmother, but it didn't prevent frequent trips by the family each way.

Granddaddy Pete had run off from his home in Ohio when he was a teenager and never talked about his upbringing, but he was eloquent about conservative business ideas. For example, he thought teacher unions were dangerous to public education, because they didn't put the students first. He was a member of the New Orle-

Charles E. Roemer, "Granddaddy Pete"

ans Country Club, with his portrait hanging in the dining room as a former president of that organization.

Granddaddy Pete loved to play tennis, and he would drive up on to Scopena Thursday night in order to play Friday and Saturday. To extend our playing time, and to accommodate Granddaddy Pete's schedule, Dad installed high intensity outdoor lights on the tennis court. Granddaddy Pete could play until midnight or later on Saturday night before his Sunday morning return to New Orleans.

Dad liked to play doubles, and he would partner with one of my younger sisters to take on my brother and me or my Mom and my brother. Dad's role in tennis changed in 1956 when he injured his ankles in a terrible airplane accident on Scopena. As a result of his accident, his ankles were fused, and he walked in a restricted manner. But it didn't stop his tennis playing. He became a terror at the net, poaching in a doubles configuration. He developed a slicing serve to match.

When Dad decided he could no longer be competitive as a single's player, he announced when we were in high school that he would play doubles tennis only, and that he would play with any partner and be the victor.

Concrete makes for a fast tennis court, so as Dad got older and slower, he built an adjoining court made of layco, a form of clay, a slower, more susceptible surface to slices and spins usually hit by Dad. The competitive tennis doubles games of Scopena were to become a thing of legend in the Roemer family.

The grandkids of Scopena still play tennis on those courts installed long ago. And the competitive spirit among the Roemer children and Mom and Dad started on the tennis courts lasts with me to this day sixty-something years later.

✳ ✳ ✳

Dad liked to give back to the community. He was elected (by the users) as president of the Bossier Rural Electrification throughout the 1950s. He fought the monopolistic tendencies of the city-oriented, investor-owned utilities and made electric energy practical on everybody's farm. He always talked about how Bossier REA brought electricity to Scopena when he was a boy, and had transformed life on the farm. It was one the reasons that Dad was always a Franklin Roosevelt Democrat. President Roosevelt had started the Rural Electrification Administration at the height of the Great Depression. That's something Dad never forgot.

Dad also served as president of the Bossier Farm Bureau in the 1950s and 1960s, although he found the experience less than fulfilling because he thought the organization included too many non-farmers who were members because of the cheap insurance.

In the 1950s, there was no doubt who was the boss at Scopena: Budgie Roemer. He made all the decisions of what to plant and when to plant. He made all the hedging decisions on when to insure the price of a crop in the future. You had to understand the price movements world-wide to understand when to act. We missed some price spikes in cotton, but he didn't care about anything but a fair price for the crop. Like any great hedger, he took the emotion out of the decision. To hedge (sell early in the year before the crop was made) took great skill and courage.

I heard the hedging consultants in Memphis say that Dad was the best there was at hedging the price of cotton or soybeans. Not only did he know the conditions of the crop in the United States, he knew the conditions of the crop in Egypt and in China, and he knew the demand for cotton in Europe and in America. He protected Scopena during periods of high price volatility in the market and stagnant demand for cotton in the United States.

There was no doubt that he was father of the family as well. He had the decisive opinion on school priorities, on where the family spent vacations (almost never in the same place twice, although the West was Dad's, and my, favorite place to see), on how the family was organized for the trips, and on which college we attended. We all went to Boston to college. Dad insisted that we leave Louisiana to see how the world outside Louisiana worked. He thought Boston was the best educational center in the United States.

The Roemers were a big family with a lot of members. We were all equal as family members, but Dad was the most equal.

Since I was the oldest child, Dad gave me special responsibilities. I felt that he expected more of me. I would ride around with him at an early age (beginning at five or six years old) when he performed his duties on the farm. He also relied on me to get certain jobs done on the farm when he could not trust anyone else as much.

Dad's inclination was not to trust someone completely that wasn't "family." As a result, I saw things that a young kid wouldn't have normally seen: workplace rebukes and confrontations, situations that required decisive action.

As a consequence, I expected more of myself than did the typical six or seven or eight-year-old kid. I had manly responsibilities, and I accepted that. I was more serious about things in general, and I didn't tolerate whining or excuses. The conversations that Dad and I had in the cotton fields were memorable and had a lasting effect; they reinforced that no excuses attitude.

He told me that life was wonderful but tricky, and it came with no guarantees. The way to combat the vicissitudes of life was to be prepared for anything so that you could react decisively to gain all the positives possible. He said over and over that most people are not prepared for either good news or bad. As a result, he said, most people could not harvest the maximum good from a situation.

Dad loved competition. The tennis court showed that. He said it made you better. He always pushed us to do better and to be better. He used to compete with each of us. The family was the center of his world. It became Dad's reason for being. It became his reason to grow Scopena. It became the reason to have his children excel at school and to have them go to well-known colleges far away from Louisiana. "Family" was everything to him. Competition was the way his love to his family showed.

A very special memory that I have of my father was a night in early June of 1960. He sat with Mom, Punkin, Melinda, Melanie, and

Danny, my three sisters and brother, on the front row of the Bossier High School football stadium to hear me give the Valedictorian speech at my graduation. I don't remember a word I spoke in those thirty minutes, but I do remember looking the fifteen yards across at my father and family, and thinking how much I loved him, but how old he looked. Dad was thirty-six. I was sixteen.

Dad and I would butt heads and disagree on many issues from graduation night forward. I guess we were both hard headed. But I loved him, and he loved me, and that would never change. I still remember that moment some fifty-plus years ago, just like it was last night.

Dad was one of a kind; he was highly competent, highly individualist, and innovative in his leadership and fathership. Of all the people I've ever known, he was the most unique. That uniqueness began with the woman he chose to marry and stayed married to for seventy years: Miss Juliet Adeline McDade.

6

Miss Adeline

Mom was the petite, youngest child of Ross McDade and his wife, "Mama," or Ethel.

Mom was born on Christmas Day 1923, a couple of months younger than Dad. She grew up on McDade plantation, owned by Granddaddy Ross McDade at McDade, Louisiana, about seven miles south of Scopena. She grew up with two sisters and an older brother. Aunts Ethel and Emily and Uncle Fuzzy were beloved kinfolk, with Aunt Emily becoming particularly close to the Roemer family.

As I mentioned, Mom and Dad met at Elm Grove School and got married in 1942, before Dad entered the Army Air Corps. During the war, Mom stayed at home with her parents until after the birth of her first son, me, in October 1943. After Christmas of that year, she joined Dad at Kessler Air Force base in Biloxi, Mississippi, where he taught navigation to air corps cadets.

In 1945, after Dad was discharged and enrolled in LSU, they moved to Baton Rouge. There, they had their second child, Margaret (Punkin), who was stricken with spinal meningitis at an early age. Margaret recovered with no ill effects, and the couple had a third child, a healthy baby boy, Franklin Daniel (Danny) in 1946.

By this time, Mom had developed into a beautiful young woman. Standing 5'1" and weighing 92 pounds, she let her light brown hair grow long, down to her waist. She wore it straight, often pinned

Adeline Roemer in front of the McDade rent house

with a hairpin atop her head. Mom continued to have children, Melinda and then Melanie, the final child in 1950, making a total of five.

One habit that Mom didn't change with the delivery of five children was the drinking of four or five bottled Cokes each day beginning early in the morning when she first arose. She never smoked, and she would have a social cup of coffee occasionally. But a bottle of Coke always accompanied her in the office.

From the beginning, Mom was a full partner with Dad in operating the farm. She was the inside person of the team, doing the books, scheduling the services like spraying or cotton harvesting for neighboring farmers, keeping the office running smoothly, greeting visitors, maintaining the parts department for farm implements, running the second shift of the Scopena gin, making sure that the families of all the Scopena workers had access to quality health care, and providing for the lunch meal for the plantation.

One of the jobs that Mom took on at Scopena outside the office was that of operating the second shift of the Scopena gin when needed. She had gained experience on her father's gin at McDade years before. Looking back, I never knew a woman ginner except Mom. In operating the gin, she decided which cotton to take next in line (cotton house or trailer), the condition of the cotton she was ginning next (damp, dry, filled with sticks and leaves, or clean), what to do in case of a gin fire, how to supervise the gin stand men, how to maximize the efforts of the press men, how to organize the trailers in the gin yards for access to the gin, and much more. It wasn't heavy lifting, but it meant getting the most out of your men and being prepared for changing conditions (a wind shift, showers or snow, and fire at any time).

At the gin, she worked from 6:30 p.m. to 2:00 a.m. about twenty nights a year. It was an awesome responsibility. Dad would go over after supper on the long nights to help her. She had the support of her men, and they worked as a unit.

Mom gained her crew's support from years of experience at running her Dad's gin at McDade when she was a teenager. She knew cotton, when it needed special handling and when you could run wide-open. Her crew told me that they felt that she was the best ginner that they ever worked for.

During an age in the 1950s when women's lib was something that happened elsewhere and you would read about it in the newspaper, Mom operated the gin like it was hers. It was more than running the second shift. She scheduled the first shift as well. Arthur England, who ran the first shift, checked with her each morning around 5:30 to get his commands for the day as to cotton order and any special instructions for the day. Mom was in charge of the gin-customers, special directives, pay requests—and everybody knew it and thought nothing of it.

Mom also spent countless hours listening to Dad's dreams of making Scopena work better. He never made a major decision—whether to buy a new property or a new piece of equipment or whether to plant a new crop or stick with the old stand-by cotton—

without talking at length with Mom.

Besides strategic planning, her most valuable contribution to Scopena, I'm convinced, was to help handle Dad's lack of people skills. He often engaged in verbal battles with neighboring farmers, always with smaller farms than Scopena, and often wrong, Dad thought, in some conflict over a fence line or some squabble over the use of a commonly shared lake.

Dad wouldn't care about the use of the lake for fishing or hunting. He was concerned about the use of water in the lake during the dry season. When Dad would draw down the lake by pumping water out with huge mobile pumps, it would affect the lake levels and the farmer would complain. Then he and Dad would bow up with shouting matches and loud cussing battles. Dad refused to back down. This was his cotton that was being affected, and pumping his water from the lake was his right. If someone had to miss water skiing for a month in July so he could irrigate his cotton crop, so be it.

Mom would get in the middle of the fight. She bargained with the irate farmer at the other end of the lake, and said that we would use the lake as a last resort, that we would pump water for a maximum of six weeks, and we would give the farmer use of the full lake for forty-six weeks out of a year. She said that she thought she could get Dad to sign a paper stating that.

The lake farmer agreed to that, and she got Dad to agree, but, Dad said, "only if it started this year." Dad signed, because of Mom. The other farmer was a customer of Mom at the gin, and he remained a major customer, although he seldom spoke to Dad again. Mom had averted a disastrous loss of water for the crop because she had people skills, even if Dad did not. Time after time, in dispute after dispute, Dad fixated on right and wrong. Mom focused on the people relationship. When Mom got involved, Dad would end up having his ass saved. Mom, not Dad, was critical to Scopena's success in those situations.

A prime example of this happened in the summer of 1958. Late on a July afternoon a thunderstorm struck over the main house and office of Scopena. It poured a monsoon of rain. Sheets and sheets of water came down. There seemed to be no end to it. Dad and I were in the office watching the flood and shoring up from the rising sidewalk water from entering the office by the use of towels. It must have been a Saturday because we were absolutely alone in the office.

I remember that we put towels against the two entrances to the office to hold back the water accumulating there. It was quite an adventure for the two of us. We were manning the fort, and we were proud. The thunderstorm passed, the skies cleared, and the crises of flooding in the office passed.

But we then noticed that the front yard had flooded. The tennis courts were under a foot or more of water, and the yard itself had been inundated. This was not good for the health of the grass in the yard obviously, so Dad remarked that we should do something about it.

He walked out to the shop—about two hundred yards behind the office—and got a mobile pump that was on the back of a pickup truck, and drove the truck and pump around to our house's front driveway next to Highway 71 South, the main thoroughfare in south Bossier Parish.

The traffic on Highway 71 was easing by, heading slowly north and south in the rain, and Dad set an aluminum discharge pipe from the pump, which was in the front yard water, to the edge of the highway, so the water could escape from the yard to across the road. The traffic could ease through the water that the pump forced from the yard over the highway.

Nice. "Neat and safe," Dad said. We left the mobile pump in the front yard, and he and I rode in the pickup truck back around to the office.

Minutes later, we heard a knock on the office door.

When I left Dad's room in the interior of the office to answer the knock, there was a man in the uniform of the Louisiana State Police standing there. I didn't know him. He had his "mounty" hat on and seemed all business. I noticed that trooper lights were not on in the

State Police car behind him and he was by himself.

He asked, "Who in there has turned the aluminum pipe with water running across the highway on?"

I said my father and I had.

He said that we were in violation of State law in causing a safety situation of Highway 71 with the pumping of the water across the road. It was dangerous, he said, and it must be discontinued immediately or someone was going to jail.

My father came into the room about this time and asked "who is going to jail?" Dad answered himself, saying that nobody was going to jail and that we would discontinue pumping the water across the road immediately. He further said that safety wasn't an issue because cars on Highway 71 had slowed naturally because of the rain, and we would only pump water while it rained.

The trooper stammered a second, took off his hat, said thank you, and turned to his car.

Dad went out to the pickup truck with me, and we drove to the front driveway, took down the pipe from the highway edge, and turned to shut off the pump.

Before he could shut off the pump, someone yelled from the front porch that Dad had a call from Memphis about hedging the cotton crop, so we returned immediately to the office. Dad said as an aside to me that we would return in a few minutes to make sure the pump was turned off and secure. It was safer to let it run in place than to precipitously stop it because of the safety requirements of stopping the pump.

So we left the pump running in place, but removed the discharge from crossing the highway to run in the ditch beside the highway, and returned to the office to take the Memphis call. The running pump was not sending the water across the highway. It was just recycling it into the yard.

The trooper, who had hung around in his car to make sure Dad had done what he said that he was going to do, waved in recognition as we returned to the office to take the call. All was well.

The call lasted between one and two hours, because the Memphis broker thought the market was making a move down, and he wanted his hedges in place. Dad listened because this was an important telephone call in the cotton commodity world.

When we had finished the call and were about to return to the front yard and the pump, I heard a knock on the office door again.

I noticed when I went to the door this time that the uniformed state trooper was standing there with the outside lights on his car all flashing like he was going to arrest somebody.

He shouted, "I told you to stop that water crossing the highway. It's running full speed." And he'd drawn his gun and pointed it right at my father who had come out from behind his desk with his mouth wide open.

Dad tells him to put down his weapon, because his son and he stopped the water an hour ago, and that something must have happened out of our control, and that if he didn't holster that weapon, he was going to have to use it.

My whole life passed before me. I can remember putting the pipe down from the highway edge, and leaving it running in the ditch while we took the Memphis call. No matter what it looked like, we had not disobeyed the state trooper.

But the trooper didn't change his expression and neither did Dad.

Mom stuck her head in about this time and asked what the problem was. When told it was disobeying a State Trooper about pumping water across the highway, Mom said not so. She had seen Albert Lyles, a farm worker, passing the aimless spraying pipe, returning it to its place pumping flood waters across the highway. That had happened about thirty minutes before, and she had said good job to herself, because she felt the pipe had jarred loose. No one had told her any different.

The trooper put his weapon back in the holster and said that no one was going to jail and he said he was sorry for the altercation and he would be on his way with the understanding that the problem would be corrected—quickly and permanently.

Dad had been on his way to escalating a people situation into one about guns and confrontation. Mom saw that it wasn't about the gun; it was about respect for the trooper's order.

Dad was not mean-spirited in any way, but it seems he always took the confrontational path. When she could, Mom tried to find a better path for him: a path of resolution and peace. Mom taught us kids about working with others while Dad was insisting on obedience and right and wrong.

Dad felt that the State Trooper had been wrong and shown poor training. I never asked Dad if he found out anything about the trooper in question when he became head of the State Police as commissioner of administration for Governor Edwin Edwards sixteen years later. I would never forget that standoff in the office that Saturday afternoon. How circumstances had pushed Dad to where he wasn't comfortable; and how Mom, as usual, had found a way to save the day.

Another thing that Mom and Dad participated in together was Scopena, the business. The business of the farm had to be considered first with them both, whether it was Saturday or Sunday, the scheduling of school activities, or the timing of the annual vacation. There was never an unplanned off-day at Scopena. Monday or Saturday, it made no difference. When the family met or was together for some other reason, we discussed Scopena business. It was all consuming.

In addition to all these chores and detailed farm-related activities, Mom had the responsibility of raising five hyperactive children. She made sure that each of us fulfilled our chores but also made sure that we had plenty of fun activities: playing tennis, riding horses, and taking advantage of the swimming pool.

Mom had developed a love for swimming in college at Northwestern State University in Natchitoches. In 1951, she got Dad to build a huge pool at Scopena between the cotton gin and the house.

The pool went from three feet at its shallowest to eight feet in the deep end. It had no diving board but was forty-two feet long with concrete shoulders extending out from the pool some ten feet. During the long, hot summer, it brought the family together for

Adeline and Budgie at Elm Grove High School in 1938
(Budgie, first from left in back row; Adeline, center in front row)

swimming and card games, canasta was a favorite, and dominos.

The pool had an additional feature that the kids and Mom loved: a fifty-foot slide that extended two feet over the pool's shallow end. All of us enjoyed the rush of sliding into the pool head first, especially on your back. The slide could be quite scary, but was safe and no major injuries occurred.

A quiet woman in many ways, Mom was never at a loss for words when defending her beliefs in education for her children and in advocating for her community. She was a wonderful mother in a different world. Her community was Scopena, and while she allowed Dad to be the titular head of Scopena, she was irreplaceable as the people-person in times of need. She could charm a skunk out of his pen. Dad couldn't, or wouldn't.

7

THE BIG HOUSE

Our farm was called Scopena plantation. But it had none of the grandeur stereotypically associated with the plantations of past times. Take our house, for example. It was a basic ranch-style home connected to the office. It was about three thousand square feet on a single floor. The office added another four thousand square feet to the house measurements and Mine's additions to the south end of the main house added a total of 2,500 square feet.

The no-nonsense style reflected Dad's view of the world. It didn't have the grandeur of GranDad's house at McDade. It was a single story and very utilitarian. It was to live in, nothing else. It wasn't a statement like some of the houses in South Bossier with grand columns and multiple stories. It wasn't for entertainment or for parties. The house was home—that's all.

There was a door from the office into the kitchen, so that the men could go to the kitchen for coffee or biscuits without disturbing anyone. The kitchen was at the northern end of the house, with Formica counter tops skirting a large stove, refrigerator, and freezer. There was plenty of room for standing and drinking coffee—which was something we kids weren't allowed to do growing up. Farming men, white and black, in the kitchen drinking coffee, is what I remember growing up.

The rest of the house led away from the kitchen, to the south.

Back of the Scopena house (present day view)

Originally, the house was built with three bedrooms, two bathrooms, a dining room, and a living room. The dining table was unique. It was a butcher's table—thick, wooden, bulky, with enough room for fourteen, even sixteen, people, Mom at one end, Dad at the other. It had a blackboard at one end over Dad's head. I'll talk more about that later. The dining room had some cabinets along the wall abutting the kitchen for holding eating utensils, but the room contained nothing else but the big butcher-block table. The table wasn't some frail work of art. It was heavy and sent the signal that it was there for one purpose: eating.

The girls had the bedroom at the far end of the house on the left-hand side of the central hallway. Mom and Dad had the master bedroom next to the girls' bedroom. The word "master" attached to the bedroom is too grandiose. It was really just an extra-large bedroom.

The boys' bedroom was to the right of the central hallway and was the last room in the original house. It had bunk beds for Danny and me and was filled with books and games for the two of us. I remember a fold-down, plywood table that contained an elaborate train set that Dad built for us one Christmas.

My grandmother "Mine" built on to the house after the death of her husband in 1954. She added a dining room, a living room, two bathrooms, a kitchen, and two bedrooms to the original house. It was an addition to our house, so everybody kept their bedroom.

So we had two kitchens and two dining rooms in the house: the original one at the front of the house that served as the main dining room with the butcher-block dining table and where we ate breakfast and lunch, and Mine's kitchen in the back where we ate supper at night.

Mine's house was extraordinary to an eleven-year-old kid like me. She had cork floors, for example, and they were heated! In 1955, who had heard of such things?

The living room in our house was right off the dining room, through an always-open entrance. It was a typical living room where we celebrated Christmas every year with presents under the tree. On Wednesday nights the living room would be turned into a card room where Mom and Dad would play canasta and bridge with neighbors. Mom often held her after school, home-study sessions in the living room. Books were a big part of the farm house. Mom and Dad were avid readers and all the kids picked up the reading habit at an early age. Classic books were in prominent display among the many bookshelves, but there were also popular books, encyclopedias, and popular newsmagazines like *Time*, *Life*, *U.S. News and World Report*, and *Sports Illustrated* when it was first published in the mid-1950s. We had built-in bookcases in the living room, all along the hall that led to all the bedrooms, in each of the bedrooms, and in Mine's house. The books remain there today after the kids are gone.

The living room was forever changed when Dad bought a slate-based, huge pool table in 1954 and had it placed in the living room. It was a monster and led us all to spend hours playing pool and billiards.

The living room was the home of the entertainment center of the house: the radio. There was no television. We didn't get a television until I was a senior in high school, or maybe a freshman in college. But we had a radio on which we listened to the farm report every morning or music every night when there wasn't some topic that we were debating.

Granddaddy Ross moved to Scopena in 1959 when his house at McDade caught fire and was destroyed. We built a single bedroom on to the main dining room at the north end of the house to accommodate him. He felt right at home until his death at the age of ninety-two in 1969. He could be involved in the happenings at Scopena, yet he could retreat into the privacy of his own room at any time. He loved the arrangement.

8

THE COTTON GIN

Probably the most prominent part of Scopena was the cotton gin. The gin had the name "Scopena" painted on the roof. It was the most important and expensive piece of equipment on the farm, costing $1 million some seventy years ago. The gin was housed in a tin-sheathed building, four stories high. The gin was actually a plant designed to take raw cotton from the fields and process it into baled fiber for use in spinning mills and fabric shops up in Memphis, Baltimore, Chicago, and other points north.

It consisted of a series of sucker pipes, conveyer belts, and gin stands that separated the lint from the seed and trash. It was noisy. It was complicated, and no two gins were exactly alike. It took a ginner and six or seven men to operate a gin.

Scopena had two gins, one at the farm itself, and one at Curtis, about five miles north of the other. The Scopena gin was relatively new, and it served about ten thousand acres of cotton. The Curtis gin was older and slower, and served about five thousand acres each year.

The gin was an amazing collection of equipment. There were only two other gins in competition with Scopena in south Bossier Parish. One was on an old plantation about six miles away in the town of Elm Grove—Elm Grove gin. The other was Granddaddy Ross's gin at McDade—McDade gin. The Scopena gins had the advantage of being more modern and bigger than both.

Scopena gin (present day view)

The farmers would bring the unginned cotton to Scopena in trailers that contained three to five bales. The raw cotton came straight from the fields and contained seeds, trash, and dirt.

"Bale" is the name for the finished product of the gin: the amount of cotton ginned and wrapped in burlap of bundled, seedless cotton lint, weighing about five hundred pounds. To process the raw cotton, a man would use a pipe to suck the cotton off a trailer into the gin for it to be processed. The gin would heat the raw cotton to make it dry enough to run through the lint stands, which consisted of tens of thousands of steel teeth on a shaft that spins hundreds of revolutions per minute. These teeth separated the cotton lint from the seed, sticks, and trash in the cotton.

The cotton lint then was blown to the gin baling unit where it was formed into bales of cotton. We would store the bales on a platform to be loaded daily onto a train to Memphis. That's where we usually sold our cotton. The cottonseed, having been separated from the lint in the gin, was conveyed to the delinter from the lint stands for further processing.

The delinter stood separate from the gin and removed the small amount of the lint left on the cottonseed by the gin. The lint was a fine fiber that we sent to a factory in Chicago where it was turned into mattress stuffing.

The bales at the gin were numbered at the press, and that number was attached to the bale permanently with a tag. That bale would be known by that number until sold to its end user. A cotton sample also was taken at the press. A man with a razor sharp knife cut the sample from the bale so it could be taken to Scopena headquarters. Mom then sent the sample to the government grader in Memphis by special postage to be graded by color (gray or white or somewhere in between), length of fiber (1 inch 1/32 or 1 inch, or 1/16, etc.), and quality of cotton (fair, fair to middling, strict middling, or middling). The result determined the minimum value of the bale—the price per pound that the government guaranteed. It could be valued as low as eighty cents per pound or as high as $1.20 per pound. Most bales were around a dollar per pound. The government grader had a very important effect on the price of cotton.

Dad graded one out of every ten samples himself. He had special equipment and lights to do that. Dad watched the grades every day to look for any prejudice in the Memphis grader. Dad didn't expect the Memphis grader to agree with him. He just wanted the error to balance out over the course of the crop. If he thought he saw some skewing of the grades, he would raise a rhubarb and ask for another government grader. There were a few conflicts, but none resulting in the slowing down of production.

Interestingly, Dad, by closely watching the cotton grade routine, was well known and not well liked by the government inspectors, and I believe he served Scopena and Scopena's gin customers well by getting better cotton grades for them than they would otherwise have earned. I can't prove it, but that's what I believe. "Always watch the Government at work," he told me.

A detachable label from the tag identified the sample, so the bale would have the same number. Another detachable label gave the ginner the proper number of bales ginned that day and their identity. Behind the gin complex (about ten acres) were soybean and corn storage and drying facilities. We stored our entire corn, soybean, and sunflower harvest there if necessary. The storehouses provided insurance against having to sell these crops at the height of harvest when prices were at their lowest.

We usually hedged our crop for a specific price long before we harvested the crop. But two out of seven years, the hedge was not a good one. So we bought back the hedge and harvested our crop, brought it in to storage, dried it, and held it to the offseason, when no grain was available and the price was much higher than during harvest. This strategy, not available to most farmers, made Scopena substantial extra money, because the cotton or grain wasn't sold at the height of the harvest season.

We sold the cotton under contract to a buyer in Memphis each year. The buyers would visit the plantation to look at the crop before they bought it, and they would always inspect the gin on their visit. The Scopena gin always shone brightly on these visits, because it was massive, modern, and clean.

Some years ago, the ginning equipment in Scopena Gin was sold to a gin stand needing some additional equipment. The building still stands as it did in the early 1950s, as if it is ready to start ginning this September. But the gin stands and all the equipment are gone. The great Scopena Gin and the memories buried in its pipes and wires and wagon and presses are forever departed.

9

THE SCOPENA SHOP

In between the gin and grain storage facilities stood the Scopena shop. It was a large, long two-story building that had storage space on the second story. It was the hottest place on Scopena in the summer and coldest in the winter because it was open-ended and covered in tin. It was like a big airplane hangar with the second story left open. It also was the gathering place for Scopena regular workers when a 5 or 6 a.m. wake up rendezvous was the social order of the day.

The gin operated during harvest time (September until January), but the shop operated throughout the year. You could always find a huddle there working on a problem or trying to get a new piece of equipment ready to operate.

But the shop was more than a year-round center of activity. It was the social hub of the plantation. Everything and everybody—business meetings, equipment meetings, many crisis meetings, and some planning meetings—went through the shop.

Men would stand in the shop beginning at 5:00 a.m., Monday through Saturday. When the weather was cold, they surrounded a barrel that had been turned into a roaring fireplace. With their hands extended over the fire, they would talk about the day to come, the weather, and the scores from the sports world from the day before. High school basketball and football and major league baseball were the lead subjects. Sometimes they would talk about projects that had

Scopena shop (present day view)

to be worked on or operations they would tackle in the days ahead.

These were not the most important meetings held at Scopena—those were held at 6:00 a.m. in the office with the supervisors—but they were the best ones. The talk at the shop informed everyone of the biggest needs that day. It might be a tractor with an engine smoking because of an oil leak. It had to be checked. Or it might be a mechanical cotton picker that was not operating properly. It had to be recalibrated.

Anyone could attend the shop meetings. As a small boy, I found this shop meeting and its conversations to be most stimulating. I attended the meetings at the shop every Saturday morning during the school year and every day in the summer time. I learned where the problems on the farm were and where the activities of the day were to be centered.

The shop manager was named James Boyd, and he was a complex genius. Mr. Boyd—I always called him that, even after I became governor—could fix any kind of equipment needing repair and could build just about anything. At Dad's request, he made a trampoline for my seventh Christmas that was huge and lasted for fifty years, long enough for all the kids and grandkids to bounce away on it. It was cast iron and substantial. He designed it with skids on the bottom so a tractor could pull it around to the front of the house on that first Christmas day, much to the surprise and joy of the Roemer kids. The skids also allowed the trampoline to be pulled to different parts of the yard later. Dad said that Santa had built the trampoline in the shop and asked him to drag it to the front yard.

The only trouble with Mr. Boyd was he was difficult to get along with and would take direction only from Dad. Many a time I remember Mr. Boyd refusing to advance work in the shop until Dad would arrive to consult with him and get his understanding on the matter. Come to think of it, Mr. Boyd and Dad were a lot alike: good with people, but better by themselves. In short, they were unafraid to stand alone. I never found out why Mr. Boyd was so beholden to Dad, but he was. Perhaps they recognized in each other kindred spirits.

I remember one more thing about Mr. Boyd. He was a champion curser. I heard words and phrases from Mr. Boyd, the likes I've never heard before or since. For some reason, I've tried subconsciously to imitate Mr. Boyd in his cussing as the years roll by. Hard as I try, I'm still an amateur in comparison. (Note that I admit to being a pretty good curser to this day, and Mr. Boyd gets 99 percent of the credit for that.)

It was at these shop meetings that I first wanted to smoke when I was seven or eight. The men around the fire all smoked. It was the habit that grown-ups wore best I thought, and I wanted to be a grown-up.

The men gloried in smoking, forming a community of their own. They laughed and jabbed their cigarettes in the air to make points. They lit each other's cigarettes. They borrowed cigarettes from each other. They coughed. They blew large clouds of smoke. They were always about to light a cigarette or about to put one out.

They all had a pack of cigarettes rolled in their sleeves or in their pocket front. They had Camels, Lucky Strikes, Chesterfields, Marlboros, Winstons, Kools, or Kents. One guy had a Prince Albert can of loose tobacco that he used to roll his own. They were so cool; I wanted to be one of them, too.

My brother Danny and I would sometimes get the makings for cigarettes and smoke when we were out riding our horses beginning when we were around twelve years old. When I got to Harvard, I bought Winston Lights and smoked when I studied or when I bullshitted with roommates. I remember using the cigarette like the men in the shop: to emphasize a point or to brandish it as a rhetorical weapon at one of my conversational partners. My brother never became an addicted cigarette smoker. He was athletic and played on the tennis team at Harvard, but the real reason I believe that he never became addicted was because he never went to the shop meetings.

I continued to smoke off and on beginning at sixteen for forty years until I quit a few months before I got married to Scarlett at the age of fifty-eight. I never enjoyed smoking as much as I did back at Scopena, before the roaring fireplace with the gang of workers and supervisors at the shop. I'd sneak a cigarette when Dad didn't show up for the shop meetings, and I was feeling brave in front of the other men. I wonder if anybody ever told Dad? They kidded me about it, but Dad never mentioned it.

I went back to the shop fire when I was home from college, when I was seventeen or eighteen, but it wasn't the same. The conversations were more stilted than I had remembered. I got a sense of the passage of time there. It was the first time that I ever had that feeling that perhaps the men considered me more of a boss, now that I was a college student.

There were large commercial scales adjacent to the shop to weigh loads of corn, soybeans, sunflowers, cotton, and cattle as the trucks carrying the produce came in. Scopena had two such trucks and trailers, which carried grain and hauled cattle to market or from one section of grazing land to another, in their own parking space on the back side of the shop.

Dad designed the scales ingeniously so that they were built into a roadway next to the office. You would drive the truck and trailer onto the ramp containing the scales, park, hit a button, be weighed, have the ticket automatically be printed, and then drive away to your destination. No waste, no bother, and you had an official printout of your cargo's weight and the time of day.

The other major operation working at Scopena was the grain complex (corn and soybeans primarily, but sorghum and sunflower seeds as well). It contained six storage tanks of 25,000 bushels each, which were interconnected to a heating system capable of drying the grain. There were a series of elevators and distribution arteries that could unload, off-load, or dispense grain in whatever mixture and from whatever tank you desired. They were great places to climb on or to hide in when I was growing up.

It was a very sophisticated operation, and the equipment was rugged because in the mid-1950s Scopena relied on its hybrid seed corn and soybean grain crop to secure a portion of its total revenue. Cotton accounted for another 70 percent of the revenue. Cattle were about 10 percent.

Scopena had about one hundred people (supervisors and workers, white and black) living near the headquarters. Their houses were small, with three rooms on average, but clean. Some houses were near the big house, where our family lived. Others were next to the shop, and some were next to the levee near the back of the headquarters. There were about sixty houses on Scopena; all the same size except for the big house. The remainder of the workers lived in private houses up and down Highway 71 or in Scopena housing not at the headquarters—at McDade or Hopewell or Elm Grove.

Besides the shop, the gin and the delinter, and the storage and processing facilities for grain, seed, and raw cotton were the major parts of the Scopena facilities. In addition, we had seven airplanes that sprayed pesticides to eradicate harmful insects from the cotton. They took off from a grass-mowed airstrip of more than a mile in length.

The runway was located just north of Scopena's main office, running east and west from the fuel and mixing tanks located by the main office to the levee a mile away. The primary plane was a bi-wing of two sizes, either a 220-hp Stearman or a 450-hp Stearman. Scopena's customers favored the bi-wing Stearman. Its two wings gave it the ability to put insecticide in tight corners of the field thanks to its high rate of climb. Besides the Stearman, we had a single-wing Piper Cub used by Dad to fly over the place to observe how things were going.

One of the biggest causes of crashes while spraying cotton fields were highline wires at the end of the field between telephone poles. The pilot of the spray plane could not see the high lines, we discovered. We solved the problem by hanging a plastic marker on the highline wires between the poles at the start of a season.

The mixing tanks for the preparation of the poison insecticide were located at the eastern end of the runway near the airplanes' tie-down spaces. They were in a large shed that contained barrels of insecticide, a mixing tank, and a water well.

The mix master would prepare the poison in the correct mixture and pump that mixture into the proper airplane. A plane would have to return to the runway every hour to refuel with diesel and to reload a mixture of pesticide. The poison utilized was mostly methyl parathion and toxaphene—a highly dangerous mixture—or DDT. The insecticide was usually a liquid, but sometimes it was a powder, applied as a dust. The shed to mix the poisons was located near the Scopena office because the office had the instructions for the ingredients for each batch of poison for a particular customer.

There were eight rooms in the office where the business of the farm was conducted. This is where the supervisors would meet in the morning about 6:00 to drink coffee and plan the day's activities. Dad had an office there, as did Mom and other supervisors. That is where the radio and the radio operator were located. The office was a simple construct built out of wood and was attached by a hallway to the kitchen at the north end of the big house where our family lived.

The offices had concrete floors and linoleum flooring. It was a sanctuary from dirt and dust. Mom, who was in charge of everything that had to do with the office, made sure it was kept relatively clean. The offices of Scopena and the big house were warm, peaceful places with a lot of people passing through.

Outside of Scopena, the world was cordoned off by race (black and white), but not in the office. That world was divided into two parts: Scopena clients (those who used some services provided by Scopena) and Scopena employees (those who provided the service offered to clients). About one-third of the Scopena clients were black. Although the largest customers were white—those who had the largest number of acres on their farm—you could never tell color by the service rendered to the client. The services were truly color blind. A lot of things counted about a customer of Scopena, longevity being the most important. It was one of the many lessons that I learned at Scopena: never worry about someone's race when there was a job to do.

After breakfast and getting the kids off to school on the 6:45 a.m. bus, Mom would spend the day in the office working on the books, collecting debts, paying bills, and doing the non-field work required of farmers by the federal government, such as gathering cotton samples from each bale ginned. She ran the office and often handled the shortwave radio. Its signal stretched the length and width of Scopena.

Mom was into books and the knowledge therein. She made sure that books were a daily part of her children's life at home. She also introduced books to the main office at Scopena. She featured three books each week in the office. The books were displayed for clients and employees alike. They could read them in the office at their leisure or check them out for three to five days to take home, like a library. The books were always checked out it seemed.

So the office at Scopena was used by clients to gather insecticide application schedules, get ginning tickets, arrange cotton trailer pickup and delivery, pick out books, and drink coffee and gossip. There was a lot of visiting in the office between the customers of

Scopena and the neighbors of the farms near and far. A lot of the discussion centered on cotton, but they also talked politics, the weather, and sports. The office at Scopena became a community forum to the farmers in the area. The books helped.

The community forum can sometimes turn bad, as it did in November of 1963 when President John Kennedy was shot in Dallas. A distant neighbor who was in our office as the news of the president's death was announced, said something like "it's about time." Dad got up out of his chair and slugged the guy, knocking him to the ground. The man never returned to Scopena.

BOOKS AND HOME SCHOOLING

I went to public schools in the nearest town, Bossier City, about fifteen miles from Scopena. A lot of a young person's life is lived at school. Mine was no different. From the first day, I rode the school bus to school. It was a 6:45 a.m. departure and a 4:15 p.m. return. We weren't all in the same grade on the school bus. First-graders and seniors and everybody in between were all together for about an hour each way each day. It was the only place in school we were together. Many a day, I learned more on the school bus than I did in the classroom: what was happening in the community, what was happening in the various grades, what was happening in the outside world, and what everyone thought about it. If you listened carefully you could hear parents speaking through their children. The school bus was a mobile classroom for community social interaction.

To have a senior talk to you about a girl that he wanted to date, or a girl that he wouldn't date, was awesome. When you were older, to have a first-grader tell you what scared him and what he avoided on the school grounds was funny and a little sad. But to have them all there and to share in their prejudices and dreams, fears and hopes, was so neat.

School was organized by grade and by class within that grade, but on the bus it was organized more naturally by where you lived or by the interest in your conversation—a whole different structure—

unique, unlike the school scene. In school, you were a sixth-grader or a tenth-grader, but on the school bus you were an LSU Experiment station kid or a Scopena kid or a trailer park kid. You chose where you sat on the school bus. The school organization was artificial, by grade. The school bus was family.

I rode the school bus from first grade through graduation my senior year—all eleven years. I began first grade at Bossier Elementary, but midway through the year, our new school, Waller Elementary, opened, and I remained there through seventh grade. Waller was the newest school in Bossier Parish. It too was in Bossier City, but a couple of miles closer to Scopena, on the eastern side of the city. From my graduation from Waller's seventh grade until twelfth-grade graduation in 1960, I attended Bossier High School. The schools were all-white, even after the Supreme Court's *Brown* v. *Board of Education* decision in 1954. Even the school bus system was segregated. I can remember a cluster of black kids standing at Scopena in the adjacent spot as we whites were waiting for our 6:45 a.m. bus. And their school was next door to the white school, Bossier High School. It made no sense at all. It was stupid. It was segregation.

Getting educated at school was not enough for my parents. We also did a form of home schooling, although nobody called it that back then. As I mentioned, Mom had several responsibilities at Scopena, including paying bills and getting the government's paperwork done in a timely fashion, but her most important job was to educate the children.

She would tie her long, beautiful auburn hair in a bun and get to work with us after we got off the school bus at 4:30 p.m. She tailored a lesson for each of the five children. We all studied in the same room for ninety minutes, before it was time for our chores and then supper at 7:00 p.m.

The principles of education were strict and blunt. You were expected to learn to read early in life, and you had to read everything that was assigned to you and write a report on it. We read the local newspapers daily, the *Shreveport Times* and the *Shreveport Journal*.

We read *Time* magazine and *U.S. News and World Report* weekly. We read the farm bureau journals monthly.

Mom sent off for correspondence courses for us. One that I remember was from Baltimore. Called the Calvert School of Instruction, it was particularly good on geography. After studying it, we could name every nation on Earth and where it was located. I remember Africa being a problem because the countries kept changing names and shapes. We also studied history, literature, world conditions, and math. Math was Mom's first love, and all of us kids became advanced math students at an early age.

Mom was a small, thin woman. But she dominated a room with her personal command. A gifted teacher, she made the lessons come alive. And she made you do your work. You wanted to please her. She was also a strict disciplinarian, using one sharp strike with a twelve-inch ruler to get the attention of a misbehaving child.

Dad and Mom were readers and had a wide range of classical and non-classical books in bookcases that lined the hallways of Scopena and one wall of the living room. Many of them were history books; some were popular fiction selections from the book of the month club. Many of the books are still there today, standing guard at the gates of knowledge.

I remember the encyclopedia that we had: the *World Book*. There were about twenty volumes of the *World Book Encyclopedia* in our set. There was a volume "A" and volume "B" and "C" and "D & E" and so on through volume "X,Y,Z." I read every page of every volume. They were so exciting aninteresting. There were so many things in the world, so many places. I couldn't wait to leave Scopena to see them. It wasn't that Scopena was a bad place. It just wasn't New York or Chicago or Boston or Paris or London or Beijing.

One of the most exciting days of the year was when the annual *World Book* supplement came to keep the encyclopedia up to date. The "1954" supplement and the "1955" supplement kept me mesmerized. There was so much new information in the world every year!

The *World Book* is still there on the book shelf, I notice. I wonder if the grandkids still refer to the encyclopedia when there is research work to be done? I wonder if the annual supplement still comes that magic day in May or June? I wonder if the supplement of 2017 would interest the children of 1955? I wonder if there is a young person in 2017 aching to escape Scopena?

The one set of books that Dad and Mom insisted we plow through were the Harvard classics, a set ranging from Locke to Jefferson. I remember the day I finished reading them and writing my final book report on the classics. Dad gave me fifty dollars and told me that "focus" was one of the keys to success and that I had showed focus in reading the classics. He was proud of me. I was nine years old. I guess it was quite an accomplishment. But what impressed me most was the fifty dollars. That was a fortune to me then.

One of the most interesting books that Mom required us to read was Gibbon's *The History of the Decline and Fall of the Roman Empire*, originally published in 1776. I remember the feeling that I had when reading about the Asian hordes nibbling away at the Roman Empire. Nothing was permanent. Nothing could be taken for granted. Years later, I had to write about the book for a class at Harvard. It was an easy assignment because I had read and analyzed it when I was seven or eight.

One thing that didn't rob us of our time was television. Although Shreveport had a television station (channel 12—CBS), we did not get a television set until either my senior year in high school or my freshman year in college in 1960. I can't remember which. It's amazing how much time you have if you're not watching television.

I saw my first television in Houston in 1950 when walking down the main street with my mother while on the way to visit my Uncle Fuzzy, her brother. I still remember the image—a cowboy on the range. It was fascinating and so enticing, but having no television growing up was the gift of time to all of us kids. We got to spend time with each other and with Scopena. Television can be like a baby sitter these days, and it can also be a substitute for life. It was no factor at all for us.

As I mentioned, reading taught us the power of focus at an early age. Dad emphasized it over and over again: focus, focus, focus, and focus. When we were confronted with a crisis or a challenge, the solution was to focus. Someone had probably dealt with a similar crisis in life years before, he would say, what did they do? What could we learn from history? That knowledge was found in books. So it was in books that Mom and Dad found many of their daily lessons.

It wasn't just "focus" that Dad and Mom thought was found in books. "Speed" was found there as well. If you can be both the fastest and the most prepared, you will be hard to beat. It was the same speed that some people get from accessing Google today. Books were my Google back in the day.

Books were a record of what others had done in similar circumstances, such as the measures taken by cotton farmers to protect their crop during the great Mississippi floods in the early twentieth century. If you had the proper history book, you could enhance your speed and improve your performance. By employing speed and focus, you were more likely to succeed.

When both my brother Danny and I were accepted into Harvard years later, the admissions office noted the pace of our learning skills in their letters of acceptance. "Advanced and deeper" were the adjectives they used. That was Mom, and we owe her a great deal.

II

THE BIG SKIP

Mom's home schooling operation worked too well. By third grade, school was no longer challenging for me. Then luck intervened. At the beginning of fourth grade, my teacher, Miss Faison, decided to take a new assignment for the next school year. She would teach the sixth grade instead of the fourth. She had an idea: I would skip the fifth grade and move up to sixth grade with her. If I skipped with her, it would help me with the adjustment. My parents asked me what I thought about skipping the fifth grade. I loved the idea. Man, to miss a whole year of school and have it approved by everyone involved. What could be better?! And so I skipped. It was 1952, when I was nine, that I went from ending the fourth grade to beginning the sixth.

The problems seemed likely to be minimal. It was the same school and the same teacher. What do they teach in the fifth grade? Geography? The Calvert School classes were already teaching me that anyway. Math? It was always my easiest subject. There would be social issues and adjustments like making new friends, but I was pretty flexible and adapted easily. It helped not seeing the kids outside of school each day. They were city kids with neighborhoods and activities there. They actually had neighbors. I was a country boy, an outsider. I usually didn't see another school mate until the next day at school. Other students later worked at Scopena in the summer

Butch in the fourth grade at Waller Elementary

months, and occasionally one or two of my classmates would sleep overnight at Scopena, but that was rare. I was used to no neighbors, and that fact helped me in skipping grades. It minimized the daily adjustment I had to make.

Skipping grades had another effect on my life: I changed names. I had been called "Butch" ever since I had a memory, although I don't know why. My mother was not smitten with me being called Butch and asked me to assume another nickname. This discussion had been going on for several years in the family. Mom said that "Butch" as a name didn't fit. She added that I would be called "Charles" as an alternative. Nobody liked that because there were too many Charleses in a family filled with Charles Elson Roemer's.

Mom wanted me to try "Buddy." She never said where she got it from, but she said it wasn't too far from Butch but was a step up in class. I believed that Mom knew best. She said that we would implement the name change at school when I skipped the fifth grade. In the fourth grade, I was "Butch." When the sixth grade started three months later, I was "Buddy."

There have been all kinds of tales about where Mom got "Buddy." My favorite is that she took it from Buddy Holly when he had started his famous singing career about the same time in Lubbock, Texas. But the origins of "Buddy" could just have been a southern thing. Like Paul Theroux points out in his book *Deep South*, passersby casually called him "baby, honey, babe, buddy, dear, boss, and bubba." Mom could have picked a sound she liked from hearing it for all her life. That's my best guess.

I gave a speech once at Texas Tech University in Lubbock, and they had heard the rumor about my name. So they took me to the grave of Buddy Holly. It had a concrete guitar, which I thought was neat. They asked me if I had been, in fact, named after Buddy Holly. "No," I replied. But the truth is, I don't know where she got the name. She just liked it, as far as I know.

When summer ended following fourth grade, I rode the school bus to Waller elementary as a fifth-grader, or at least that's what everyone thought. But I walked into Miss Faison's sixth-grade class to begin my year—as Buddy. On the way back home, I explained to the students that I was now a sixth-grader named "Buddy." They thought I was spoofing them somehow. They came around eventually on the name change, but it took the better part of a year.

It is already a red letter day to skip a whole year, but to compound that action by changing names was awesome to me. Mom knew what she was doing. My new sixth-grade classmates generally weren't familiar with the old name of "Butch." The school was large with 1,200 students, and only a few of them knew me as Butch. So when I said my name was "Buddy," they thought that was it. Same school. Different classroom. Different classmates. Different grade. Different name. It was a whole new world just one grade apart: Butch in the fourth grade, and Buddy in the sixth.

I remember meeting some classmates years later who referred to me as Butch or Butchie. I could tell that they knew me in the fourth grade or before. Thinking about that makes me a bit nostalgic for my first nickname. It's been years since anyone has called me Butch. I kind of miss it.

At college, good friends called me Buddy or Charlie. Some classmates called me Chuck. I went by Buddy during my years in Congress and as governor. Given the choice, I would have picked Buddy, not Butch, not Charles, not Chuck, and not Charlie, although I have been called all those names at various times.

12

HORSES

In 1952, Dad and Mom bought six Shetland ponies from a farmer in Alexandria for the kids' Christmas that year. They let us know that Santa had brought the ponies by leaving six bridles under the Christmas tree that morning. We were excited when we found the bridles. But who were they for? Dad suggested that we go outside to the front yard and see.

There they were, tied by rope to stakes, contentedly chewing grass. We were so excited. Christmas could not have been better. These were not show horses; they were working ponies that had to be fed, watered, brushed, and combed, which is what we kids did each and every day. We rode the Shetland ponies bare back. That we could cling to those narrow shoulders while the horse was racing at full speed seems remarkable to me today. The ponies were multi-colored; painted by nature in white and brown. In truth, the ponies were stubborn and difficult. It took a while for us to fall in love with them. But man they were awesome.

Dad purposefully bought Shetland's because they are small. All of us ended up being bucked off many times—the Shetland ponies were not an easy ride. But injuries were rare since you were close to the ground when you fell.

We named them after the characters in *Peter Pan* or an Indian tribe. Danny named his "Apache." My pony was already named

"Wendy." There was "Tiger Lily" and "Tinkerbell," too.

Once at the end of fourth grade, I made plans with my buddies to ride horses to school. My friends—Jimmy Tharp, Richard Johnson, and Robbie Hucklebridge—spent the night before the ride at Scopena. We left at about 6:00 a.m., to make the eleven-mile ride in time for the first bell. The only eventful happening on the journey to school was the passing of a Kansas City Southern freight train when we were halfway to town. The engineer apparently decided it was neat seeing four kids on horseback so early that Friday morning. So he blew his whistle. The horses were so startled that we had to dismount and hold their bridles until the engineer stopped. After a while the ponies quit bucking and regained their composure. Upon arriving at Waller Elementary, we staked them with steel rods to pasture in the grassy field behind the school.

My kids and grandkids don't believe that I rode my horse to school. I did. Not often, but enough to officially log it. It was a wonder in 1953-1954 and caused enormous community attention. Among fourth-graders, I became "famous" with a front-page write-up in the school paper.

We rode the horses literally thousands of hours from Scopena to my Granddaddy Ross's house at McDade, to school in Bossier City, and round about the plantation. The only time I was ever hurt while riding occurred in the summer of 1954 when I was ten years old. I had a group of friends down to Scopena for a Friday night sleepover. There was Robbie, Richard, and Pete Hendon. Around noon on Saturday, we had an early lunch and decided to ride our horses back toward the river away from the house. After riding on the sandy beaches of the Red River, we turned back to the house about five miles away. I was on Wendy.

We rode along the top of the levee to return to the Scopena office, as we often did. Of course, someone had an idea like young boys do that it would be fun to race the horses back to Scopena headquarters along the top of the levee. After much jostling and shouting the race was on. At two hundred yards, I was in the lead by more than a

Shetland ponies at Scopena

head with three ponies right behind me.

I don't know exactly what happened. Wendy might have stumbled, or maybe I just slipped. We were riding bareback after all. In the excitement of the race, I fell on the rock hard levee top.

Horses go out of their way to avoid hitting an object on the ground so, although they were running full speed, the other horses jumped and dodged me as best they could. That caused them to throw Richard and Pete. In the midst of the confusion, one of the tangled horses landed squarely on my right arm, pinning it against the ground. I could tell it was broken by the way it hurt and hung limply at my side when I got to my feet.

I jumped up behind Robbie on his horse, and we rode back to Scopena headquarters about two miles away. There, Mom took one look and said we had to go to the hospital in Shreveport. We climbed into the car and away we went to the Highland Sanitarium.

Dr. Goslee met me in the emergency room, set my arm, and insisted that I spend the night for observation. I spent several weeks in an arm cast, but there were no lasting effects. Dad grumbled that I needed to stop racing or learn how to ride better, or some words to that effect.

It was the only time that a horse really hurt me while riding bareback for hundreds of hours and thousands of miles, until ten years later when I was bitten on the chest by a mare in a pasture protecting her newborn foal. The mother horse was perhaps threatened by something I had done that morning. She had never charged at me before. I think it was the fact that I had gotten between her and her colt.

Turning on me suddenly and unexpectedly, the mare charged from about twenty-five feet with her head extended toward me, like a battering ram with bared teeth, aiming at my throat. I threw my hand up just in time to divert her bite. She ripped my chest just below my throat. I was knocked sprawling and had to go to the emergency room. It took three weeks to recover, but I was very lucky that day. Between a Mama and her baby is not where you want to be.

13

The Levee

Running through the western edge of Scopena—where the gin, the shop, the office, and the big house are located—is a levee 25 feet high and 50 feet wide at its bottom and 20 feet across at its top. It is imposing compared to the flat cotton land that surrounds it. The levee was built in the late 1920s by the state of Louisiana to help prevent flooding in the spring, when rains from up north swell the Red River. The river forms the western boundary of Scopena.

The Red River begins in the western edge of Oklahoma and the northern boundary of Texas, forms the border between Texas and Oklahoma, and turns south to form a small part of the border between Texas and Louisiana before flowing into the Mississippi River below Alexandria. There is a Red River in Minnesota at the headwaters of the Mississippi, but our Red River flows quietly during much of the year in Texas, Oklahoma, and Louisiana. It springs to a wild ride of flood waters only every few years. The flooding occurs usually not because of snow melt but from heavy rainfall in southern Oklahoma and northern west Texas.

Scopena sprawled on the east bank of the Red River off and on for thirty miles when it was at its biggest size in the 1950s, and floods could be a threat to the cotton crop in its earliest, most important growth stages, during March, April, and May when it was just planted. The levee was designed to protect the crop from this spring flooding. The levee ties into the system of levees reining in the Mississippi River, into which the Red River flows sixty-eight miles below Alexandria. The levee is maintained by the Bossier-Bodcau Levee District and the Army Corps of Engineers.

In most places, the levee is green with bermuda and other types of grasses. The authorities let the levee grasses be baled for hay to feed horses and cattle and let cattle graze on the levee since the animals do not hinder the use of the levee for flood control.

You could stand on the top of the levee and see the winding Red River off to the west. There was about one half mile to a mile from the top of the levee to the river itself. Much of that land was temporary from month to month as the river twisted and turned, growing sand bars, replete with quicksand eddies.

Some of these plots of land became rich spots to grow cotton and soybeans. These parcels were called "the cut across the levee" or "Hopewell cut across the levee" or "McDade cut across the levee." They amounted to several thousands of acres across the levee in non-flood periods, they were subject to flooding every couple of years because they weren't protected by the levee.

Because the land across the levee was so important to Scopena, and because it was subject to periodic flooding, the levee maintenance board and Scopena had good relations. Periodically, the board checked the levee to insure its good condition or to cut the grass. We always cooperated with these requests and took down gates where the mowing machines operated or access was inhibited by fences that crisscrossed the levee for cattle control.

The levee was a thing of majestic size on Scopena, and it became a place of wonder and delight for those of us who grew up there. A series of small lakes on the river side of the levee were created when dirt was first dug decades before to form the levee. These small ponds or lakes became places to fish or to shoot ducks when my brother and I were youngsters.

I caught my first fish, a bream, with a bamboo pole in one of those lakes when I was six. I caught my first butterflies on the levee behind the Scopena shop. I also shot my first blackbirds on the top of the levee when I was six, with a .410 gauge shotgun. On another occasion, I hid on the far side of the levee and crept up on three teal swimming in a small pond while hunting with my .28 gauge. I rose and shot the three ducks on flight with three shots. It was something that I never accomplished again, even as an adult.

I used to take long walks on the levee when I wanted to be all alone with my thoughts. I would leave the house, walk the mile down to the end of the runway, get on the levee, and take a left or right on the levee depending on whether my walk and thinking was going to be long or short.

I would turn left if my journey was short, say thirty minutes, and loop around to the shop and the Scopena office. If I turned left, I was ready to get back, my problem having been solved.

But if I turned right, I still had deep thinking to do, and walking away from Scopena was just what I needed. It could be whether to go out for football in the sixth grade (I didn't), what to do about a B in tenth-grade speech class at Bossier High School (I worked harder and got A's thereafter), getting prepared for my student body president election speech at BHS (I blew them away), or some political decision—whether to "buy" votes—when I was running for office (I didn't.)

Looking back on this habit, I think it was a form of "bouncing," but more acceptable by family members and co-workers. The addiction of bouncing in the back seat of a car or focusing on imaginary things where I was the hero had evolved to a long walk down a runway and a levee.

The levee meant something else growing up. It was a place that strangers to Scopena would visit for a social outing, a scenic tour, or a view that they couldn't get otherwise in the flat land of the Red River valley. Public and private schools would call us to get permission to bring their classes down to see and feel the levee. So did civic clubs that wanted to hold a barbeque on the top of the levee, or the Jaycees who wanted to hold a party and dance.

One of the unique requests came from the pastor of a black Baptist church. As I learned later, he said that he had eight children to baptize into the faith and didn't know a better place than in one of the small lakes behind the levee. He wanted to do it on the Sunday before Easter—Palm Sunday.

Dad told the pastor that it was quite all right and that morning in the office he would leave the key to the gates that crisscrossed the levee.

We went to the early service at First Methodist Church in Shreveport. After we returned to Scopena for lunch, I soon noticed a steady stream of cars passing the office, headed to the levee.

Dad suggested that Danny and I go to the levee and see what was happening for ourselves. It might be interesting. I was ten, and Danny was eight.

He and I got our horses in the pasture, bridled them, and rode them bareback down the runway toward the levee at the far end, about two miles from the office. We saw fifty or more cars and trucks parked on the levee.

We dismounted, tied up our horses, and crept up the far side of the levee. We decided it was best if we remained unseen, so we slipped under the cars to watch the proceedings below. We thought that for some reason, they might not like us being there since they were Baptists and we were Methodists. Plus we weren't dressed for church. And there was the racial aspect, although we didn't even think of that at the time.

As a Methodist, all the baptisms that I had ever seen were "sprinkle" baptisms, where water was sprinkled out of some "Methodist" bottle. The baby did not really get wet. The Baptists baptized young adults, not children. Danny and I were there to see what it looked like. It was all a mystery to me.

We saw a large crowd of parents and grandparents, members of the church flock—maybe 125 in number—gathered around the small lake. We were only fifty feet from the crowd, but unseen. The pastor was standing knee-deep in the water. He had a Bible in his left hand and to his right in the water was a young assistant pastor. The pastor was wearing what looked to be a white robe over his pants. Before him on the bank of the lake stood eight young people that were joyous in their singing and clapping in rhythm, along with everyone else. We could tell that they were going to be baptized.

The preacher was talking to the young candidates when he called them out one by one to join him waist-deep in the water. "This could be another little Mary," he said to one. "This could be a Joshua," he said to another.

Each youngster was smiling as the preacher took him or her into his arms and prepared to dip them into the water.

The preacher was in his sermon voice the whole time, so we could clearly hear him from our spot on top of the levee. "Does this little Mary or does this little Joshua takes Jesus into his heart? Does this Peter receive the Christ as the only god in earth or in heaven? All we know is that this person accepts Jesus Christ as his lord and by doing that will someday walk with God hand in hand to the Promised Land. Look at little Sarah. Praise be to God."

And with that the preacher took the child and dunked her below the surface. When he lifted the child to the surface again, he said, "Jesus, this soul is yours. Make her whatever you need in the world. It could be James or Joshua or John or Peter or Sarah or Mary or someone who washes the feet of the lord or someone who commands mighty armies. We don't know. We do know this person and whatever they do will be yours. Amen, Jesus. Amen."

The crowd exalted to high heaven with every baptism. Eight times they made enough noise that heaven must have heard their cries as the preacher dunked eight little Marys and little Joshuas. Danny and I were transfixed in our hiding spot. We had never seen anything like it. We Methodists weren't used to a baptismal ceremony that included immersion in the water of a lake. But it wasn't just that. It was the joy in the crowd. It was the sermon of the minister. It was the rapture of the children.

As the festivities were ending, Danny and I glanced at each other, an unspoken signal that it was time to go. We scooted backward from underneath the car, raced to our horses on the far side of the levee, mounted, and rode as fast as we could toward home. We found Dad and told him what we had heard and seen. He just said that he respected the Baptists. It was private. It was so special, so sacred.

While observing what was happening down below, we felt, as did the crowd, that the height and bulk of the levee somehow kept the world away, making the baptism almost seem like a secret ritual. As a result, I think, Danny and I never talked about that day.

We parted the curtain and saw the joy of parents and grandparents and common church-goers. The levee had given them quiet grace.

The event confirmed to our young minds what Dad had said all along in the supper table discussions at Scopena: blacks were human beings like the rest of us. The only possible difference between us was the quality of education, and that had nothing to do with color. Nothing. It only had to do with evil notions of men.

The levee was to be a place of riding and walking and horse races, of going to fishing holes, of separation from the world that was hustling to its own beat, and of protection from the floods of the mighty Red River. But for that Palm Sunday in 1953, it was a mighty cathedral of God.

14

TORNADO

My biggest house-bound memory was a storm in 1952. Most summer storms blew in from the west with rain and sometimes hail, blasting the house at right angles. Looking back, the house held up surprisingly well over the years and kept us safe and dry. But I thought our good luck was going to run out one early summer day in 1952. I was eight, nearly nine years old.

June had been hot, and this late June day was especially hot and humid with thunderstorms building throughout the day. I was working in the fields but had returned to the house that afternoon to get a baseball cap to wear in the hot sun. Looking out of the boys' bedroom window, I noticed that the sky had turned ominously black except for flashes of lightning in the dark sky. There was no noise—and there was no wind. Just quiet. I must have sensed that something was afoot because I kept staring out the window.

Then I saw it. About a mile away—on top of the levee—I saw a funnel cloud. It was small and black, and it was headed right for the house. It blew over the equipment sheds and feeding troughs in the field next to the shop. I saw the wind peel off the wood planks and various sidings of the small barns in its path. And the tornado kept heading my way. Soon, it was less than two hundred yards away. I couldn't stop staring out the window at the twister. I was transfixed. Everything was moving in slow motion. It was coming right at me, and it seemed much stronger than I had originally thought.

The air was blowing a gale and the noise was earthshaking. I thought the funnel was going to hit the west side of the house. I dived to the floor and pulled the blanket off the bed to cover my head. Obviously, a blanket would have been no protection. However, with the storm right on top of me, I couldn't think of anything else to do. As I waited for disaster to strike, I thought about how I hadn't fully lived my life yet. I thought about how my family and friends would miss me but hadn't seen everything I was capable of achieving. I would die before I made my mark in the world.

But the tornado veered northeast at the last possible moment. It missed me. It destroyed the chicken coop-garage immediately to the west of the house. Just leveled it. There were no cars in it, but the chickens inside the coop were thrown in all directions. Most did not survive.

I don't know how or why the house was spared. I did not see the tornado turn north and west. My head was buried in that blanket on the floor of my bedroom. But turn it did.

I jumped off the floor after about thirty seconds when I realized the tornado had missed me. I ran outside to survey the storm damage. I was so happy that I kept jumping up and down for joy. I had survived. It was a miracle as far as I could tell.

Under a deep yellow and brown sky, I surveyed a bunch of dead chickens scattered about the backyard, a path of debris from the farm equipment yard to the edge of the house. About ten minutes later, quarter-sized hail began to fall, and this lasted for fifteen minutes.

Afterward, I examined the tracks of the twister, leading up to the house and then veering away. During the cleanup, I found out that nobody in the house or office had seen the twister when it came at us and then turned abruptly away. They had been performing other tasks. They had heard what sounded like an intense summer thunderstorm—a storm that happens two or three times a year at Scopena. Little did they know that that thunderstorm had contained a mighty twister.

As I stood surveying the scene, it was as quiet as it had been loud a few minutes before. And it was like the earth glowed. Everything moved in a surrealistic manner. People seemed unconnected to what they had been doing. It was like everything was in a dream state. People seemed to walk in slow motion. There was no traffic on Highway 71 in front of the office. At least that's the way I remember it more than sixty years later.

Truly, it was a miracle at Scopena that day. I never saw another tornado at Scopena again, or anywhere else. And I had been spared to live out my life.

I've seen the television shows on the Weather Channel the last few years depicting the guys and girls who go out in the Plains States—Oklahoma, Kansas, Nebraska—and search for storms. I have no desire to do that on my own, because I have been way too close to a twister.

15

CHRISTINE

Back to the kitchen. It was the center of the house and was run by two large black women: Christine Lyles and Romie Lee Henderson, with Christine being in charge. Christine lived in a small house next to ours, right around the corner from the back steps of the kitchen. Her husband, Albert, was one of the main tractor drivers and was a valued member of the gin crew. Romie Lee lived by herself in a small house in the Scopena quarters, about one-half mile from the office.

Christine was clearly the boss of the kitchen. Any man who came there for a cup of coffee, a slice of bacon, or a scrap of food had to acknowledge Christine and get her permission. Christine was a large woman, with oversized arms and an oversized appreciation for the joy of life. She was good with the kids. She would keep us the few nights that my parents had to go to town. We could get away with mischief like stealing cookies or cornbread that had been prepared for lunch or a special occasion. She always defended the kids' thievery to Mom and Dad, saying we were "just being chillen." She cooked for us Monday through Saturday, and Sunday, too, when we ate at home and not at my grandmother's or at Morrison's cafeteria in downtown Shreveport after church.

Above all, Christine was a great cook. She had no formal training. She had grown up on Scopena and worked in the kitchen at the

Percy "Money" McCraney and Chrstine Lyles

house that had stood there before Dad built our place. That was a much smaller operation than Scopena became. Christine tried recipes from prior cooks and attempted recipes of her own in the new kitchen. Mom, Dad, and the men told her what worked. And before you knew it, Christine was the acknowledged cook for the Scopena kitchen. She was twenty-nine when we moved to Scopena in October of 1949.

The main meal she cooked was lunch—mounds of fried chicken, corn bread, black-eyed peas, corn on the cob, salad tossed in giant, wooden bowls, chocolate crème pie, and glasses filled with sweetened iced tea. She cooked pork chops and roasted chicken and other things, to be sure, but her fried chicken—golden brown with a crispy crust—was better than any I ever had anywhere.

She cooked breakfast as well—with eggs any style; bacon, cut thick by the butcher, Dad wouldn't have it any other way, and fried to a slight curl; hot chocolate; big glasses of milk; oatmeal steaming in china bowls; pancakes; cinnamon toast by the stack; and various cold cereals with strawberries and peaches. For supper, she prepared smothered pork chops, steak, fried catfish, or meatloaf.

I rarely saw Mom cook a meal at Scopena, and I never saw Christine eat at the big table.

One of the things that Scopena featured was fresh vegetables and fruit. We had an interest in a farm that raised vegetables that were harvested every day and taken by truck to market. That farm operated in south Shreveport about ten miles from Scopena. "Money" McCraney, the black man who operated it, brought the fresh produce each morning to Scopena. There were tomatoes and greens, onions and squash. There were strawberries and peaches and watermelon and cantaloupe—something, every day.

Money was not quite an employee. Dad set him up as an independent contractor and financed his operations. As a result, Money had his own produce store in Shreveport. He retained all the proceeds. In return, he delivered fresh produce to Scopena at 9:30 every morning, in lieu of paying interest on the funds lent to him by Dad.

Money did this every morning that I was growing up on Scopena and for years afterward until his death in 1995. Money, a small, light-colored, distinguished man, had two children who helped him with his business. They went on to get degrees from LSU and become business leaders themselves. They were both hired as state employees when Dad became Louisiana's commissioner of administration, the governor's top appointee.

Money was a lifelong friend of Dad's. The reason for the friendship was that Money grew up on Scopena and became friends with Dad when they were both children. The friendship turned into a financial and business arrangement between the two men. I didn't realize it at the time, but the relationship between a white man and black man was most unusual. But it was well-known by the business community of northwest Louisiana.

Christine stayed on duty at the Scopena kitchen after all the Roemer children grew up and went off to college.

16

SOLVING THE WORLD'S PROBLEMS, ONE MEAL AT A TIME

Supper was the quiet meal at Scopena because it was just family at the table. But it was at this "quiet" meal that the family had deep discussions about the issues of the day and our position on them. These were real discussions with points outlined on a blackboard. Dad managed the show, but Mom and all five kids participated. There might be tears and anger. But slowly we would come to a consensus.

The blackboard was essential at the nighttime supper discussions. We would eat at 7:00 or 7:30 p.m. Dad used the time to teach as he led us through the discussions for the evening. Sometimes the discussion was heated, and Dad would be on his feet for what seemed like the entire supper. At other times, the debate was more subdued. Dad would remain seated and become just a voice with an opinion. Supper varied in length from thirty minutes to two hours.

Supper lasted late into the evening when Dad felt the need to cover a specific lesson or address an ongoing topic that had everyone charged up. The lessons addressed a variety of subjects—all at the whim of Dad, although he was always open to a question or a possible topic from one of the kids. It could be an article from one of the daily newspapers, the *Shreveport Times* or the *Shreveport Journal*. It could be a lesson from the farm. Or it could be about where our next summer's vacation should be. It could be a history lesson about the founding of the United States. It could be about money—how to

The butcher-block eating table with Mom at one end, Dad at the other, and Margaret, Mine, Danny, Melinda, and Melanie in place

save it, how to manage it. (Dad loved the lessons of Napoleon Hill, a renowned national investment advisor.) Or the focus could be other personal habits that he felt were important to being a good citizen, such as reading the newspaper daily.

"You must be well-informed," he would say, as he asked us questions from the day's news. Everyone was expected to participate. I realized that my little sisters, Melinda and Melanie, were growing up when they started asking questions at the supper table in the late 1950s.

One of the things that Dad believed in was communication. Not just talking and listening to the average citizen—he was an advocate of "democracy" as the form of government America should practice. He railed constantly against fascists and socialists and their inevitable power-grab for take over of our democratic government, but he liked the ability of each family member being able to communicate with organizations—church groups, civic clubs, police unions, etc.—directly, when we got the opportunity.

Dad believed so much in the power of communication in each of us, that he signed up the whole family for a six-week Dale Carnegie course on public speaking. Mom, Dad, all the five kids, and Cookie, Judy, Randy, Charlton, and David, our wives and husbands, were signed up for the course. And this was in the late 1960s before any of us were running or had run for public office. Simply put, Dad thought we had a civic duty to give our views to our fellow men in an organized, Dale Carnegie-way.

But it was before that, in the 1950s, that we started serious discussions at the supper table with each person expected to contribute and participate in some way. Little did I realize that Dad was preparing us for leading church class, for the school board, for the police jury, for Congress, and for the governor's office. Truly remarkable.

No alcohol or wine was served at lunch or during supper. We drank water or iced tea, unsweetened or sweetened with real sugar. I was not a type 1 diabetic yet. When I got the disease in my twenty-ninth year, after I had graduated from college, I could no longer use the Louisiana cane sugar in my iced tea that I had enjoyed at the Scopena table. And alcohol was never a viable option for me either, whether I was a diabetic or not. Dad didn't countenance it, and I didn't like its taste.

Meals at the lunch table were just as memorable during summer months when we didn't have school and were at home. There were guests for lunch every day: farming neighbors, equipment salesmen, crop-duster pilots, friends of Mom and Dad from town or from church. You never knew who would show up. There were also always three or four people from Scopena who were working on one of Dad's special projects. The projects changed every day. So did the people, as a result.

Regardless of the crowd gathered at the table, Dad led the discussion. It often would get passionate, prompting Dad to direct the overheated party to calm down and drink more of that sweet, iced tea. Dad was usually careful not to dominate the conversation. Often, he just listened. I can still feel him holding back, in order to give others a chance to contribute.

I remember he often would tell me as we rode around in the Jeep after lunch that the lunch-table comments were not indicative of what the community feelings were. He felt that our friends were elevating their comments to adjust to the special circumstances of Scopena: the presence of white and black people at the table, the quality of the discourse, the lack of a real thought being unusual.

We didn't tarry over lunch. One hour was the limit as there was work to be done. But while there, Mom and Dad treated us kids as adults who were expected to hold and to express our informed opinions.

At first, the guests didn't take kindly to being called out by a ten, eleven, or twelve year old. But the rules of debate would prevail. Everyone at the table was expected to have opinions on sports, on LSU, on tennis, on politics, on world matters, on the conditions of the mules, on the Shetland ponies, on how to kill boll weevils, on the latest political rhubarb, and so on and on.

The spirit, quality, diversity, and inclusiveness of debate at Scopena at the lunch table during the summers of the 1950s have never been matched anywhere else I have ever been.

And I have eaten lunch with a couple of presidents, with congressmen by the score, with senators by the dozen, with Wall Street moguls, with business tycoons (Donald Trump, for example) with foreign potentates, with movie and sports celebrities, and with Harvard students and professors (including Margaret Mead, John Kenneth Galbraith, and Henry Kissinger). While I was governor from 1988-92, I attracted all sorts of guests for free lunch at the governor's mansion, including Ron Brown, the wonderful head of the national Democratic Party, just before I switched parties in 1991 to become a Republican. Others included Lee Atwater, the fiery head of the Republican Party from South Carolina, and Bill Clinton many times when he was governor of Arkansas. He'd talk about running for president. Funny, he never talked about Arkansas, but his conversation was always stimulating.

Nowhere was the conversation as profound, as fun, and as stimulating as those debates over lunch in the big house at Scopena. Ask anyone who participated—Alphonse Jackson Jr., a black man who went on to become a great state representative; Jim Leslie, an advertising executive assassinated years later by the order of the Shreveport police chief; Leon Tarver, who went on to become president of Southern University; Johnnie Horton, a country and western singer and his singing buddy, Claude King; David Melville, a cotton authority at the LSU Red River Valley Experiment Station (his son, David, would eventually marry my youngest sister, Melanie); Ben Sour, who was married to mom's first cousin (Billie Elston) and was a friend of the family; Stan Tiner, a friend and editor of the *Shreveport Journal*, who went on to win the Pulitzer Prize while head of a Mississippi newspaper; Virginia Shehee, who became the first woman to be elected to the state senate without succeeding her husband; and Nalda Averett, my uncle, who married my mother's older sister, Aunt Emily, and who farmed cotton just south of us.

A subject that generated deep discussion at the lunch and supper tables in the mid-1950s was the question of bomb shelters for private homes. The Cold War was hot, and it was possible for a family to have a shelter underground to protect itself from a nuclear blast. Should Scopena have one?

Bomb shelters were one of the topics that carried over from the lunch table to the supper table when someone asked, "What about the people who lived in housing on Scopena? Should bomb shelters be provided for them, too?"

I hadn't thought about the other people on Scopena. I had just thought about my family, and I wanted us to build a shelter. But thinking of others caused me to change my mind. The debate raged on for weeks. We argued over whether the food supply should last one day, one week, one month, or longer. We talked about how to dig underground shelters when water existed just a few feet below the surface.

One night after a full discussion we called for a vote by all on whether or not we should have a bomb shelter for us. We couldn't build a shelter for all the families of Scopena. Mom said that we owed it to the family to build the shelter and that we should build it ourselves, not asking any help from others who wouldn't be protected.

I argued that we couldn't hide the shelter; that the other families would know that we were building a shelter for us and not for them. It was a terrible thing to do I said, and it was against everything we stood for at Scopena. I further said that I didn't want to live if the other Scopena families perished.

The question was defeated 2-5 with Mom and one of the girls in the affirmative. We asked if any of the losers wanted to continue the debate, and Mom said that she thought we should leave the question open in case something should change in the future.

We never built a bomb shelter for ourselves or any of the workers at Scopena, but we came close. At least we talked about it—at length.

My guess is that conversations like ours happened all across America, maybe not in the same exact circumstances, but with similar choices. It would have taken fifteen or more shelters to protect all of Scopena's permanent workers, and that's not counting the neighbors and friends beyond Scopena. We decided that it would take millions of dollars. So we chose to be involved as citizens, and to stand with our country politically, to deter nuclear missiles with the threat of mutual destruction and a strong military. It was a good, hard fought decision. And we stuck with the workers of Scopena.

17

DEBATING INTEGRATION

We also discussed civil rights at length. The discussions lasted days and days and days, and it was a subject brought up multiple times around the family table at suppertime. Although we mentioned "civil rights" issues at lunch, the discussion wasn't meant for deep talking and resolution. That sort of deep thinking was reserved for members of the family at the evening meal, where luncheon strangers were not present. Looking back, the discussion of civil rights was almost too personal, too controversial, to be held at the lunch table in front of guests.

Civil rights was the issue of the times. Interestingly, some sixty years later the discussion of race continues unabated in America. Looking back, the debate at Scopena was not about the question of integration—we didn't see how America could work at its best divided by color—it was more about the best way to get it done. The Declaration of Independence was quite clear on the subject, and Mom and Dad were very clear on it, as well: all men were equal.

One thing that we didn't talk about was our failure to provide equal employment for blacks at Scopena. Blacks were better off at Scopena than they were in the community, but we still had a culture where blacks were kept subservient to whites. This discrimination was observed in small ways—hat in hand when addressing a white overseerer—and sometimes in big ways—having to go to poorly funded black schools of public education.

Blacks were treated as second-class citizens in most places, even Scopena, when I was growing up. If you were black, it was difficult to vote. You had to watch a movie in the balcony of a theater or from the back row. Bathrooms were segregated, as were drinking fountains and restaurants. So were public schools. Not surprisingly, the schools that blacks attended were poorly funded and not as good by anybody's criteria as the "white" public schools. Schools were separate and not equal. And in so many ways, so were our lives. It was years later that we found out that our black friends had gone to schools without a book for every subject, often without separate classrooms for individual grades, and in buildings that were so run down that they didn't fully protect the students from falling rain or freezing winds.

It was odd having black friends like Junior Duncantell and Albert Lyles who were about the same age and had the same interests—baseball, riding horses, the river, bees, yet we never discussed the differences in our schools. It was as if we understood they were being mistreated, but that if we didn't question them openly, it would somehow all go away.

There was a different set of rules for black people. If a black man stopped to fix a flat tire for an unaccompanied white woman, he couldn't have any conversation with her unless it was very formal and very proper. A black man who ignored these rules could lose his job or put his life in peril.

Some politicians thrived on depicting blacks as inhuman, and ordinary people used the "n" word in everyday language.

My parents felt that citizens of America should be treated fairly and be fully protected under the law, so things were different at Scopena than elsewhere in the south. We had black supervisors, and we had white supervisors. A white man ran one shift at the gin, and a black man ran another. They were paid the same. Of course, it all began with Dad. I never heard him use the "n" word. Not when he was mad nor in casual conversation. I can say that growing up I never knew any other white man like Dad. Blacks ate at the lunch table and were encouraged to debate ideas just like the whites.

What was so interesting about the treatment of blacks by Mom and Dad is that they gained nothing from their actions. There was no political benefit; they held no political office. They were just farmers running a large plantation, and the blacks had few other places to work. But there was something in their relationship that caused them to treat people right, regardless of color. Maybe they wouldn't have acted that way alone—who is to know? But together they acted differently from their neighbors and, as a result, taught their five children a lesson in race relations.

We supported a black man for Congress—with a financial contribution, signs on our property, and bumper stickers on our vehicles—in 1966. His name was Leon Tarver. Whites were aghast at the audacity of Dad backing Leon. I heard people call Dad a "nig--- lover"—not to his face, but when he wasn't around. He supported Leon because he liked his mind. (Leon became president of Southern University years later.) He was young, barely thirty, and energetic. He had a business background and was president of J. S. Williams funeral home—the largest funeral home in all of north Louisiana. Dad thought he was the perfect candidate to represent our district in Congress and that Leon's color was an asset in reaching nearly half the people in the district. Dad also thought that his intellect and business experience would help him with the other half. He should have won the race decisively, according to Dad.

Dad was wrong. He had let his heart influence his political judgment, for Leon lost by a landslide, and Dad was derided by many because he supported a black man. Something was to come of the racial hatred that campaign generated, fortunately. Leon Tarver became a lifelong friend of the Roemer family.

I was to win the same seat in 1980, two years after the retirement of the longtime Congressman, Joe Waggoner. He had been sheriff in 1966 and strongly opposed Leon's candidacy. Publicly, he called it "audacious." In private, I'm sure he described it in harsher terms. In 1980, Waggoner worked against me—hard—when I ran for Congress. I wonder why?

My parents taught us that we did not use the "n" word, even if we heard it from customers every day. We heard it from some blacks. We certainly heard it in school daily. But my parents taught us that color was irrelevant in differences among people. I grew up in a different world when it came to racial attitudes.

I am not saying that there was no difference between workers and management at Scopena. There were racial and social issues that divided whites and blacks. People went to different schools, different churches, and different football games in town. Differences existed in the real world, but at Scopena, unlike the rest of Louisiana and the South, race was not the deciding factor in your status in the organization or in your pay.

Take baseball, for example. The sport was very popular across the South. American legion teams with high schoolers played in nearby small towns, including Minden, Homer, Haynesville, and Springhill. Young adults also played baseball in semi-pro leagues.

Scopena was the only place I knew that played baseball on an amateur basis with whites and blacks playing together. It was no big thing for us, but it stood out in the community as one of a kind.

We began playing baseball at Scopena when I was eleven. We often played on the tennis court, using the court as the infield, with the backstop at one end as home plate, and the chicken-wire fence on the other end as the home run wall in the outfield. But if it was being used for tennis, we used the baseball field in the pasture by the equipment shed on the other side of the shop.

I made myself captain of one team. It included blacks from Scopena and white boys from neighboring farms. Danny and Dad had the other team. It, too, had black players from Scopena and white players from other farms. In other words, both teams were fully integrated. We played ball once or twice a week as work permitted in summer when school was out and baseball season was in full swing.

New players played for each team for various games, and we tried to ration the new troops between the two teams so it would be even. There were many spirited arguments about the rules and about the contests. The only no-no was to try to hurt someone. We played regularly in the 1950s, until I went off to college in 1960.

It's odd that we played baseball at Scopena when school was out, on fully integrated teams, and none of us asked why we went to separate schools.

We knew that it was different, black from white. Scopena did not ignore that. Life at the farm made up for some of that difference, but it didn't go all the way. Many of the blacks lived with their families in the quarters at Scopena in four- or five-room, bare-boned wooden houses built in a row. Many families living in the quarters grew gardens on land around their homes. The land was made available without restriction by Dad, and there was always a garden blooming. These gardens were very important to families and Dad let the farm equipment like tractors, discs, and cultivators be used in the gardening.

It has been said that the black man who was "uppity" could suffer from a late night visit from the Ku Klux Klan. I don't know that for sure, but I do know that some men who visited Scopena to talk to Dad said they were members of the KKK. They lived out in the hills of Bossier and Webster Parishes ten or fifteen miles away, and they asked if he had a range for testing guns. He said no, that the only guns allowed on Scopena were for hunting quail, dove, and duck, and that strangers were not allowed to shoot because it was an operating business. They left.

So the KKK was around when I was a kid. There was no doubt about it. But Dad stiff-armed them and mentioned it to me only one time. As they were leaving Scopena after one of their visits, Dad nodded in the direction of their pickup and said to me, "Be careful, son. There go small minds that can hurt people. Be careful."

It was against this backdrop that early during our discussions about civil rights, we decided that full integration was legal, constitutional, and desirable. The only question was how to get there. That's where Dad and Mom became practical and aware of the community. Some of us—the kids—had no such reservations. "Do it now" was our theme. Dad and Mom were more conservative in that they wanted to challenge the causes of segregation. Integration would follow, they believed.

Some of us argued during the mealtime debates that people of color should be treated as citizens in every way. They had helped fight our wars. They contributed as workers and owners of businesses. There was nothing in our view that should limit a black person's full citizenship. Not the constitution, nor the practical existence of everyday living.

The only thing to ultimately limit a person of color, we thought, was education. The funding and the lack of emphasis on education limited blacks from becoming full and equal citizens. We had to turn that around, we believed. Equal civil rights would follow.

From our farmhouse in the Deep South, we believed that equality of education was the essential first step. Education was the key to future progress, for blacks and those with redneck prejudices. This would lead to full citizenship regardless of color. We knew of the lack of education on behalf of young farm laborers on Scopena, and we came to understand that those attending the black schools in our parish were not getting a good education. Full, unified public education was the beginning answer, we thought, one that everyone would see and support.

We failed to see that it would take years and years to achieve school equality. This would not be accomplished with the passing of a law, or by a presidential decree only. It would take death and destruction and much time for this to happen. The stain of racial prejudice had, and has, spread across America and, to erase it, countless acts of personal confession and personal courage will be required.

Years later one of our own, my son Chas (Charles E. Roemer IV), became president of the Louisiana Board of Elementary and Secondary Education for eight years, in charge of K-12 public education for the entire state of Louisiana. My daughter, Caroline, became head of the public charter school movement in Louisiana, not only establishing charter schools as an alternative education for public school children in Louisiana but insisting that charter schools provide openings for blacks, too.

Both Caroline and Chas participated in the public school revolution in Louisiana some twenty-five years after I was governor. I could give them almost no political assistance in their battles, because my political time was long gone. They did it mainly on their own. And no two people have done more for public education as have Chas and Caroline in that quarter century. Their Poppa is proud of them. Who would have expected these developments when we were debating public education at the supper table at Scopena sixty years before? Those roots run deep through their mother (Cookie) and father (me) to my Mom and Dad and the discussions at Scopena.

In our discussions years ago, I realize with hindsight, we failed to see the necessity of citizen equality first. We failed to see the powerful thirst for equality that would rise above practical, more gradual steps to integration and equality. We came to the opposite conclusion: that education had to lead. We believed that equal rights in citizenship would inevitably follow thanks to blacks having been taught the principles of full citizenship in an unsegregated, unified, equal education system. There was a method to our madness.

Martin Luther King was right all along: civil rights in America is mainly a spiritual and moral issue. You don't treat people as equal individuals because it's the legal thing to do; you do it because it's right; you do it because it fits your moral code.

It's interesting that the Supreme Court's *Brown* decision in 1954 addressed schools first, just like we thought it should. But we learned a lot in the next fifty years, about the racists' resistance to any progress on integration. The real driver in the struggle would be school desegregation. All else would follow from that. It's why the racists and the bigots fought school integration so hard, so long.

I remember when the *Brown* decision was announced to the

country. I was eleven. We were on vacation, somewhere in Texas coming back from the Grand Canyon in Arizona, when the radio announced the ruling. Dad pulled the car over, got out and yelled at the top of his voice, "At last! At last!" He was so excited.

When he got back in the car, we asked him all kinds of questions. What was the Supreme Court? Were they a Louisiana court? Who enforced what they decided? He laughed and said that public opinion was the force of their opinion and the American belief in the law was the power in their judgment. He said that President Franklin Roosevelt had tried to overturn the Supreme Court by packing it with his supporters, but he had failed. He said that it was the most powerful court in all the land and that's why he was so happy. In American history, no one had ignored the United States Supreme Court successfully. We were a nation of laws, not of men.

If he had only known how long the school battles would continue. Decades later, the uneasiness over public education continues. I don't think it can be disputed that much of that uneasiness and delay stems from racial bigotry.

Louisiana has not shown much leadership on the battlefield of school integration. Progress for various reasons has been painfully slow. My step-grandfather, Vernon Mayer, had been very wise in 1954 when he warned that in spite of the *Brown* ruling, the state of Louisiana would delay the implementation as long as it could, rather than advance as rapidly as possible. Bossier High School, for example, did not integrate until 1964, fully ten years after the Supreme Court decision.

Louisiana did not have a governor who emphasized the need to integrate the races until Edwin Edwards won a razor-tight primary race for governor in 1971. His statewide campaign manager was Dad.

Edwards's faults are well known. But he did include blacks in his administration in significant numbers for the first time in Louisiana since Reconstruction, and his policies on state jobs and construction projects were inclusive of black citizens. I continued those practices as governor.

Louisiana has made little progress in civil rights or public education since Edwin Edwards. That is one of the many reasons I think that Louisiana has grown in population at only 1/8th the rate of Texas. There are of course many reasons for this disparity: tort laws in Louisiana that discourage investment; no personal income taxes in Texas; better public schools and higher funding for education in Texas. But the one area that Louisiana under Edwards developed a better, more attractive record than Texas was black participation in public life.

Looking back over time on the *Brown* v. *Board of Education* decision, I can see that racism is a powerful force in America. It seldom is overtly obvious, but it always lies just below the surface. It needs to be called out wherever and whenever possible.

18

A Crazy Program

We talked farming and new crops at the lunch table. We talked about the inefficiency of government, particularly the annual cotton program where the government paid you not to plant cotton. We thought it was a crazy program. Pay you not to plant cotton! My Dad said that only the U.S. government would do something as stupid as that.

Every year in June when the crops had been planted and had come up or not, I would go around with a government inspector (usually one of our coaches or gym teachers from high school, like Mr. Smith or Mr. Burtman—it was a good summer job for them), and measure with a tape to determine how much acreage was going to be used that year to grow cotton. Dad assigned me the task of going with the agents because I knew where all the fields were located. Plus he knew that I understood where the cotton was stunted from excessive rainfall or from bad soil composition in each field.

You would pick out the weak cotton stands where the cotton was stunted. A weak cotton stand meant the cotton wasn't healthy or had less than a desired number of plants growing in the field. We had to plow those spots or fields up. The plot of land that had a weak stand of cotton wasn't going to produce a good crop of cotton anyway. The crop that was left was designated as crop land and was the farmer's official acreage for the government program. It was a trick—plowing up the crop after it had already failed—that all farmers used to game the system.

For Scopena, it was a big deal. If we had 1,200 acres free of cotton—plowed up—at $200 an acre, we received a check for $240,000 for not planting that cotton. The trick was to plant your allotment and more and see where the cotton did not come up strong and healthy. You measured the cotton that showed symptoms of weakness and then you would subtract that number of acres from what you were originally allotted to that plot of land. Then you would plow up the weak cotton and let the government pay you for it. You ended up with the strongest possible crop. People with extra land used this tactic. It was legitimate and successful, and made the cotton program an absolute joke.

Let me give you an example. If the government said that you had a one hundred-acre allotment of cotton, and you planted 120 acres and measured thirty of the acres as having a weak stand, you could plow up the thirty weak acres and still have ninety acres of strong cotton. Because you were in the federal cotton program, you got paid for reducing your acreage and yet because you over-planted, you got the strongest cotton left standing when you plowed up the weak cotton. That's what Mr. Burton and Mr. Smith did—officially measure the land that was to be used to grow cotton.

This was a game that farmers had perfected. Here's another one: the skip-row game.

Cotton needs room and hot weather to grow. Rather than plant every row with cotton, farmers took to skipping a row. They found that if they planted only two of three rows with one row unplanted, they would increase the yield of plants adjacent to the skip. Some years the yields would increase so much that they made as much cotton on skip row cotton as if they had planted every row like conventional cotton. And what's more, the government let them count the skipped row as acreage untilled; so the smart farmer with adequate acreage got his full payment for skipping a row and suffered no drop off in production. In other words, the farmer got credit for not planting the skip row in his allotment calculations and received payment for that blank row.

It was a federal program that made no sense because it didn't reduce cotton production and stabilize cotton prices for the farmer naturally, as it was purported to do. Instead, the government paid the farmer for land where either the crop had already failed or the farmer had deliberately skipped a row to increase production. No anticipated production was lost.

Over the lunch table, Dad used to talk about this program. It started during the Eisenhower years, and Dad thought it was a stupid program with good intentions but foul results. He said that it was the reason he could never be a Republican. They were so stupid that they didn't know farming, and they didn't know the character of the man behind the plow, who would beat the government at every opportunity and think nothing of it.

I asked him one day whether we should take the money from the wasteful federal program. He thought a moment and said "yes." The government was just giving back what it had stolen from successful farmers in other situations—estate taxes, cattle assessments, etc. Further, members of Congress could change the law any time they wanted to, and they would do so when they stopped talking and started listening. Dad would testify before Congress the next year about how crazy the federal cotton program was and how it ought to be changed. It was.

The other day, I met the son of one of the football coaches at Bossier High School who measured how much acreage we would be using that year to grow cotton. His Dad had passed away several years ago, as had mine. He started talking about the memories that he had from his father's measuring cotton for the federal government on Scopena.

He had been a small boy and would ride with his father in the summer to pull the chains to measure the cotton. He said he remembered being helped by two young boys, one in a pickup truck and the other riding a horse. He was talking about me and my brother Danny.

He reminded me that his father had thought the program was a joke, costing the government money and failing to reduce cotton production. Everybody knew of the futility of the cotton program in the field, except the politicians in Washington, D.C. It still took them five years to change the farm program. Dad enjoyed those five years as much as any he had in agriculture, because he could make fun of the federal government. Plus he got paid to not plant cotton that he was not going to grow anyway.

The son telling me that he had accompanied his father at Scopena to measure cotton reminded me that I had started to drive a pickup truck on the farm when I was seven or eight years old. I taught myself. Scopena was so large and my duties required me to cover so many fields that I taught myself how to drive a five-gear stick shift International Harvester pickup truck before I could see over its steering wheel.

Mom made a big pillow for me to sit on so I could see where I was going, and Dad attached blocks of wood on the brake, gas, and clutch pedals, so I could reach them. I practiced in the cow pastures and pretty soon had the hang of it.

The truck quickly became essential for me to conduct my business activities at Scopena. I was a careful driver and a good one, and I drove everywhere when I was barely half the legal age of fifteen.

I thought nothing of it at the time—driving at eight. It was just a convenience. Driving made my life a lot easier and more useful. Dad didn't let me drive to town until I had my license at fifteen, although he did let me drive the ten miles between Curtis and McDade on Scopena business.

19

SUMMER VACATION

When I broke my arm in 1952 when my horse fell, it was painful, but I was happy, because we were to begin our summer vacation car trip in two weeks. The vacation always took place during a narrow window of time, when the cotton crop was "laid by." That is when the cotton has three to six weeks to finish blooming and growing until it is ready to be harvested. By then, it has been irrigated. It has been sprayed with insecticide. It has been fertilized. It has been hoed.

When that process is complete, the cotton is defoliated (its leaves are removed) and harvested two to four weeks later. That period of waiting is called "laying by" and usually happens in the last weeks of August. "Lay-by" is an important time to a farmer, because there is little planned activity in the cotton fields. The farmer, for the first time all year, has some time off where no land or crop has to be prepared. He can just wait on the crop to come in. Spraying the cotton occasionally for insect control was the only scheduled operation happening on the farm.

Throughout the 1950s, we used this period to take a vacation together, just before school resumed and summer ended. These were real vacations—not to go to the beach, or to visit grandma, or to take a weekend off to go to Dallas or New Orleans. Loading five kids, Mom, and Dad in a late model Oldsmobile for a fifteen-day adventure was a real vacation.

The kids would have our designated spots in the car. The smallest child would be in the front seat with Mom and Dad. The other four kids would be on the back seat, with two on the floor board and two on the back seat itself. That would give us each a place to play or read. When there was something to see, we would share the side windows to look.

We planned the trip months ahead and would try to go somewhere new. We always drove, and when we went west the first hurdle was to get across Texas, which took a day and a night. There is no other way. There was nothing that we wanted to see in Texas, except west Texas, so we would drive all night, that first night, on the way to Carlsbad Caverns, Yellowstone, the San Diego Zoo, or San Francisco, the painted desert, Mexico, the Four Corners country, Canada, South Dakota and the Corn Palace, or Wind Cave or Tipanogus Cave in Utah. We also went to Capulin volcano in New Mexico, my favorite place in the whole wide world. I liked Capulin volcano, because it was only one day from Scopena and it was just the opposite climate—six thousand feet high, not sea level; dry pasture land, not swamp and bayou; and mountain-desert, not woodland.

Before departing, my parents always got an AAA map of the route we'd take, with the recommended route marked in red. Dad would drive, and how far or how long was up to him. He liked an early start and a late stop. And each of us worked at seeing America all the hours in between—no shopping, no lollygagging, no resting, no side shows or frivolous undertakings. This was vacation, Roemer family style!

Each of us had jobs on the vacation, and we took them very seriously. Margaret was in charge of making sure we followed the route shown on the map. I was asked to take pictures one year. I promptly forgot to put film in the camera. When one of my sisters noticed that I was taking a lot of pictures day after day without changing film, I was relieved of my picture-taking duties permanently. I was secretly pleased not to have to listen to the girls argue about what pictures I should be taking. They never could agree. Fired as the picture man, I became responsible for lodging.

We never planned a stop or accommodations. It was strictly when we felt like stopping. We usually had a single goal for the day, such as seeing the giant redwood trees in northern California, for example. But we had no timetable or reservations along the way. We did it like that because Dad didn't want to arbitrarily tie us down in a spot.

Our vacations were life experiences, free and easy in deciding whether we liked a certain place and how long we chose to stay there. In our many years of taking a family vacation, we never missed a sight that we wanted to see because we didn't have room reservations. Not once that I can remember. It was the power of flexibility. Dad thought that "flexibility" was a key to success, right up there with speed and focus.

The family vacations out west were living proof.

I was the person responsible for flexibility when it came to accommodations. I enjoyed that role. We would pull up to an out of way place with a well-lit vacancy sign and with seven people in the car (five children, don't forget) at night. I would walk inside to do the negotiations. I began doing this when I was eight. It was always negotiation at the motel. I don't ever remember us taking the advertised room rate. What would the fun be in that?

I would ask for a discount because we were tired and had not planned to stop. We could all sleep in one room if it had two beds, I would say. Two of the children counted as one because they were so young. My Dad was a WWII veteran and should be honored, I'd add. My Mom was battling five kids. And we so much wanted to see . . . "Crater Lake," for example. I almost always got a discount. If not, we moved on. I wish I could congratulate Dad and his war record for the discount. But I think it was Mom and the thought of those five children that brought out the best in people.

We were so lucky. No one ever got hurt on our many adventures: hikes, excursions, swims, campouts. The rooms were not so lucky.

No room could survive a night of the Roemer children. Pillow fights. Shower fights. What do you expect from five kids to a room on vacation? Cooped up in that car all day and then released into a big hotel or motel room that night? We always stayed in a motel so that we could park on the outer edges and leave early the next morning while other guests were sound asleep. We didn't do permanent damage to a room, and we didn't do deliberate damage. But you knew the room had been occupied. We always left so early that I didn't know motels served breakfast to guests until years later.

One trip out west stands out because of the ending back at Scopena. One of the things that we kids had to do beforehand was to get somebody to do our chores. We had front yard mowing (about three acres of yard), tending the bees, feeding the chickens and rabbits daily, taking care of the ponies. On and on it went. On vacation, you usually got somebody on the farm to do it for you. Either one of the field hands or a member of their family would do it for five or ten dollars or whatever you negotiated. We all had a few dollars from selling the harvest every September from the twenty-five pecan trees in the front yard. We would sell these pecans in town and use the forty or fifty dollars apiece in profits to go to the State Fair in Shreveport every October and also to pay farm employees to do our chores while we were on vacation.

On this particular trip, I forgot to make arrangements for my rabbits. I don't know why. I loved them. It may have been dealing with a crisis about insecticide poisoning that kept me busy until our departure. I may have been so excited that vacation time was about to begin. But no excuses, I forgot. The rabbits were of various sizes, eight beautiful creatures in a hutch under a roof next to the shop, not far from the back door of the house. I changed their water and fed them daily. They were in individual cages that I cleaned regularly.

While on vacation, I was busy with sightseeing and daily accommodations, and I didn't think about rabbits or dogs or horses at all. If I thought about them, I shoved that stuff to the back of my mind.

But when we were coming back after fifteen days away, I began to think of the things I had to do when I got home. Check on the rabbits and their care was one job that jumped into my mind. For the first time, it hit me. A cold chill went up my spine. My heart seized up. For the first time, I realized that I had failed to ask Mel, Tommy Lee, Albert, or Christine to take care of them. The rabbits were alone without me. Maybe someone heard them begging for food and water? They were right there next to the shop. Imagine what the days were like for the rabbits when it hit them that I had forgotten them.

Within a day of home, I began to imagine that I had asked one of the Scopena crew to fill my shoes and take care of the rabbits. I got quiet. I was in agony as we traveled across north Texas. I was hoping against hope that I had asked somebody in the rush to leave and the excitement of travel day or that, failing that, somebody had noticed them in their cages and given them food and water.

When we pulled up at Scopena, everybody went running in all directions. They were so happy to be back and see the dogs and the horses. Me? I went running to the rabbit hutch.

They were there. They were quiet—all eight of them. They had starved to death. It wasn't pretty. No water. No food. Twisted in their cages. Sunken ribs. Sunken chests. Hollow faces. Flies buzzing all around. I can still hear the buzzing. They had been dead for several days. What had I done? Killed eight innocent rabbits. None of the farm workers had noticed them because the rabbits were quiet in their cages, and the cages were out of the way, so the bustle of people coming and going from the shop wouldn't frighten them.

I told Dad and Mom and each of my siblings what I had done. I apologized. I prayed forgiveness. There was no forgiveness in my mind. I lived with it for a long, long time. It didn't help the rabbits.

When I was governor, on several occasions I had to decide whether to approve the execution of a prisoner who had been condemned to die by the jury and who had undergone all his appeals. In each case, I talked to the killer and to the victim's family. In each case, I thought he was guilty and deserved to die. But I would be lying if I didn't say I didn't think just a little about how I was responsible for the deaths of those eight rabbits decades earlier. As a result, I would look at the case just a little closer to make sure I hadn't missed anything.

20

PAYDAY

As I mentioned, 95 percent of the two hundred workers at Scopena were black. Field pay was seventy to ninety cents an hour for the eleven-hour work day, for whites and blacks alike. Supervisors got an extra twenty cents an hour. Men with skills—tractor drivers or gin operators, for instance—were paid one dollar per hour or more. Pay was dirt poor, but the men had few options beyond farm labor. The wages were what other farms paid in the surrounding areas, except for the bonus for supervisors.

Scopena supplied some necessities to workers that neighboring farms did not, such as work shoes, work clothes, decent family housing, and access to good medical care that was free. The workers got care from the same doctors as did the family, but their hospital care was at the charity hospital in Shreveport.

The workers picked up the shoes and other essential items at the company store, Scopena Grocery. The store was what you've always heard a company store to be: relatively expensive, limited choices, and a lot of sales on credit that tied a man unknowingly to the company. The store was located along Highway 71 just north of the Scopena headquarters and was managed for Dad by an old cowboy who wore a ten-gallon hat. His name was Slim Waldrip. His wife Beattie helped him run the store.

Slim was a friend of Dad's. He and his wife were regulars at Mom

Workers in a Scopena cotton field

and Dad's Tuesday night canasta games at the big house. Slim ran the store as if it contained his own private stock of vittles and whiskey. He could be contrary in his attitude and loud in his disagreements. Not once in his life was he wrong. Slim provided employees their necessities as required by Dad, but he also provided credit to the men's families to provide them non-essentials, such as dresses and dress shirts.

Credit was central to the function of the store. In fact, credit is why it existed. The men made so little money that they became dependent on the credit extended them at the company store by Slim. They would settle up with the next paycheck. Their credit balance was always known at payday. Dad and Slim used the extension of credit as an enticement for a few key employees. Other employees paid their credit charges as billed.

The interest rate paid by the workers on their store credit was always low (half of the prime rate or 4 percent, whichever was lower). But Dad thought the principle of "interest" was important for the men to understand and to hold them accountable. In truth, the logic was flawed because Dad agreed to forgive the interest, and even the store credit for most workers, when it became a financial burden. Dad tolerated Slim's fussing and fuming about credit and interest rates, but in the end the happiness of the men came first, so the working men would win out.

What Dad did not forgive was the credit and interest owed Scopena's store by workers from other farms. Ours was one of the three general stores available for miles around, and while Scopena workers were protected from the financial pressures of high credit and high interest rates, other laborers were not. Thus, Dad provided a not too subtle advantage of working at Scopena.

Laborers were paid in one of two ways, depending on the kind of work they did. Day laborers—hoe hands, corn detasselers, hay balers, and cotton pickers—were paid in cash at the end of each day. We paid the regular workers at the end of every Saturday.

There were occasional arguments, but the pay procedure was straightforward and known by everybody. Daily workers got a dollar cash in the morning, and if they quit before lunch, then that's all they got. But if they stayed at the job all day, they got a day's wage, usually five dollars. If they quit after lunch, they were paid depending on how many hours they had worked. For the salaried workers, it was a different system.

Saturday was settling up day for the men who worked the tractors and other farm equipment at Scopena. These men were on the payroll and worked for a higher rate than day laborers—ten to twenty-five dollars a day compared to five a day or less for cash laborers. The men would line up outside the office after work ended on Saturday, and Dad or I would go over their paycheck with them. The paycheck was small with sixty hours of work on a robust week at $1.20 to $4.00 an hour for a supervisor equaling $72 to $240 a week typically, minus five or ten dollars per payday for repayment of debt or store credit.

Many times the guys would want to borrow money. If a guy was dependable, you would lend him five, ten, or one hundred dollars and charge him a low rate of interest. Basically, we forgave a loan if he continued to work satisfactorily for a period of time. The loan forgiveness policy added a cost of about ten cents an hour to the cost of labor, we figured.

I remember the excitement in the air surrounding settling up. Those that had no work on Saturday or had time off that day were usually drinking beer or wine to excess when pay time came late Saturday afternoon. There was always whooping and hollering going on. It was payday.

Dad treated each of the men as an individual. Each received his pay for the week. Some would thank Dad and go out the door satisfied with their check. Some would have a question about hours or pay rates. Dad would check the log book where the men's work had been logged each day, and show them what it said and where they stood.

Sometimes the log record wouldn't settle the question, so Dad would arbitrate. Some men wanted to work in a different place, irrigation rather than plowing, for example; some men wanted to borrow money to buy a car or build on to their house; some wanted to pay down store credit. Occasionally, some wanted to borrow money and would not say what they wanted it for. Dad wouldn't let them have it. For example, Dad denied a loan to a man named Robert one Saturday because Robert wouldn't say why he wanted to borrow the money. Robert returned on Tuesday saying that he needed to borrow three hundred dollars to get married. Dad granted the loan. Robert and his bride remained married beyond their time at Scopena. In fact, they were still married some fifty years later the last I knew of. By then, Robert had retired from working as a corporate security officer in Shreveport.

At some point when I was seven, Dad let me begin sitting in each week on the payroll discussions. The process fascinated me. I soon realized he was preparing me to take over the responsibility, despite my young age.

I was only eight when Dad turned it over to me. He felt that I was prepared. I knew the worth of the men, the hours they had spent on their tasks, their dependability, and their worth to the organization. Strange as it may sound, my age was not a big issue because the men knew me and saw that I had responsibilities of my own by working every day after school. Plus, I was the boss's son.

The payroll job was another of Dad's efforts to have me assume responsibilities at a young age. He believed that young people could handle adult responsibilities. All they needed was experience, and the way to get experience was to do the job, under an adult's supervision. Dad thought there was no substitute for acting like an adult. And Dad consistently gave me jobs normally done by adults.

The workers tested me, to be sure, but they tested Dad, too. I had plenty of "if I don't get this, I quit" moments. But I survived by handling the men just as I had seen Dad handle them for more than a year—with quiet reserve and dignity. No request was too small to be considered. No question went unanswered. No item of concern important to them was unimportant to me.

The men appreciated something else: I valued them a great deal and demonstrated that by how I treated them. When the men had a problem with my age, they would see Dad for a few minutes. He always resolved the issue by supporting my judgment. Always. As long as I can remember, Dad treated me as a man, and expected me to be a man no matter my age.

21

MOISTURE METER BOY

As you know by now, my parents believed in exposing their children to new ideas, concepts, and activities at an early age. So I was eight when Dad gave me my first formal farm work at Scopena, beyond my payday responsibility. I became the moisture meter reader. That called for me to measure the amount of moisture in the fields to see when it was time to irrigate the cotton or, occasionally, the corn fields. You could do this in part by observing the fields as farmers had done for thousands of years. When it didn't rain for ten days and the weather was hot and the plants started burning—the leaves would look wrinkled and crinkled—then you wanted to irrigate.

But Dad wanted a more scientific way of measuring moisture, and he wanted to know when the fields first needed water. In other words, he wanted to act before you could see the signs that you needed to act. Speed was critical to the decision on water. He wanted to avoid the stress on the cotton plant. Our goal was to irrigate a field within twenty-four hours of determining it needed water. He thought if water could be applied when the cotton needed it and not before, this was efficient in terms of operations and was most advantageous to the cotton plant.

Irrigation was expensive. Pipes had to be strung in the field to be irrigated and moved every six hours around the clock. The pipes were heavy, filled with irrigation water, and moving them required at least ten men on a shift, plus a foreman.

The irrigation crew also was responsible for maintaining the main pumping engine that sucked the irrigation water from the canal or lake. In addition, there were constant blow-outs in the lines or with the sprinkling heads.

Irrigation was a full-time, hands-on task. You didn't just turn on the pumps, let them irrigate for a couple of hours, and return to go to another field. You were constantly moving a line, trying to finish irrigating a field before you moved on to the next one.

You didn't want to irrigate if you didn't have to because of the cost, but when it was time to irrigate you wanted to put the water on the plant as soon as possible so as to minimize stress on the crop and maximize yield.

Scopena's irrigation system was handicapped by the topography of the land it farmed. Its fields had not been leveled by machines to put a slight fall from one end of the field to the other so they could be flood irrigated, as many fields in Arizona and California are. This type of irrigation was relatively easy and inexpensive, but did not suit Scopena's many fields. So we had to irrigate ours by pipe. That was difficult, very labor intensive, quite expensive, and very slow.

To enjoy the benefits of irrigation, while at the same time lowering the cost of the operation compared to those benefits, Dad desired the best, most up-to-date information on the moisture in his cotton plants and discovered a company that produced moisture meters that could tell where and when the cotton fields were ready to be irrigated for maximum gain. I know of no other farmer in Louisiana who used moisture meters.

This was revolutionary in terms of gathering scientific information about the status of the crop and taking the guess work out of the irrigation decision. It was yet another critical management policy implemented by Budgie Roemer.

So we implanted moisture meters, five feet into the ground every forty acres in the spring, to determine the needs of plants and their root system every few days, and to see whether the plants were stressed. My job was to get the dozens of readings every few days, and in conjunction with the meteorological forecast, determine which fields needed water, how much, and when.

The company manufacturing the equipment sent a man to Scopena to train us. It lasted a week. Dad, a field supervisor, and I took the training. The company rep said I was the youngest person he had ever trained, but I found it quite easy, even at the age of eight.

At the peak of the growing season, we had 50 to 150 stations to read, measuring about six thousand acres. That covered all of the cotton and corn fields that were close enough to the water wells, the lakes, or the river to allow for irrigation. Corn required more water than cotton, but both were vulnerable in the hot Louisiana summers.

We were the only commercial (or private) operation in Louisiana that had moisture meters to give an early signal for crop irrigation. This was like so many things that Dad did at Scopena (hybrid seed corn, plantation-wide radio communications, geese for crop weed control, moisture meter readers, and aerial application of seed, fertilizer, insecticide, and defoliate to name a few of his groundbreaking ideas) that were ahead of all other farmers in the area.

I did the work on horseback, and it would take me all day long. Moisture was important in the summertime when the sun was hot and available water evaporated rapidly. The fields were far flung, so I rode my horse great distances. I would call by radio and let the headquarters know when a field was ready to be irrigated. When I had finished reading the meters each afternoon, I logged the results on a large, green blackboard in the Scopena office. I constantly updated these charts. I also recorded the information on map charts of the various fields.

I learned that not all fields required water at the same time. Fields with sandy soil developed nonvisible signs of stress long before clay soil, for example. Clay soil on the other hand needed more water than sandy soil when it was under drought conditions. You wouldn't have known these things under the old "look and guess" routine of the non-scientific approach. Dad's knowledge of the land combined with the meter numbers gave us an advantage in the critical mysteries of cotton irrigation.

Other farmers in the area knew that I was learning the process of water management at Scopena during this period, and they would drop by the office when I logged my findings each afternoon. My knowledge about the numbers I logged reflected my understanding of the system in which I had been trained as well as Dad's tremendous knowledge of the land.

Our cotton yields confirmed that. Timely irrigation in the proper amounts improved our cotton yield by up to 300 percent, we found. Scopena's cotton yield was the best in Louisiana during eight of the next nine years after we installed the scientific moisture meters.

22

THE HOE FIELD

I can't think of a cotton crop before 1960 without thinking of the hoe hands. They worked in the fields from about May 15 until July 15, chopping away weeds and grasses so the cotton would grow strong and unhindered.

The hoe hands did not have homes on Scopena, but were brought to the proper cotton field from Shreveport at 6:00 each morning, Monday through Friday and a half day on Saturday. Contractors would provide the buses to transport the hoe hands. There were up to two hundred hoe hands each day, and on some days more than three hundred. There were some adults, but primarily they were high school students or elderly people. For many of them, the summer break was an opportunity to toil in the hoe field and earn some money. They were paid a dollar for lunch, in addition to five dollars at the end of the day. They worked a ten-hour day with an hour break for lunch.

My first job in the hoe field was to train new hoers in the kind of hoeing that we required for the day. I could demonstrate that within a half hour. I began overseeing the training during the summer when I was nine years old. Dad had taught me how to hoe and train others to hoe.

Some fields required "thinning" of the cotton where cotton had grown too thick in a certain field. The cotton grew on a trunk or stalks like a tree. If the stalks were too crowded when they grew from the ground, they would inhibit vigorous growth of the other plants and weaken their ability to produce cotton. These cotton plants in a field were called the cotton stand, and to maximize production we wanted the stand to be just right—not too thick, not too thin.

To do this thinning operation required our continuous oversight, because if poorly done, the cotton left in the field would be insufficient to support a good crop. Production would suffer. Or if the stand was not chopped adequately, cotton would be too crowded and sickly. Production would suffer.

Some fields required a scorched earth approach where all weeds and grasses would have to be chopped out. Some fields had a small amount of grass and weeds, but had one infestation, like vines, and the hoeing had to focus on the type of weed that we wanted to eliminate. I would usually visit the field to be hoed on the day before and determine the type of hoeing required.

After I would train the hoe hands, I would walk the fields to be sure they were doing the job correctly. Hoeing was easy if done right. The hoe was relatively light, and the blade sharp. Several men walked the fields with files to keep the hoes sharp. If I found someone straggling or failing to chop certain weeds, I would re-train him with a warning that he needed to improve. If he didn't, I told him, I would have to let him go. When I fired someone, I would tell him he could try again tomorrow, but he rarely returned. I would fire one or two workers each day, but I remember the number reaching fifty once.

For those fired, I would give them the wage earned and that would be computed at the hourly rate for the day's labor. That rate was usually fifty cents per hour plus a dollar for lunch. The work period was from 7:00 a.m. to noon and from noon to 6:00 p.m. Out of the eleven hours, ten were in the cotton field, and an hour was for lunch.

We gave a minimum of one dollar to a hoer regardless if he got fired in the first minutes of the morning. Dad figured that he deserved a dollar for showing the initiative to come down to Scopena. His approach was not typical. Other farms gave no pay for a partial day.

A bigger issue than having to fire workers was having them wilt during the work day. Although the hoe was not heavy, you had to constantly move it while you were walking down the row under a scorching sun—temperatures averaged in the 90s in June and near 100 degrees in July and August. There was no shade.

Fatigued workers would lean on their hoes or return to the bus that brought them to the field. If they could not continue after resting for a few minutes, we provided their per diem salary for the work performed and gave them a place to rest in the shade of the bus until the bus took them and the other workers home at the end of the day.

To provide relief, we paid a separate group of workers to deliver ice-cold water to the hoer's in five-gallon pails. We encouraged the hoers to drink plentifully with long-stemmed ladles when the water bucket passed by every few minutes. We would provide the water and ice in fifty-five-gallon drums on a truck following the hoe field operations.

I always felt that the job of water boy was the toughest in the hoe field because a five-gallon water bucket weighs forty pounds. The water boy carried two buckets at once to balance his load. That's eighty pounds of water at a time.

I also used the hoe field to practice my speaking. There were hours of walking to determine if the crop had been hoed correctly. You would walk behind the hoe hands to see if they were doing their job. These long walks behind the hoe hands were at times in places where the hoe hands were hoeing at present and at times where the hoe hands had hoed earlier in the day and had moved to another part of the field. In these instances, when there was no one present, I could speak like I was giving an address to the legislature, and no one could hear me.

What great practice for me! I spoke for hours with whatever audience I invented in my mind and could start and stop whenever I wanted. I gave countless speeches, practicing stories of various sorts and making whatever points I wanted to make. I knew I was going to get off the farm, I just didn't know how or when. I had picked politics as the way to go when I stood on my own. I don't know why I picked politics, but I wanted to be prepared when my chance came.

Supervising the hoe field gave me a chance to work on my ticket away from Scopena. It's funny looking back sixty years ago, how practicing speaking in the hoe field was a little bit like bouncing in the backseat of an old car in that my mind could transport me to a different time and place where I could move an imaginary crowd wherever I wanted.

The hot July days quickly passed to autumn thanks to my speech-making in the cotton fields.

We started a lunch wagon for the hoe hands in June, July, and August. It was Dad's idea. It allowed the workers to stay in the field for lunch rather than lose time by going into town. Most hoe hands refused to bring their lunch from home, so all hoe hands received a dollar for lunch. Most hoe hands spent part of their dollar on a sandwich and their choice of iced drinks. Each morning, my three sisters, my brother, and I would prepare the sandwiches for lunch that day and sell them to customers in the field. We charged a nickel, a dime, or a quarter, depending on the type of sandwich. The sandwiches were ham and cheese, bologna and tomato, Vienna sausage, salami, or roast beef, which was the most expensive at a quarter. We called the lunch wagon the "pop wagon."

My siblings and I worked as a team early each morning to prepare the sandwiches. We had a mustard line on one half of the sandwich and a mayonnaise line on the other half. Some bread required spiced mayonnaise on both halves of the sandwich. We would apply the roast beef, ham, or salami. Next, two of the girls would place a clear plastic wrapping around each sandwich. Danny would add the desired store-bought items in big cardboard boxes (sardines, Vienna sausages, saltine crackers, cigarettes, snuff, and hard candy). He also placed the soft drinks in huge, galvanized, eighty-gallon wash tubs filled with cracked ice.

Danny and the driver of the pop wagon that day would pick up the food and sundry items and soft drinks at the Scopena store, where we had a credit line. I would settle up with the store manager every week until one of the girls got old enough to take over that task. The store items and the pop wagon would swing by the house to pick up the sandwiches we had prepared, and off to the cotton fields we would go.

Mr. Boyd, the shop manager, had engineered the pop wagon to maximize efficiency. The wagon was a large wraparound platform that could fit behind a tractor or truck with a trailer hitch and stay in the equipment shed until hoeing season arrived again.

Given the summer heat, the workers clamored for the chilled cans of Coca-Cola, Pepsi, and RC Cola at a dime apiece. We also sold cigarettes, peanut patties, and Baby Ruth candy bars. One of the girls, usually Melinda, worked the change box for the pop wagon. There was usually change for every customer from the one dollar that they had to spend for lunch. It was a madhouse with up to three hundred hoe hands wanting service all at once and with each of the four children telling Melinda the needed amount of change, but there were usually no arguments. All five of the kids knew how to serve the food and drink, so we got it to all three hundred hands pretty quickly.

Dad always had every angle covered. To ensure that we kids would enthusiastically work on the pop wagon, he designated that the profit would go into a college savings fund. We each set up our own bank account. Thus, we worked three hours daily during the summer and made between three and five hundred dollars collectively each week, or about three thousand dollars each year. Not only did the pop wagon make college money for us, it provided a service for the up to three hundred workers stuck in the fields, unable to go to town in the time provided. We had a monopoly in the pop wagon.

We didn't realize it then, but hoeing was a dying practice. By the early 1960s, new chemicals appeared that killed weeds and grass without hurting the cotton. By 1964, the year I graduated from college, the hoe hand had become extinct on Scopena, the victim of modern chemical technology. No more great speeches by me, just out of hearing of the hoe hands.

23

RUNNING AWAY FROM HOME

When I was seven or eight, I developed a bad habit of running away from home when something there didn't go right. Maybe it was a test to see if I was still loved. Would someone come for me? Would they miss me? There was also a world out there that I wanted to see and sometimes I would feel trapped in the life there on the farm. Texas, New Mexico, Arizona, California—these were the places that I wanted to see; these were the places where I would be appreciated; these were the places that my talent could shine and not be hidden under a cotton plant. Maybe I was just rebelling, but I wanted to leave Scopena at times and sometime that feeling was overwhelming. It would never be an argument that preceded my departure. I would be upset at some decision made by Dad that affected me. Rather than confront Dad with it directly, I would swell up, pout, and, on my own time, run away. It happened three or four times over the course of a couple of years. I knew Dad was going to come find me. It was, in a sense, a game.

The drill was always the same: I would slip out of the house right at dusk or dark. I sometimes carried a small suitcase that contained a t-shirt or two, a couple of pairs of underwear, a change of shirts, a pair of blue jeans, and a pair of socks. I would even put my piggy bank in the suitcase. I didn't save my money for the escape. Don't forget that in my mind, it was a game.

After slipping out the back door, I walked quickly down the runway to the levee at its far end, turned right, and proceed for a couple of miles in the gathering darkness. I then walked to the river and its border of willows.

Dad would always come get me. Mom would stay at the house and watch the other kids while Dad drove in his Jeep back on the levee to find me. He wasn't subtle. He would blow the horn on the Jeep and cry out my name, over and over again.

When I first heard him, I would hide in the darkness. But eventually I would step out to the levee and reveal my presence. Sometimes Dad had driven a mile or so past me down the levee or down the river bank. It was dark, so I could just see the lights on his Jeep and hear the faint sounds of his voice crying out, "Butch? Butch?"

I would let him know I was ready to go home by standing exposed on the levee or in a clearing of the willows. He would stop the Jeep when he saw me finally or when he'd hear me calling, "Dad? Dad?" He always had a big smile on his face and would pull the Jeep over right next to where I was standing and say something like, "Do you need a ride?" or "Do you want a lift?"

He'd hug me and ask what was wrong. We would then talk about what had upset me. Usually it seemed petty by then, and I would tell him that and he'd laugh and say nothing was unimportant if it got between the two of us. We would come to an understanding by talking it out where we stood in the dark on top of the levee or on the banks of the Red River sixty-five years ago. I can still remember the sounds of rushing water, fish jumping in the river, and barking coyotes.

He'd say, "Let's go see Mom. She's missing you, she is worried about you. Let's go put her mind at ease." There was no such thing as a cell phone then, so we had to drive back to the house to tell Mom. When we got to the house, the other kids would be playing or studying depending on the time of night. Sometimes they didn't even know I had run away from home.

If they knew I had run away, they got real quiet when I walked into the room and saw Mom. She always held out her arms and would hug me for a long time. She would say, "Welcome home!" in a big voice as she held me. The other kids would then continue playing or studying or reading or listening to the radio. Life would go on. It's as if they expected me to run away every now and then, but they also expected me to come back.

Dad was different from other men in many ways—his racial attitudes, his treatment of me as if I was a grownup, his innovative agricultural practices, his aloofness from his fellowmen—but his attention to the time spent in being an active father was always felt and appreciated by me. I remember no times in my life where we were closer than those times when he would drive in the dead of night down the levee to search for me, a lost little boy.

One day my time as a runaway little boy came to an end. I'd just celebrated my tenth birthday, and I was feeling for some reason a need to escape the farm that day. Texas was in my brain. But this time, rather than run away in the direction of the river and the levee (west toward Texas), I would head east for the woods between the house and a big tract of land that we farmed, called Oklahoma. When safely there, I would reverse directions, loop north, and double back toward Texas to the west going around Scopena.

I don't remember what the beef was at home, and I forget why I decided to run away to the east. I do remember thinking that Dad and the Jeep wouldn't be able to find me this time. In fact, I left a note beside my bed for my mother saying that I loved her and that I was going to walk to Texas (about twenty miles away, twenty-five with the circuitous route I was taking) and catch a ride to California from there. I also wrote that I was not going down the levee or to the river but was starting in the opposite direction this time. This note was quietly telling Dad that the rules of the game had changed.

When I left, I carried my trusty small suitcase and slipped out the back door of the house. I walked through the office, maybe hoping that somebody would stop me and ask what I was doing. But no one saw me. I walked out of the office unseen. It was late afternoon on a summer day, not yet dusk.

Rather than turn my usual direction west down the long grass runway, I turned east, walked across the large front yard and tennis court to the two-lane highway, which I proceeded to cross. I then crossed the railroad tracks into the pasture that was on the other side. From there, I slowly walked the length of the pasture to the edge of a thick forest. I entered it and had a two-mile walk ahead of me to Oklahoma, a large tract of cotton land owned by Scopena. Since no one had seen me, I felt secure that I would actually carry out this runaway plan. The game had changed. I was excited.

The forest was dark when I entered even though the sun was shining brightly on the pasture outside. It was quiet, too. You could hear nothing except the chatter of squirrels playing in the tree tops and the whistles of red wing blackbirds and doves fluttering in and out of the woods. I felt very alone, less than two miles from home.

It was an old, long-established forest with pecan, oak, sycamore, and maple packed into its thick cluster of trees. It had no scrub brush under its main canopy of trees. So, even though it was dark and quiet, you could see one hundred feet ahead of where you were walking. Plus, there was a trail that went through the forest. I had been there before.

At first, I enjoyed the rush of freedom, out of sight of all and unseen by anyone, especially Dad. It was easy walking, and I had escaped all notice.

But then I began to think that since I had traveled from home in a different direction than I usually took, Dad couldn't find me unless he found the note I had left for Mom, which said that I hadn't taken my usual route. It didn't say that I had taken the Oklahoma woods route, but surely he would guess that if he read the note. It was less than an hour from when I had run away from the house, but I began to worry. What if Danny destroyed the note for some reason? I would go unfound.

Suddenly, I heard a strange sound. Something was scratching one of the trees. I stopped and listened but couldn't spot the source. As I turned to walk away, I saw a yellow flash out of the corner of my eye.

There on a low hanging limb about twenty feet behind me was a bobcat. He was stretched out on the limb and making no noise except one claw was raking the limb on which he rested. He was about fifteen feet off the ground on a sycamore limb. He was as still as death except for that one claw. He stared right at me with large yellow eyes as he raked.

He was about three times the size of the average male house cat, and he was a dirty yellow in color. The tip of his tail was a light brown.

I had ridden or walked through this forest a dozen or more times before and had never seen a bobcat before. I had read about them in nature books, and I knew north Louisiana was subject to an occasional bobcat sighting, but it was rare. I didn't know anybody who had ever seen one. At least, they hadn't told me. When I see them in zoos, I always stop and take a close look and remember the color and size of that bobcat. And I'm drawn back over time to that tree limb in a runaway woods in a Scopena forest.

I stood still for what seemed like an eternity. I didn't say a word. I didn't hear another sound in the forest. The squirrels had stopped playing. The blackbirds weren't flying or calling. The doves had gone quiet. I remember there were no sounds. The bobcat looked me over, never moving, eyes unblinking.

I didn't know what the clawing meant, but he didn't seem disturbed in any other way. He seemed relaxed on the limb. He was stretched out and calm. He didn't hiss or show flashes of a temper tantrum. He just watched me as I stood there quietly on the forest floor, less than three miles from my house and less than twenty feet from his resting place.

He was the first to move. Rising slowly from his resting place, he sank slowly off the limb to the tree trunk, leaped to the ground, and hurtled in the other direction through the forest. Gone.

I remained where I stood. The only thing that moved was my jaw. It had dropped wide open and was still hanging there. All thoughts of running away from home left me. I wanted to tell Danny and Punkin, and Mom and Dad about seeing the bobcat. I wanted to tell them about how the bobcat had stood its ground and how he had looked me over.

It was an animal in the wild, not in a zoo someplace, trapped in a cage with other wild things. This one was free. It was the first wild cat I had ever seen like that: free and natural.

I turned to return to home. I wanted to go home and tell my story. It was summer and still daylight outside the forest, although late in the day.

I gathered my suitcase and hurried through the forest edge and through the pasture. I saw a couple of men going to the Scopena store after work. I waved and kept on toward home. When I got there, I quietly went unseen into the house and went to my room.

My brother was there and so was the letter that I had left to Mom. It was unopened. My secret runaway was never detected. I told Danny and Punkin about the bobcat, and they loved the story. I told a little white lie about going through the woods to take a shortcut to the Oklahoma field. I didn't mention running away.

I never ran away from home again. I guess I had reached the age where running away wasn't the thing to do. Getting old; isn't that what they say?

24

THE PRICE OF PROGRESS

On July 4, 1954, the world at Scopena changed. An era that had dated to the Civil War and earlier would now end.

Two giant cotton pickers arrived that day on the back of railroad flatcars straight from a factory in Illinois. They looked like monsters, on those Kansas City Southern rail cars on America's birthday. They were red and shining in the sun. I remember because it was a sign that something basic was changing at Scopena. I was ten years old.

In time, the machines would take the place of up to two hundred human pickers of cotton. These workers had not been permanent employees of ours, but were day laborers transported from Shreveport each morning in buses that arrived at Scopena about 6:30 a.m.

Machines that could pick cotton on two rows simultaneously were a huge advance over the antiquated single-row pickers they replaced. The single-row mechanical harvesters had been slow and difficult to operate and calibrate. They made hardly a dent in our need for workers on a daily basis. It had been this way before the Civil War on Scopena and thousands of cotton farms throughout the Deep South—dependent on hand-labor for the harvest of cotton.

The day laborers who came to Scopena each morning were young and old, but almost all were black. They were paid for each one hundred pounds of cotton they picked from three dollars a hundredweight to five dollars a hundredweight, depending on the time

Cotton harvester in a Scopena cotton field

of year and the picking conditions. The price for picking cotton was posted daily in the harvest field. A whole crew at Scopena provided for their care, training, water, and feeding.

The elimination of a major workforce didn't happen in a day or overnight. It took three or four years, as the performance of the mechanical harvester became more and more reliable.

Old habits die hard, so the hand cotton pickers were still around in some numbers for us three years later. By the time that I went off to college in 1960, we needed only one bus with fifty workers. When I returned to Louisiana for good in 1967, all the hand pickers were gone.

As I stood there that summer day in 1954 when the cotton pickers arrived, I didn't think about it as being anything other than progress. I didn't think about the hundreds of people who weren't qualified or equipped to find work in the marketplace. They had no education. They had no chance. They picked cotton or nothing. Dad never mentioned this price of progress. Surely, he understood what was being lost. We did not discuss it at any of our family meetings over the lunch or supper tables. Like so many things in our life, it just happened.

What happened to all these people? Some were retrained. Some got other odd jobs. But most retired from the workforce and became welfare recipients, I'm sure. I would see some of them hanging on street corners when I went to town.

There they resigned themselves to a life with no prospects. When they recognized me, they would wave and whoop and holler. But when I talked with them, they would admit that nothing was happening in their lives. They would ask about Scopena and talk fondly of working on the farm even if it was only a day-labor job. Each one appreciated the dignity of work, even though they were trapped in poverty and found themselves in the hopelessness of technological obsolescence.

You got the feeling that although their lives were threatened by the advance of technology and the force of mechanization, they were oblivious to what was happening. It was almost as if the safety net of government welfare had clouded their ability to see that they were being made unnecessary in the workforce. They were the last to know. That's not unusual in life: the people most personally involved in changing condiditions are the last to know that conditions have changed.

Look at a collapse in oil prices. The rough-neck is the last to know when prices fall. The rough-neck has to lose his job; then, he realizes that the market has collapsed. Until then there is no warning.

What was the price of progress? Welfare at permanent levels; hopelessness in the job market; the exposing of an education system that had been educating poor blacks insufficiently for more than two hundred years?

What resulted was mass migration to California, Illinois, Michigan, and elsewhere in order to get factory jobs. Los Angeles, Chicago, and Detroit gained millions of migrants from the Deep South during the 1960s and 1970s as farm mechanization gathered speed and swept the land. I saw it begin at Scopena in the 1950s. Although I didn't know it and we didn't talk about it then, it caused Scopena to change in a dramatic way. The human cotton-picker had gone the way of the dinosaur, and there was no going back.

My friends went to California, rather than to Detroit, as it turned out. Years later, when I had a congressional office in downtown Shreveport, and an aged Scopena hand or a member of a family that had lived in the quarters years ago paid a visit, I would ask "where you coming from?" California would be the answer, seven times out of nine.

25

BASEBALL WITH GRANDDADDY

Ross McDade was my mother's father, and he lived on a cotton plantation of his own about seven miles south of Scopena on Highway 71 South. The town, a general grocery, and the post office were all called McDade. He was a tall (6"1'), silver-haired man who was up in years when I first knew him. He had three girls and a boy and a longtime wife, Mama, as she was known by all.

Mama was known to play the piano in social and church circles. It was always fun to go to McDade and see Mama and Granddaddy and eat Mama's fine cooking. Granddaddy was seemingly oblivious to Mama's cooking or piano playing, though. He sat at a card table in the living room playing solitaire by the hour, or he was out reviewing the crops and making sure his foremen were doing their jobs. Or he was playing pitch (a form of gin rummy) at the McDade general store, which was located 350 yards from his grand house. He saw himself as an overseer. He never got his hands dirty.

His only son, Ross, had won fame as a golfer, winning the state amateur and state professional championships. He had moved to Texas as a young man to head a small finance company. Granddaddy's three girls—Emily, Ethel, and Adeline, my mother—grew up at McDade and ended up marrying local men.

Granddaddy ran for sheriff of Bossier Parish years before I was born. He was defeated by the incumbent sheriff soundly in a bitter

Ross McDade, "Granddaddy," reading the newspaper

campaign. Granddaddy took to wearing two guns after his defeat—not one, but two—saying that one gun wasn't enough. The election showed, he said, that he had more enemies than he had figured. He was quite a character.

At McDade, Granddaddy Ross was king. He had amassed about 1,100 acres of cotton and a few cows. His plantation stretched back about a mile to the river. His main source of revenue was the annual crop of cotton, which he had picked by hand, and the cotton gin located at McDade. The gin was smaller than Scopena's and not as modern, but it ginned the cotton harvested on about five thousand acres around McDade.

He lived in a lavishly built southern mansion that was a single story, with a wood-planked floor. It had four large bedrooms and a front stairwell that led up to a fine front porch that went across the whole front of the house. The front yard was home to six beautiful pecan trees.

You could converse with Granddaddy when he was playing solitaire at home, but it had to be about baseball. He studied the box scores in the newspaper every morning. In fact, he knew baseball statistics better than anyone I've ever known. He would have been very good at a game popular now, but impossible in the 1950s before the internet: fantasy baseball.

He especially loved the Shreveport Sports, a professional baseball team in the Texas League. The Texas League had teams in Texas, Louisiana, Mississippi, Arkansas, and Oklahoma. I think he owned a small piece of the team. Texas League teams were part of the major league farm club system, so all the players were trying to climb to the big leagues after they spent one or two years in the Texas League. The quality of baseball was good.

I was a baseball fan myself, and a special treat beginning when I was about ten in 1953 was to go to some of the Sports games with Granddaddy. He would call Scopena after I arrived home from school around 4:30 and see if I had homework that would keep me from going to the game on a school night. If I didn't—and I rarely did—we were on. In the summertime he called in early afternoon for a game that night.

He called on a party-line phone that was connected to six other customers in the McDade area. When you made your call, you never knew if anyone else was listening to your conversation. Granddaddy would speak loudly when he called me. I was never sure that he spoke loudly because he wanted the neighbors to hear or because Scopena was located seven miles from McDade, and the longer the distance, the louder you had to speak, or so Granddaddy thought.

He would pick me up in his Packard automobile about 5:30 in the afternoon at Scopena, and we would drive straight to the Dandee's restaurant in Bossier City, along Highway 71, about one and a half miles past the entrance to Barksdale Air Force base. Dandee's was a family diner with a large room for dining. It was the kind of place featured in the television show *Diners, Dives, and Drive-ins.*

The choices were smothered pork chops, hamburgers, cheeseburgers, hot dogs with chili and beans, chicken sandwiches, cheese sandwiches, and chocolate shakes and malts. We loved stopping at Dandee's. Everybody knew us there, and over time they found out that we were headed to watch the Shreveport Sports baseball game. If I ordered a Coke for my meal, Granddaddy let me get a chocolate malt for dessert, and we would take it with us.

Finishing at Dandee's, we would drive up Barksdale Boulevard through Bossier City and across the Texas Street bridge to the Shreveport Sports' baseball stadium. It was about a fifteen or twenty minute drive through downtown Shreveport to the stadium, which was in the black section of town.

The Texas League was segregated. It had no black players until long after I stopped attending games with Granddaddy. Jackie Robinson entered the majors in 1947, but the Texas League I think integrated only in the 1960s, as the league was embedded in the heart of Dixie.

In spite of segregation, the Shreveport Sports always drew a large and enthusiastic crowd of black fans. Unlike today, when pro football is king, baseball was very popular then with the average sports fan, in part because tickets were affordable, at about two dollars per reserved seat.

The seating was segregated, of course. Blacks couldn't sit in the white section along the first and third base lines and in the second tier of stands on either side of home plate. They were restricted to the grandstands in the third or upper deck section of the ballpark.

I had occasion to go to the black section late in the stadium's life, long after Granddaddy and I quit going to the games, on a day when no game was scheduled. It was a Shreveport Chamber of Commerce "get to know Shreveport" tour. I was amazed at how the black fans had a good view of the field. Maybe they were laughing all the time at the stupidity of the white folks who had forced them to sit in the best seats in the house.

The first thing we did after arriving at the game was purchase a scorecard and then we headed to the hot dog stand. Our stop at Dandee's for pre-game food didn't prevent us from getting a hot dog and chili, a large soft drink (I loved RC Cola), and a giant bag of peanuts. I can taste the peanuts now. We sat on the third base side of home plate. Granddaddy taught me how to keep score. The scorecard kept us informed how the players had done in previous at-bats. We were a vocal force along that third base line with that information. We would support our individual ball players and razz the players of the other team.

Sitting with us in our gated section of the infield stands were a number of friends and baseball fans from Shreveport. They remained friends of mine and supporters of my political campaigns for years. When I would see them at a political rally or a chance meeting on the street, we loved to reminisce about those old ball games, years ago.

We had such a raucous good time in that section along third base. We were so close to the opposing players, as well as with members of our own team. I remember in particular an outstanding young outfielder for the Cleveland Indians farm team, either from Dallas or Fort Worth. He hit two home runs in his first two at-bats against us. We didn't let him forget it, riding him unmercifully for the rest of the series.

I won't forget how he took the ribbing. He didn't say a word. He just turned to us and smiled. He hit five home runs in that three-game series and made only one out. He was the best outfielder we ever saw. He was called up to the big leagues before his team returned to the Shreveport Sports' stadium. His name: Rocky Colavito. He went on to become one of the top sluggers in major league baseball, as he hit 374 home runs.

After the game, Granddaddy and I would visit with our players and with Bonnaeu Peters, the majority owner of the Shreveport Sports. About thirty minutes after the game's final out, Granddaddy and I would walk to the back of the parking lot, pick out the Packard in the dim light, and make our way to the bridge that brought us to Bossier City and eventually home.

Granddaddy's old mansion was built of pine and that proved to be its undoing when it caught fire one night in 1962 while I was at college. It burned to the ground. Mama, his wife, had passed away from a heart attack in 1961, so Granddaddy Ross moved to Scopena and spent the remainder of his life there until he died in 1969 at the age of ninety-two. Mom died in 2016 in her sleep at the age of ninety-two also. I guess there was a genetics connection. They can talk about all the advances in medicine they want to, but in the fifty years since Granddaddy Ross passed, Mom, his daughter, passed at the exact same age. Medical advances had not bought one extra year of life.

26

A Shooting

In the early 1950s, a family lived on the back of Scopena in the cut across the bayou. They owned about eighty acres right in the middle of our farm but wouldn't sell it to Dad. So he leased it every year to grow cotton. There was no problem with the negotiations on the lease, and Scopena enjoyed farming the property right in the heart of the territory it called its headquarters site.

They were good people who didn't have much money. They lived in a shack with tin and broken bits of timber from the river bank nailed to its side. It looked like what it was: a patchwork house. Dad offered to buy their land and let them remain in a new house that he would build. They would accept Dad's offer, but by the time that the papers would be drawn up, they would change their mind and Dad would have to negotiate all over from square one.

Alcoholism was a factor in the off-again, on-again negotiations. Some days they were so drunk you couldn't even understand what they said. Dad just steamed, but because he had leased the land for long periods, he managed to tolerate them.

As an aside, I learned a powerful lesson about untreated alcoholism from this family. The family had three brothers. They were in their forties and fifties and all alcoholics. But they looked seventy-five. They could be the nicest neighbors in the world when they were sober: thoughtful, funny, engaging. But when they were drunk, they were paranoid, fearful of the future, uncertain of the past.

The key lesson here from Dad is to not be an enabler or to tolerate the addiction, but to be a truth-teller, insisting on professional treatment and action.

One spring, the family had a mama pig, who delivered about six babies. Beginning soon thereafter, the momma and daddy pigs took the piglets into the surrounding cotton fields, stripping the cotton of leaves and thereby robbing the plants of the ability to produce bolls. The family of drunks had a fence around its home site, but they didn't maintain it, allowing the pigs to roam free. Dad warned the head of the family several times that they needed to control their animals. He said that pigs and cotton don't mix.

I was with Dad one day when he discovered the pigs outside of the fence and in the young cotton fields around Sunny Point, about a mile from the family's home. The pigs had done extensive damage up and down the cotton rows. Dad was furious. I was nine and followed everything Dad did, so I was furious, too.

We rounded up the pigs and drove them home. The head of the household was on his front porch. Without ever getting out of the Jeep, Dad shouted to him that he had found his pigs in our cotton fields and that it must stop. I will never forget what Dad said then. "I promise you this," he said, "if I find your pigs destroying my cotton again, I will shoot them dead—every one of them. Be warned." The man just nodded his head.

In one sense, it was unfair what Dad said because the man was drunk and wouldn't be able to remember it. But one thing was certain: I had never seen Dad that angry before. I asked him whether he was serious. He said yes, that idle threats were not part of his repertoire. He said that he had warned the man multiple times. And he said that the man could solve the problem with a simple repair to his fence.

Dad said that the family was deliberately releasing its pigs into our cotton fields, and he wouldn't stand for it any longer. He found proof of their intent the week before when Dad sent a gang of workers to repair the fence, but the family ran them off the property. They didn't want it repaired, Dad believed. They wanted their pigs to range free in our cotton fields. It was good eating at no cost.

Without a word, Dad placed a rifle in his Jeep that day. That was new. Dad was not a hunter.

Two or three days later, Dad and I were driving across the top of the levee on the back of Scopena. It was the Levee Cut about a half a mile as the crow flies from the drunken family's homestead. He saw something and stopped. It was the eight pigs—six piglets and mama and papa—munching and rooting on the cotton plants at the other end of the field.

He stopped the Jeep and got the rifle from its stand in the Jeep. He sighted on the hogs and took aim at them. One by one, as he fired, they squealed and hit the ground dead. Not just one papa or mama hog. All eight hogs.

When he was through, Dad didn't celebrate or brag or say anything. We drove in silence the three miles back to the Scopena office. There, he went inside and wrote a check for eight hundred dollars to the head of the drunken family—one hundred for each pig. A fair price, Dad thought. He mailed it that day. When I mentioned the incident to him a couple of days later, he said that he expected a man to do what he said he was going to do when he was in the right.

Several months later, one of the brothers passed away. As a result, the other two sold their interests to Scopena. I never heard about the pig incident from them. Maybe the alcohol affected their missing the pigs for a day or two. Maybe the check for eight hundred dollars, which they cashed, made them think that they had sold the hogs to Dad.

It sounds cruel thinking back about it. It wasn't the pigs' fault that the neighbors lived drunken, unruly lives. But that didn't matter. Dad had made a promise, and he stuck to it. So the pigs had paid for it with their lives.

Dad never mentioned the incident again. Nor did I ever mention it to anybody. I have thought about it a thousand times since then. It was an internal life's lesson for me: say what you mean and do what you say. And the lesson was delivered in such a graphic way that I never told a soul, until now, when Dad and the family of drunks are long gone.

27

A Pig Skinning

Dad would let me stay home from school some days if something noteworthy was happening at Scopena. One cold, drab day when I was in fourth grade, I stayed home from school for a pig skinning. It was a sight to see.

The hog was huge—it weighed over a quarter ton the Scopena folks estimated—and was not happy about moving from its pen behind the house, where it had been getting fat for more than one year from kitchen scrapings, to the killing pen. There, three old men and two younger men wrestled the pig to the muddy ground. The hog was squealing as the men grabbed for it. The hog was tough to wrestle down because it sensed something bad was happening, I guess. It moved quickly for its size. Its more than five hundred pounds shook with anger or fright.

Finally, the workers gained enough control to kill the hog with a blow from an axe to the back of its head. They lifted it with a winch until he hung head-down from his hind feet suspended about eight feet in the air. Behind the house by the water pump the workers were planning to use a big pot of boiling water to wash and skin the hog. It was a cast iron pot that had been used for washing clothes outdoors in the days before we got a washing machine. I remember watching the men build the fire to boil the water.

Wearing rubber gloves, the five men scrubbed the hog with running water and then dried it with rags. They lit rags attached to long poles and burned the hair off its hide. When the hog was clean and the hair removed, the workers gutted it and then sliced the hog into pork chops and slabs of bacon and the skin into cracklins.

There were about a dozen spectators (me, Danny, Punkin, and several of the black kids from the quarters, who had skipped school as well). We didn't make a sound. Silently, I guess we showed respect for the hog.

The five men took great care in their work, one chopping and the others assisting, and were given parts of the hog for their efforts. They seemed to know the role that each one had played, and they split the hog accordingly. The kitchen at Scopena took the rest. And the rest of the hog was more than half the meat. We ate pork chops and bacon from that hog for weeks and weeks.

I remember other activities on Scopena that are long-gone like hitching the mules to pull the ditch digger to drain fields. The mules could pull the ditch-digger in the mud and rain where a tractor would get stuck. I don't know what the management does now for excess rainfall on the crop fields. Maybe just wait until the tractor can work again, and lose part of a crop while you wait?

Hog slaughtering and mule hitching were long-ago functions common at one time. Now, they have joined the forgotten buggy and whip that the farmer has seen the last of.

When the men were finishing their work that day, I remember Dad saying that we might never see such an activity again. He was right. In the sixty years since that day, I have never seen any kind of pig skinning at Scopena or anywhere else. Dad was so perceptive to have me, and Punkin and Danny stay home from school to watch a brief glimpse of passing history.

28

Detasseling Corn

Scopena had been growing corn from the late 1940s. We sold the corn for human consumption at local grocery stores or for cattle consumption as a feed crop on the farm. It was not a big crop and never took more than one hundred to two hundred acres of our land. Cotton was the prime revenue producer at Scopena.

But in 1951 an associate of Gran Vernon's in Illinois proposed that Scopena begin growing hybrid seed corn for their corn operation in the Midwest. The parent company, Funk's Hybrid seed corn, was looking for a producer of corn seed that could meet their stringent growing standards. In turn, they would pay well for the corn seed— at least three times the price as that paid for regular corn.

Despite the higher payment, it was not an easy decision for Scopena, for growing hybrid corn was much more expensive than growing regular corn. First, Scopena could use only a select type of corn seed, bought from the parent company at a very high price. That price averaged four times the commercial rate for seed.

Second, Funk's required Scopena to agree to grow the hybrid corn relatively weed-free, an expensive standard. This was hard to do in the South where weeds (Johnson grass, purslane, morning glory vines, and ragweed) were a natural part of every field. A commercial corn operation generally ignored the weeds beyond plowing the fields.

In addition, we would have to irrigate the corn during a drought. Irrigation was so expensive in the South that we rarely irrigated corn and only irrigated about 40 percent of the cotton acreage. Cotton earned so much more for farmers than did commercial corn usually. The rigorous growing requirements of the Funk's contract changed all that and made the hybrid seed more valuable.

Irrigation each year was necessary in Funk's plan, because their contract called for Scopena to produce a bountiful harvest every year. In hybrid seed corn, Scopena couldn't have a crop failure because the mother company had to have seed every year. So irrigation was mandatory, even for corn.

Finally, to grow hybrid corn, we would have to detassel six rows out of eight. Tassels grow out of the top of the corn and provide the pollinating strength of the plant. There is one tassel to every corn stalk. The tassel is the male source of pollination in the corn system. You had to remove the tassel from some rows in the hybrid seed corn system. In fact, out of every eight rows of corn, you leave only two rows with tassels (males), and six without (females).

To make sure this process worked, hybrid seed corn had to be detasseled, which meant pulling tassels from the top of a female plant that was eight to ten feet tall. Detasseling six of eight rows was very labor intensive, and you had to do it before the tassels dried out and started to produce pollen. Because the tassels dried out and can mature at different times, the corn fields had to be detasseled at least twice.

To reach the high corn to pull the tassels, a worker needed a place to stand and to move down the row of corn. The job required two people per row to not miss any tassels. Since the machine enabled you to detassel six rows at a time, and you would need two people per row on the detasseling machine to pull all the tassels, that would be twelve detasselers per machine. We had eight detasseling machines at Scopena, with one used as a spare and seven fully loaded. That meant we had a minimum of eighty-four detasselers at any one time in the corn field.

Nature does not grow any crop uniformly, so the tassels did not sprout where they could all be pulled at the same time. So the detasseling machines had to make at least two passes over two to three weeks so the workers could strip the tassels from the six female rows.

Taking all the pluses and minuses in the equation, Gran Vernon and Dad decided to plant a small patch (135 acres) of hybrid corn and agreed if it were profitable to sharply increase production under Funk's requirements the following year.

The first year of production was in 1952, and it was quite profitable. A key reason was that Dad conceived the idea of using geese in the fields for weed control. Nobody used geese in the fields except Scopena, so he didn't get the idea from talking to another farmer. Nor did he get it from a trade journal. I asked him one day. I had to do a report in school on the subject of geese to control weeds. I figured I would call the person or company who had given him the idea, and I would have my report for school.

To my surprise, Dad said that he had gotten it from reading a book on ancient times. In the middle of the book, he said, the author mentioned how the ancient Egyptians raised long-staple cotton to the envy of the rest of the world. They had used geese to control the grass and weeds in the fields. Dad decided to use geese for weed control at Scopena for cotton and corn, and Gran Vernon swiftly agreed. It was a startling and innovative idea that had value for about ten years, until the mid-1960s when new chemicals started to destroy grasses and weeds in the corn and cotton fields on their own. The cost of the geese was one-tenth the cost of human hoe-hands.

We got about four hundred five-month-old goslings on special order from a nursery in Texas. They came to Scopena in the flat bed of a long, enclosed trailer. They were calm, but curious when we herded them off the trailer into a holding pen in the equipment yard next to the shop. They immediately started to attack the grass in the pen. They herded together, running first this way and then that across the wide pen. When they settled down, they drank from the water troughs that lined the edges of the pen.

After we gave them a day or two of rest, we backed a trailer with walking ramps up to the pen and herded the geese up into the trailer. We took them to the first cornfield to feed on the grass and weeds. We strung a three-foot high fence around the field made of chicken wire, light and flexible. We also placed long water troughs with fresh water—built by Mr. Boyd—around the edge of the field.

It worked like a charm. The geese ate the grass and weeds in the cornfields without harming the corn, which stood at least three feet tall. It took about a week to eat all the grass and weeds in the field. They didn't miss a blade of grass.

As it turned out, the geese were very effective in the cotton fields as well. We didn't have to wait for the cotton to grow since they did not like the taste of the cotton plant no matter the age. So while we got the geese to take care of the corn weeds, they had an even bigger impact in the cotton fields. The use of geese didn't mean we could eliminate the hoe hands, but it did mean we could cut their numbers by half.

We had an occasional goose that would fly off with a migrating band of snow geese or Canada geese. But that was the exception because their wings were weak, and they preferred to stay with their community, which provided comfort and safety rather than flying off into the wild blue yonder.

We learned to collect the geese in big transport trailers to transfer them from one field to another. Timing was critical, because geese too long in a field would eat the corn. What a racket the geese made with their loud clucking and wild wing flapping. But we could control them as they herded like cattle. At one point, we had more than 1,200 geese patrolling our corn and cotton fields. About two geese were required for every acre of crop.

The geese were another example of the innovative improvements that Dad made to Scopena compared to those at other farms in the region. No one else in Louisiana used geese in their weed control operation. Yet the use of geese allowed Scopena to meet the requirement of a weed-free corn field and to do it cheaply.

Our biggest problem with the geese was they were an appetizing meal for foxes and coyotes. When we lost too many geese in a particular field, we would post a man with a shotgun in the field at night, and in short order he would take care of the problem.

By the fourth year of production, we knew that we had a winner with hybrid seed corn. It had become a cash cow, as an old farmer would say. So we expanded production eventually to more than 2,500 acres of prime Red River valley land. It was all irrigated in a round-the-clock operation. We transported the irrigation pipes, which were five inches in diameter and made of aluminum, to a different portion of the field every six hours, day and night. During the time I was fourteen to sixteen years old, I took on the responsibility of running night irrigation. It was backbreaking work for the men, lifting those irrigation pipes to dry ground every few hours, but I had a supervisor's role so I didn't have to lift the pipe.

When we would move the last pipe about day break and see the sun creep over the horizon bringing light to the fields, we felt elated, and dragged ourselves home to sleep and do it again the next day. I still dream about that feeling of coming in to the house and going to bed when others were just coming to work. A drought, which caused the irrigation to start, didn't happen every year, but when it did, we were prepared to irrigate every acre of the corn land. Corn was not as hardy and drought-resistant as cotton we found, and therefore the irrigation on the corn proved a significant enhancement to corn production.

As we increased the acreage dedicated to corn, we found it difficult to find a workforce for detasseling. The work was grueling, hot, and itchy in the corn field. As a result, we had a lot of turnover.

At first, we used the same workforce that we had used for hand hoeing in the early summer. Detasseling started in middle to late June, at about the time that hoeing was winding down, and we thought it was a natural fit. But the working conditions were not attractive to all the hoe hands. It was much harder physically for the workers.

We had to offer more money, eight dollars a day rather than five dollars a day, but hoe hands usually were too old to do the tough manual labor of corn detasseling no matter the wage, so we had to look elsewhere for labor. We found the answer in the high schools (white and black) in Bossier City. We visited the two high schools in May to recruit students for summer jobs. They signed up for a job that paid far above minimum wage, which was then two dollars a day.

We paid fifty cents a day extra for those who provided their own transportation. We picked up the others in school buses at the two high school campuses at 7:00 a.m. There was turnover, and we were short some mornings. When necessary, Scopena workers filled in. We paid the workers in cash each day in the corn field.

Corn detasseling under normal conditions was difficult at best. Reaching for the high tassels and yanking them from the top of the corn stalk took no special skill like hoeing did, but it was physically tiring. Plus, the corn detasseling machines were always breaking down. There was a lot of standing around as a result. Pay dropped in half during those extended down times.

There was also pressure on the detasslers: no tassel could be missed. A missed tassel would destroy the hybrid structure of the corn crop. So we had to have a great deal of supervision after each round to make sure that the field had been completely detasseled.

The job became even more complicated when it rained, and the detasseling machines couldn't drive up and down the corn rows, because the rain had made the fields impassable. When that happened, the crew would go down the row on horses or mules, and remove the corn tassels from the six female rows of corn.

This animal-driven corn detasseling operation proved effective to prevent the corn from self-fertilizing, but it was an operational nightmare with mud everywhere, and horses and mules bucking to get out of the corn. We bumped the pay up to ten dollars a day during these rainy days.

Years later, I would meet students who had been employed at

Scopena on corn detasseling duty. They always talked about the challenges they faced and the obstacles they overcame. In the process, they said they had developed an *esprit de corps* and fellowship that they remembered for years to come. None of them ever had another job like corn detasseling.

As an interesting side note to the corn operations, I was mainly missing in action because I turned out to be severely allergic to corn. We didn't notice it for the first couple of years, but in year three, my eyes would swell shut when I went into the corn fields. After much testing and many shots (self-administered), we diagnosed the problem, and doctors told me to avoid the corn field. So for years, until college, I specialized in cotton and steered clear of corn.

For years, Scopena ran a sizeable and sophisticated corn operation, but in the late 1960s hybrid seed corn in north Louisiana was afflicted by a virus that caused the yield to drop more than 70 percent in a single season. The LSU experiment station next to Scopena determined that the diseased corn infected the land, which would have to lie fallow, with no corn, for at least six years.

Scopena went back to its traditional corn crop as cattle feed and for public sale as corn on the cob in the late 1970s. But we never grew hybrid seed corn again. The prospects were too uncertain given the risks of infection.

29

GRAN VERNON

I've mentioned the man who started Scopena and then took Dad as a full owner and partner after the war, Vernon Mayer, or Gran Vernon as we called him. He and I were very close, and he was close to Dad as well. Dad ran the place, but Gran Vernon handled the farm meetings required off the farm, as well as such groups as the Southern Growers Association that met in Atlanta or the Louisiana Farm Bureau that met in Alexandria or Monroe—meetings that required a Scopena presence and that Gran Vernon loved, but Dad was not comfortable in attending. It was a partnership that worked for both men and for Scopena. He was my step-grandfather, but he was treated as a father by my Dad and a grandfather by me and my siblings. I was especially close to him.

Gran Vernon and I both loved movies so we began going to the King's Drive-inn near his house in Shreveport. He and my grandmother, Mine, lived in a huge two-story house with a wrap-around screen porch in Shreve Island—a neighborhood of south Shreveport. It was from this big house that gran Vernon and I would go to the drive-inn movie on many Friday or Saturday nights. They would change the movie once a week. His wife, my grandmother Mine, never went, but he and I would get a couple of quarters from her and go to the movie on Friday or Saturday nights at dusk. We spent fifteen cents each on tickets into the drive-inn, and that would leave us a dime each to get popcorn and a Coke. The movies were such a treat with all the possibilities for adventure, action, and mystery alive in the world. The drive-inn seemed to specialize in gangster and western movies. Both were favorites of Gran Vernon and me.

Movies weren't all we did. We listened to the radio while falling asleep at night, when I slept over at Gran Vernon's home. The Lone Ranger, Sky King, cops and robbers, Perry Mason—we loved them all long before television. He told me that television was coming in 1950-51, and he said it would change everything eventually. But we'll worry about that when it comes, he would say. He died before he ever got a television set.

He also liked to fish. He and I spent many hours fishing in Cowley Lake, which was inside the levee, formed by the meanderings of the Red River behind the house on Scopena. It was a big lake of more than a thousand acres and was located more than five miles behind Scopena headquarters. One day when we had gone back to the lake to fish, we watched a momma raccoon and her three trailing babies tiptoe around the edge of the lake. They walked right by us as if we weren't there. We stayed still as they delicately walked north around the lake concentrating on fishing. The mother looked at us briefly as she taught her babies how to fish. It was early in the morning on a cool May day. Life was never better than that morning in 1952.

Gran Vernon drove often to Laredo, Brownsville, and other towns in south Texas to sell Stardel cottonseed, which he had developed with David Melville at the LSU Red River experimental station. It was a cotton seed that produced well in the weather conditions of south Texas and north Louisiana—humid and hot. Gran Vernon was well liked and extremely popular in the farming communities of south Texas, because he had been traveling that country for several years selling the services of Scopena—Stardel cottonseed and mechanical cotton harvesters. I accompanied him on the one-thousand-mile roundtrip journey several times when I was eight, nine, and ten years old. He and I loved listening to the car radio on these trips. We would listen to major league baseball (especially the

Vernon Robards Mayer, "Gran Vernon"

St. Louis Cardinals) for hours.

When we weren't listening to the radio, we would talk about school and events in the world, like how the New York Yankees were doing. What I liked most about Gran Vernon on these journeys is that he would listen when I spoke to him. He wasn't just being polite. He would really listen and would respond. Not many adults did that.

One of our secrets on trips to south Texas is that when work was done, we would pull up in a little town like Carrizo Springs or Laredo and go to a movie at night, if one was playing that we hadn't seen. How exciting that was for me, to go to a movie in a strange city and buy a popcorn and a Coke and sit with my Gran Vernon. I knew that he would want my opinion about the movie when it was over and that he would really listen. Gran Vernon was the best.

Dad continued the tradition of going to the movies when I was young, and it's odd that every time I go to a movie now, I think of Gran Vernon and Dad. It's a small thing that we were never aware of when it was happening, but by going to the movies together, we were building a bond that would last a lifetime.

One afternoon in 1954 I was at the cotton gin when something happened to Gran Vernon. He was at the delinter—a building right next to the gin—where we had long known some repair work had to be done. Gran Vernon had taken the assignment. The most important piece of equipment in the delinter was the 1,800-pound seed cleaner. It was called the delinter; it gave the plant its name. It was the piece of equipment that was most often adjusted, and it occasionally had to be replaced altogether when adjustments didn't correct the problem.

This equipment consisted of a roller of wire brushes and saws that combed the lint off the cotton, making the cotton seed slick either for planting or crushing as oil. It also yielded a fine lint that was used for mattresses and pillows in furniture.

The delinter stood adjacent to the gin. The gin sent cottonseed to the delinter to be stored for replanting or to be transported to the seed mill for oil after it was processed. The delinter removed the fine lint from the ginned seed regardless of its ultimate use. The value of that lint from the delinter was credited to the farmer as was the value of the seed either for oil or, better yet, for replanting. These sums more than repaid the cost of ginning for the farmer. So the delinter was an economically important piece of the cotton business for everyone.

The tragic day began innocently enough. Gran Vernon prepared to replace the seed cleaner (the delinter). We had one in inventory, (the order time was nearly two weeks). So Gran Vernon used a day to prepare the site and get ready for the big operation to put the cleaner in place. He had a chain wrapped around the cleaner. The chain was attached to a giant hook so that, when raised, it would lift the whole mechanism. It seemed simple.

The next day as they were lowering the cleaner in place—about an eight foot drop from the top of the beam—my Gran Vernon was lying underneath to line it up when the main chain broke and dropped the cleaner to the struts below. One second the chain was doing its job, and the next it was whirling out of control in a death spiral. The 1,800-pound cleaner landed on Gran Vernon's chest. It was as if an automobile had landed on him. He died instantly.

I was with Danny in the gin after school. Mel, one of the employees, rushed into the gin screaming, "Mr. Vernon! Mr. Vernon! Mr. Vernon!" That was all he said. The expression on his face said enough. Danny and I ran to the delinter. They told us we had to stay outside during the twenty minutes or so that it took to lift the cleaner off Gran Vernon's chest. It was my first human loss. Ironically, it happened on Dad's birthday—December 11, 1954. I was eleven. Dad was thirty-two.

I remembered a memorable day with Gran Vernon, where we watched snow geese come into Cowley Lake on a late fall afternoon, like pieces of paper dropped from heaven tumbling down. We stood there in ignorant awe. The air, cool like a piece of spearmint candy, filled with snow-white geese, falling out of the sky. And life was good and hopeful.

I wish everyone could have a day like that. You don't know how many days like that you will have when you are living day to day. But, looking back, you will have fewer of them than you deserve or that you expect.

Dad talked to me after Gran Vernon's death. He thought that the most powerful lesson was you should always tell the people closest to you that you love them, every day, because life is unexpected, and a person might be gone without you having the chance to tell them goodbye. Every time I saw Dad after that for the rest of his life no matter what the circumstances, I told him I loved him. In the last period of his life, during a twelve-year battle with Alzheimer's, he usually didn't even recognize me. But that didn't matter to him or me. I had learned the lesson after Gran Vernon's death. "I love you, Dad," I always said.

30

ENTOMOLOGIST

One job that became a big deal in my farm life was as an entomologist. That's a fancy Latin word for bug checker. At nine years old, I became the entomologist for Scopena, trained by Dad. He expressed faith that I could do the job, and that I would do it in a thorough, systematic manner, as I did when I read the moisture gauges. I would ride my horse to check the fields beginning in early June when the sandy land cotton had leaves. Those leaves were host to aphids, spider mites, and early season insects like boll weevils and bollworms that could, if not stopped, threaten to delay the growing season of the cotton plant and ruin the yield. In a field, I would check a representative sample of plants every forty or fifty acres.

The way I kept up with the insect pressure on the cotton fields was to either examine the entire cotton plant and determine what percentage of it was infested, or I checked a part of several plants and got an infestation rate overall, i.e., 10 percent, 20 percent, or 40 percent. The cotton plant was filled with nodules (squares) that grew into bolls and eventually turned into cotton. There were about 150 such nodules or squares per plant. Any insect damage to the nodule would prevent it from becoming a boll of cotton. The higher the infestation rate, the lower the number of healthy bolls and the lower the production of cotton for the field. We tried to keep the infestation rate below 20 percent. If untreated, the infestation could range as high as 90 percent. A 10 percent infestation rate was not alarming, because that was about the rate that the plant naturally rejected bolls as they formed on the cotton plant. When the infestation rate would rise to higher than 20 percent, the entomologist would become concerned by the insects found in the cotton, and begin an eradication program.

The bug checker would have to determine the infestation rate but was also responsible for determining what kind of insect was causing the damage to the cotton. Different poison was required to kill different types of insects.

For example, boll weevils were easier to kill than bollworms. Bollworms required heavy doses of a stronger poison in order to reduce their numbers.

If I found signs of infestation above 20 percent, I would put management on notice by writing my findings on a big blackboard in the office. We would then check the plants every four days instead of every seven. Doing the survey was time consuming and required attention to detail, but the health of the crop was riding on the outcome, and Dad expected a rapid response.

I would check the percentage infestation with the same plot taken a week earlier. If the infestation rate had risen above 20 percent or had doubled (for example, from 8 percent to 16 percent) I would note that it had to be sprayed by a crop duster. I would notify the person in charge of scheduling the crop dusters what was to be sprayed on the crop and when.

I wanted to be ahead of the insects, so I had two warning signs: a doubling of a low infestation rate (under 20 percent) or a reading in excess of 20 percent. I had the rule printed and posted in the office, so if I was absent whoever took my place would follow it.

I had maps printed of the individual fields that I checked, so actual infestation rates and dates checked could be given daily to Dad. I'm proud to say that he came to rely on these maps and the recorded infestation rates as he battled the boll weevil and bollworm infestations.

The bollworms were the worst infestations of all. They did so much damage so quickly, and they were so hard to kill. The bollworms hatched from the eggs of the bollworm moth in the cotton fields. After hatching, the worms fed on the young squares and bolls of the cotton plant and could destroy a crop in just a few days. They devoured green bolls, the fruit of the cotton plant.

A bollworm infestation was dangerous because a high wind can blow the moths from an infected field to a field that had no insect problem. This could happen quickly in an afternoon or night with no warning. That's why the checking had to be done every week throughout the cotton bolls growing season—late June through early September.

My adviser on what insecticide to use on the fields was David Melville, the cotton man at the LSU Red River Valley Experiment Station. Scopena surrounded the experiment station and was perfectly located for the results of the latest experimental insecticide. He would tell me what insecticide was killing the cotton pests best on the experimental station plots. That's what I would use in my spray program at Scopena. He would also let me know the dosages and frequency of the spraying, and once again I would follow that pattern at Scopena.

I was nine years old when I assumed the responsibility for determining the proper application of insecticide—from checking the crop to the type of insecticide to be applied, to the schedule of the airplane applications.

They would schedule either the airplane or a ground machine, depending on weather conditions or the number of acres that had to be covered in a single day. The plane was more expensive but much faster than ground machines, so it could cover more acreage. The plane was ineffective in high winds, however.

The bad thing about spraying for an infestation, like bollworms or boll weevils, was that the poison also killed beneficial insects—such as wasps and certain kinds of caterpillars. So once a spraying operation was started in a field, the field was vulnerable to attack by the destructive insects throughout the remainder of the season because the natural beneficial insects were killed in the first application of poison. When the field was totally defenseless against attack by destructive insects, you had to check it on a regular cycle throughout the growing season, once you began to spray, because the beneficial insects were long gone.

The poison spray was mixed in a shed on the end of the runway. Mixing had to be done carefully to get an accurate spray mix to fit the infestation of a particular field, at a particular point in time. The shed where the mixing took place contained huge vats to store the prepared poison post-mix; three fifty-five-gallon drums of poison; a large vat of fresh water; a couple of pumps and nozzles to transfer poison and water to the mixing tank; a high-speed pump to load the airplane sprayer; and a powerful pump to pull the amount of needed water from a water well hundreds of feet below ground.

It was a highly technical and precise operation to get the right poison on the right field at the proper mixture at the right time. That was my job. I not only checked the cotton and decided what poison was appropriate for the field, but I mixed the poison and made sure that it was loaded in the aerial sprayer.

One day when I was farm manager, but helping out, we were mixing a load of spray of DDT and Toxaphene when I threw the wrong electrical switch by accident. The pump became loose from the DDT's fifty-five-gallon barrel and sprayed me thoroughly. The poison washed over me like a waterfall, drenching me with DDT and Methyl Parathion and Toxaphene. It was a deadly mix of poison with short-term effects on insects (thirty minutes to one hour) and residual effects over time on insect eggs (one to three days when the caterpillar eggs hatched).

Danny rushed me to the house—one hundred yards away—and threw me with my clothes on in the shower. I undressed and washed and washed. Afterward, I rested in bed, while a doctor on call came to Scopena to examine me. Nothing came of the incident, at least right away. I did not become ill. I was lucky. We changed the pumps in the mixing shed so they would be thumb activated, to prevent future spills like the one I had.

Five months later, I became ill with what was diagnosed as Type 1 diabetes, better known as juvenile diabetes. A crucial part of my pancreas—known as the islet of Langerhans—had died for some reason. The death of that part of the pancreas means that the person is a Type 1 diabetic. Type 1 diabetes is life-long. You become insulin dependent, and your life is shortened, depending on your success at managing blood sugar, because sugar damages your veins, your nerves, and your heart and other organs.

Type 1 diabetes is typically inherited, and no one in my family tree as far as we can tell was a juvenile diabetic. Neither Dad, Mom, my grandfathers, or my grandmothers had diabetes. My brother and none of my sisters became a Type 1 diabetic, nor did my three children or their children get the disease, for that matter.

The doctor who diagnosed my diabetes could not say whether the thorough soaking in the DDT and Toxaphene mix a year earlier was to blame. I have no way to prove it, but no other explanation makes sense to my rational brain.

31

SHEP AND KING

We always had dogs hanging around Scopena. Dad and Mom liked dogs, and so did we. Our two favorites were a German Shepherd named Shep and a collie named King (see photo).

Dad had gotten the German Shepherd from a friend in the early 1950s as a puppy, and he grew into quite a dog. Shep weighed about 145 pounds and was huge and dangerous in appearance. He protected the family around the clock, particularly Mom. He lounged around the yard and office during the day, but he slept on the floor of my parents' bedroom each night. With the family, Shep was wonderful: powerful, massive, playful, and athletic. He was everything that you wanted in a dog.

He was good at commands from any of the family, but don't be someone unfamiliar and run across him alone. He nipped the postman, salesmen, and other strangers.

Shep developed the terrible habit of chasing cars that drove by the house. He couldn't be dissuaded from doing this. One night on the dirt road between the shop and the house he was accidentally run over by a car driven by a Scopena farm hand. He died instantly. The farm hand behind the wheel, came to the kitchen door to report the fatal accident.

The whole family ran from the house to the spot where Shep was sprawled on the pavement, near the weigh scales. Dad said we

King, Scopena dog,
always close to Budgie Roemer

should bury him. We got a shovel from the garage and dug the grave next to the hedges in the front yard. When we were finally done, we wrapped Shep in a blanket and carried him to the grave site. It took Danny and me both, because he was so heavy. The girls and Mom cried as they watched us. A soft summer rain fell, and we could hear the sound of the cicadas humming a nameless tune of the night. Danny and I lifted Shep into the grave and covered him with dirt. Dad said a few words about what a good dog Shep had been and how he hoped Shep was racing in a pasture lane somewhere watching after the Lord.

Then, it was just us standing there in the quiet shadows of the front yard—alone with Shep and the rain. I was fourteen years old and except for Gran Vernon, I had never known the sadness of death. I think I was in shock.

Our other beloved dog, King, was a collie. He was beautiful in a classic collie sense of the meaning: tall, thin, with a full coat of hair. Shep lived in the house with the family, but King preferred the outdoors.

King was Dad's dog. He was beside Dad throughout the day. He even climbed into his Jeep when Dad traveled about Scopena. At night, he slept in the front hall of the Scopena house. He protected us from potential intruders with a deep growl. But King was as friendly as Shep could be fearsome. He lived to ride in the front passenger seat with Dad, his colorful coat of hair blowing in the wind.

I never saw King and Shep get into a fight, although they both were male, dominant dogs fully capable of a tussle. I think it was because they had their own territory staked out, and they never challenged each other's domain. King was the outside dog, at peace with human activity that takes place outdoors. Shep was the inside dog, carefully attuned to who was supposed to be in the house and what they were supposed to be doing.

One day King accompanied Dad as usual to the back of Scopena to retrieve lost cattle. In walking the sand bar banks of the Red River, Dad got separated from King, who was doing his own thing, running more than a mile away down river. Maybe he was chasing a rabbit. No one is sure.

King started barking in distress. By the time that Dad found him more than twenty minutes later, he had sunk in quicksand, struggled in his frenzied efforts to be free, and drowned, smothered in mud. After twelve years, Dad had lost his constant companion.

Dad refused to let the Red River keep King. When he got back to Scopena headquarters, he got four men in his Jeep and drove back to the river to dig him out. They brought him home and buried him next to Shep in the front yard, next to the hedges. I don't know all the details because I was away at college, but I do know that the news of King's passing was a heartbreaking time for me in Cambridge, Massachusetts.

32

POOL AND POKER

It seemed funny to some that our book-lined living room also contained a slate billiards/pool table for family entertainment. It seemed normal to me. Somehow the two things were connected: reading and excitement meant books, and fun meant pool and also poker.

Before the living room and its collection of reference books were turned into a pool room, it was the scene of memorable card games between Mom and Dad and neighbors on a Saturday night. The four adults would play canasta or bridge in a fierce game for bragging rights for the next week. The two adults playing Mom and Dad would alternate from Saturday to Saturday—my Uncle Nalda and Aunt Emily, or Joe and Mrs. Caplis, or some other neighbor. One of the more enjoyable card-playing couples was Slim and Beatty Waldrip, who together managed the Scopena store. Slim always wore a Texas-sized cowboy hat and was obnoxiously loud when he played. Beatty somehow put up with him.

We five kids loved the card games and the banter, and we would play around the card table, the older kids reading or playing music back in Mine's house. When the pool table was imported into Scopena, the living room became the pool room, and the card table and the card games played on it were moved back to Mine's house.

Many of my friends commented that they thought it strange to bring a pool table and fill up the living room, but to enjoy life was the goal that Dad and Mom set for us, and a big way to do that was to read good books and enjoy a great game of pool, poker, or some other game that challenged your brain. Pool and billiards were not only fun, but could be played anywhere on earth by the same set of rules. The whole idea of us kids in competition with the rest of the world was exactly the philosophy that Dad preached all the time.

I became quite good at pool by playing hours and hours of the game with Danny, Dad, and friends. We had the pool table at Scopena to practice on. I played by myself for entire days. It was a slate pool table, top of the line. I never played on a better one—one that was more true, one where the roll was more certain.

I don't know where Dad found the table, but it came, delivered in a big truck one afternoon when I was about ten. It took five men to take it into the pool room/library. It replaced a perfectly fine table that was quite ordinary in comparison.

Dad had the men level the table by adding shims underneath its legs. He used a levelling instrument with a bubble gauge to make sure the table was perfectly level. Every month he would bring the gauge over from the shop to check the trueness of the table. We had such an advantage learning pool and practicing its intricacies on that fine table.

At Harvard, years later, there were eight to ten social clubs called final clubs. Fewer than 10 percent of the students were invited to join a final club. Greek fraternities were not permitted on campus. I never thought of myself as a final club candidate, because I was not a prep school boy, and I thought my sophomore year, which is the year when selected students were asked to join a final club, would pass uneventfully. A pool and billiards table served as the main recreation for the club's members, and games there were hotly contested. Thanks to the opportunities at Scopena, I was hardwired into the game of pool. Dad somehow had known that would be a part of my life.

One day early in my sophomore year, a member of the Dunster

House (one of ten houses where all Harvard non-freshmen lived) came up to me in the chow line. He introduced himself—I hadn't known him to be a member of the Iroquois final club up to then— and invited me to the club to play pool that afternoon. Come as you are, he said—I was dressed informally with blue jeans, a tennis shirt, and tennis shoes—and come to the side entrance of the club at 3:00 p.m. Knock, and you will be let in. I was still only seventeen years old.

I had played pool and billiards as a freshman in the rec center at Harvard, although I hadn't much time to play pool, but I guess my reputation as a good pool player had gotten around. So the Iroquois members had decided to get their own look at the boy from Scopena.

The interior of the Iroquois club was just like you read about in works of fiction—*The Great Gatsby* comes to mind—with quiet elegance on the inside: chandeliers and paneled wood walls. The members made it clear that they disdained Harvard's formal rules and regulations. While some were dressed in slacks and sports coats, others wore tennis shoes and shorts. I was coatless in my jeans. They obviously didn't care about my attire. They wanted to watch me play pool and see how I reacted to close examination by the members.

I smoked, as did most members I met that day, but I did not drink alcohol, as many of them did. I had a glass of Coke while I played their best members. The games were hard fought. But no one could defeat me. When someone did win a game, I had the right to challenge him to a rematch. I always won it. We talked mostly pool while we played. That was stimulating for me because it was my longest stint in a normal conversation since I had been at the university. No classes or grades were discussed; just life in general.

There was one awkward scene that day, however. A former member of the club who was now a successful businessman in Boston was visiting and insisted on playing me. I beat him. He had been drinking and didn't take well to the result, or maybe he just didn't like me for some reason. He proceeded to challenge me in front of the others.

He was loud and rude and waved one-hundred-dollar bills at me as he challenged me to a one-hundred-dollar shootout. I accepted and beat him soundly. He bemoaned the loss, saying that I didn't drink and that had given me an advantage. So I gulped down a whiskey sour to satisfy him.

That encouraged him, and he challenged me this time to a five-hundred-dollar winner take all. Even though I didn't have five hundred dollars, I accepted his challenge. I beat him silly while becoming fairly irate over the things he was saying. In thinking over the incident, he was saying what all losers say ("lucky shot," for instance, or "you couldn't hit that shot again in five years"), but he carried his comments to the extreme. Finally, three members of the club asked him to leave or to go sober up, and the tense situation settled down.

Throughout the afternoon, I had been wondering whether an invitation to join the Iroquois would be forthcoming. But no one said anything about it. I assumed that I would be formally asked to attend an "invitation" party and be reviewed for membership like all other potential members. The Iroquois invited between five and fifteen new members annually out of a Harvard class of one thousand. The unpleasant scene with the man left me thinking, however, that I was doomed for a blackball.

I was wrong. A note was inserted beneath my door at Claverly Hall several days later formally asking me to join the Iroquois club and bring my pool cue. (I didn't have a pool cue of my own. Never did. I borrowed whatever cue was at the club's pool rack.) My pool acumen became a club legend and, in fact, I was elected president of the Iroquois club when I was a junior—by acclamation. We asked Danny to join the Iroquois when he reached his sophomore year at Harvard and I was a graduate member of the Harvard Business School.

We also learned how to play poker as boys, and it, too, became handy later on. Dad spent hours with me and Danny in the living room teaching us the intricacies of the game when we were ten or so. We used matchsticks as the common currency. Dad had picked up the game while in the military during World War II. The stories he would tell about playing poker with his Army Air Corps buddies would keep Danny and me wide awake long after our bed time.

There is a great deal of luck on any individual hand of poker—the luck of the draw, for example—but, if poker is played the correct way with skill and discipline, a player can win consistently. Dad taught us boys how to get the small, winning edge in poker: count the cards that have been dealt to estimate which cards are remaining in the deck, and read the person you're playing to surmise the kind of hand he has. With that information, you could know when your hand was best and when it wasn't—usually. Sometimes a card had already been played that was necessary to the victory of an opposing player. And so he couldn't win. That was the advantage of reading cards.

Danny and I were good with math, and we could keep count of the number of cards already played. But reading other players hands took some time to develop.

The best way to read your opponent was to watch him carefully as he played. If he had a good hand, he might sit up straighter, order a drink or tinker with his chips. These were called tells, and everybody had them. The same is true about tells if the man was bluffing. His voice might change or his hands might shake. He would give himself away, and the poker odds would change to your benefit. Your chance of victory might change from one in three to one in two, and a losing night would turn into a winning one.

You identified tells by careful observation. By observing the way a hand was played when you were just a spectator or by watching an opposing player closely, you could pick up the tells of an opposing player the only way possible—by watching him.

Dad was good at picking up the tells of an opponent, because he was a careful, observant player. He watched how the hand would be played each and every time. If there was anything to be learned, he learned it. He was uncanny at judging your cards, and, as a result, I never could beat him consistently. I think it was psychological. He said that a man either had the cards or he didn't, and your job was to be right about each condition.

That is why he never drank at a poker table. Alcohol is a threat to concentration and makes you less observant. If decorum made you have a drink so as not to stand out, then make one drink last all night long. A person's chance of victory increased by being the only sober player at the table, according to Dad's simple philosophy.

Dad predicted that we would be good players because we were focused. Danny is still the finest poker player that I have ever seen. Dad didn't teach poker to the girls. I guess that was a sexist thing. The girls were developing other interests, like tennis.

Dad always said that poker was played all over the world, both to earn money and friends. Funny how that quiet practice at poker also paid great dividends at the Iroquois club. Some members of the Iroquois club that I see in Boston still ask about Danny and me at the poker table long ago. They want to know if we were bluffing when we won. The secret is to never tell them. So, we just laugh, and never let them know.

There was a poker room at the Iroquois. It had a window over-looking the main lobby, so the members could always tell when a poker game was being played in the club. During those times, no other activities were allowed in the Iroquois except television, which was in the basement four floors from the poker room, or pool in the pool room on the third floor.

Poker was a serious pursuit at the club, usually with a waiter as-signed to get drinks and sandwiches for members who played. And cigars were allowed only in the poker room. But it was fun for me, because I always won. Maybe it wouldn't have been as much fun if I had lost more frequently.

My prowess as a poker player served to draw me closer to the young men who fancied themselves as poker titans. Many of these same men supported me when I became president of the Iroquois club my junior year. You never know where political support will materialize.

I continued to play poker long after college, holding a weekly game with a group of oil and gas friends in Shreveport at the Petro-leum Club. This was a high stakes game with ten thousand dollars or more in each pot. It was very profitable to me, stemming from the practice sessions of years ago with Dad.

I interrupted the weekly games of poker to run for Congress in 1978 and again in 1980, when I was fortunate enough to win. During my first two years in Congress, I played in a weekly game in the men's locker room at the congressional gym. Only congressmen were involved, and it was a great place to do business on your congressional agenda and to develop friendships with colleagues of both parties. The buzzer system was timed to give you plenty of time to get from the gym to the floor of Congress to never miss a vote.

I also began playing in another weekly poker game that was held at a private house on Capitol Hill or in Georgetown. The congressional game was relatively small stakes with one or two thousand dollars being the range of losses or winnings. The "off the hill" game was higher stakes and included such journalists as Robert Healey from the *Boston Globe*, Bob Woodward from the *Washington Post*, Lou Cannon from the *Los Angeles Times*, Thomas Edsall from the *Washington Post*, and also Ab Mikva, a judge with the U.S. Court of Appeals, who went on to become President Bill Clinton's chief counsel, to name but a few. Just like Dad had told me twenty-five years earlier when teaching the lessons of poker, the relationships would mean money, but, most important, friendships.

The congressmen who enjoyed poker were Jerry Huckaby and Bob Livingston from Louisiana, Ron Dellums from California, and Charlie Rangel from New York. Georgia was represented by Ed Jenkins, Billy Lee Evans, and Dawson Mathis—all good players and all good men. Joe Early from Massachusetts brought a Yankee richness to the game. I mention Joe because his accent stood out among all those southern drawls. Plus he was memorable because he was so nice.

We developed quite a good friendship around our poker games, and things were fine until the second year when I made my income tax returns public by filing them with the Clerk of the House. I showed net income of twenty-five thousand dollars from poker winnings over a year period. "What if my name had been revealed?" they wailed.

I apologized for the offense, but explained that I always publicly released my tax returns. While I included all sources of income, including my poker winnings, I noted that I never identified winners and losers. They moaned. They groaned. They threatened to quit playing with me. But they didn't.

Looking back, I think the thing that they objected to most was the revelation that they might have been a big loser in a game where I won so much money. They had been telling a few people at home that they were winning all those years, yet their income tax form didn't say that. Had they been lying? Should they pay taxes on what they didn't win? They were caught in a dilemma, and their reputation suffered.

✷ ✷ ✷

One benefit came from the news article. Tip O'Neill, speaker of the house, called to congratulate me for reporting the income and asked if I wanted to begin playing gin with him. I was a "poker master" and, if he could beat me at gin, then, he was the man. He would enhance his card playing reputation. Tip was very competitive. Plus my guess is that he thought he might get some inside information on what I and the other members of the boll weevil caucus were up to.

The only thing is that I didn't know how to play gin—Dad hadn't taught me the game—but I told Tip that I would love to. After all, he was the speaker of the house. It was a little awkward because I didn't know Tip well but especially because I had voted against him for speaker. That got a lot of attention since we were both Democrats, and I was the rare congressman to break with the party game that Washington played. I didn't have anything against Tip. It was simply that he was much too liberal for my district. But I thought it was okay to be friends with him, like I would with any other member. Of course, he was even more important than just any other member. He was speaker of the house. Plus, he was a nice guy. I liked him.

I took a crash course in how to play gin. I asked a Republican congressman from Houston, Bill Archer, who could beat me at gin, to give me a lesson or two. Bill was the best gin player in the Congress, I thought. Eventually, Tip and I played in his office just about every month. He would call at odd hours depending on the schedule of the House of Representatives. It usually was a night session. We played in an anteroom just off his office. He had his calls held during the games, but President Reagan called once during an important House debate. I overheard the conversation, all big-eared. I couldn't help it.

I noticed that he was very respectful with the president, but I could tell from the call that they were on opposite sides of the debate. All Tip said to me after he said goodbye was "that's your guy. Politics." He uttered not another word, because, I guess, he figured I was with President Reagan, as I was on most issues.

Tip and I even played gin on the congressional chartered flight from Washington to Louisiana and back for the funeral of Congressman Gillis Long. Gillis was not much of a card player, but I never knew a more astute politician. He loved politics and deciphering the convoluted map of any political deal. The idea of me and Tip playing gin together on the flight to and from the funeral would have stretched him out laughing.

During my gin games with Tip, it came up a time or two that I hadn't voted for him as speaker. I told him that it wasn't personal, but that it showed the kind of political independence that I stood for and that I thought that my congressional district demanded.

He understood that logic. It was political, and it made sense to him. He did ask if I would vote for him as speaker if he would need just one vote in a tight election. I told him that I would consider it if required. That answer seemed to satisfy him, but I never found myself in that quandary. I don't think that I would have had the courage to vote for him and against my district, unless that vote would give me an advantage that would help my district.

Tip was a serious gin player and good. When we played in the antechamber off the house floor, he never fooled around or kidded with another person who might stick his head in the room to seek his advice. His full attention was on our game. We played for a penny a point, a normal betting range for a low stakes game. I would be ahead or behind $300-$500 in the month. We forgave losses to each other as it turned out. No money ever changed hands, but if the truth be told, he ended up owing me money.

Tip was good to me, putting me on the Banking Committee in my second year in Congress when the Democratic hierarchy didn't want it done because I wasn't viewed as a team player. His decision caused a big stink at the time. But Tip knew that I knew banking from our conversations at the gin table.

He was a crafty, good politician and gained a great deal from the conversation with me by better understanding the conservative wing of the Democratic Party. Just in casual discussions, he could tell whether an issue was important to me or my colleagues, or whether we might have some political flexibility on the issue. I learned that he always listened to what you had to say and tried to figure out if you had any wiggle room to come to his side of the issue.

I remember one issue that involved missiles on one of our bases overseas. President Reagan called me to lobby for the bill, which would give him the power to change the location of the missiles in certain limited cases. I was inclined to vote for the president before his call, but while making his case President Reagan used the Japanese as an example of a foreign power that he would use this against, saying that he needed the authority to rattle the saber against them if need be.

I was shocked with the president indicating that the Japanese were adversaries. He had misspoken. I stopped him respectfully and asked if he meant to mention the Japanese. I thought they were one of our best allies, I said.

The president sputtered a second and said, "no," he had been referring to the North Koreans not the Japanese. But I was shaken. He had used Tokyo as well as Japan in his pitch for additional power.

I didn't tell Tip about the incident, but I told him that several boll weevils didn't want to give missile power to the president unfettered by a congressional up or down vote. A compromise adding that language to the original bill was possible, I said, and indeed one was struck.

I can truthfully say that Tip and I seldom voted together, but I could talk to him about issues that affected my district in Louisiana, and he helped every time with sage advice. He was the consummate politician. I'm proud to say he became a friend.

33

The Crash

It was kind of an off day during the middle of the week in early August 1956, a day when cotton chopping had been completed, the dry weather for irrigation had not yet started, and the insect infestation for cotton was just beginning. It was the summertime, so school was out. I took the day off.

At about 2:00 on that hot afternoon, I was with my brother, sisters, and Mom in our backyard for a swim. I had no work assignments, so it was like a vacation day. It was typical chaos at the swimming pool, with fun fights, screams, hollers and the fifty-foot slide in high demand.

We hadn't been in the pool long when Homer Gray, who operated the farm immediately north of Scopena, came running around the corner of the house. He had been in the office to book an airplane for crop dusting. Homer was over sixty, and I had never seen him run. And the expression on his face was unforgettable. He kept screaming and screaming, "Miss Adeline! Miss Adeline! He crashed!"

It took me but a split second to realize what had happened: Dad had crashed in one of our planes. Homer pointed to the far end of the grass landing strip that was at the opposite end of the house. Homer then collapsed in a heap beside the swimming pool. Danny and I ran to the runway and then toward the far end of the field.

The runway was about a mile long. As we ran, I prayed that Dad

Wreckage from
Budgie Roemer's
airplane crash

would be all right and, as we approached the crash site at the end of the runway, I hoped that there would be no fire because I could smell gasoline pouring out of the ruptured tanks. We could see that the plane was destroyed, with the engine smashed and the cockpit collapsed. It was barely recognizable as an aircraft. It was just a pile of scrap. (See photos.) Danny and I were the first ones there, but Mom and her crew were right behind.

Gasoline was trickling across Dad's face. He was passed out. He had crashed about fifteen minutes earlier. I pushed the gas line away. He was breathing. So he was alive. I could not immediately determine the extent of his injuries. I could see that the dashboard had slammed into his chest and face. The speedometer and the altimeter had implanted where his chest was resting. I could tell that a foot was broken from where he had hit the ground because it was turned out at an odd angle. Dad was bleeding from the face, the chest, and the legs—so much so that his body was covered with blood. His arms dangled at his sides. A portion of his clothes was soaked in gasoline. He came to—a positive sign—but just moaned and groaned, over and over. He couldn't talk and he couldn't move. Thank God, Dad was alone in the plane. If there had been anyone else, he would have been dead, I believe.

As Danny and I were carefully removing the seatbelt and harness off him, the family car pulled up. Mel was driving with Mom, and three men in the backseat.

They stemmed the bleeding with bandages and cotton wrap under Mom's direction. They inched him out of the plane and into the backseat of the car. By now, Dad had stopped groaning long enough to speak gibberish. "The cropduster is trying to land. Watch out for the horses." Things like that. One of the men stayed in the back seat with Dad and Mom. Mel drove off toward Highland Hospital with the car lights flashing. We watched them drive away and then sat beside the plane and prayed and prayed.

Dad was lucky. Plus, he had good doctors and a determined heart. He had broken his ankles and suffered a broken skull that

would leave him with scars on his face and a flattened nose. He needed months to recover in the hospital and at the house. He was bed-
ridden at home for the rest of the year. Over that time, his fractures
healed. His head was misshaped a little, but healthy. Doctors performed pioneer surgery to his ankles by replacing the natural bone
with steel. He walked with an artificial rigidity for the rest of his life
but remained an avid tennis player, stiffness and all. He would contract arthritis in his fingers and hands that would bother him for
the rest of his life. He would fly again, but always as a passenger and
never as a pilot.

What had happened? Dad was by himself reviewing the crops
that day when he became distracted as he was coming in to land.
Another plane was about to take off. Somehow, in the light summer
air, Dad stalled over the end of the runway and crashed head first
from about two hundred feet. Pilot error! Or, as Dad would say: "loss
of focus." The lesson was simple, and I have been reminded of it
many times through the years: focus.

Somebody once said that there are four rules of engagement
that will bring success: focus, flexible, fast, and friendly. Focus is the
number one. If a moment is important, then focus on it. Make it important in your actions. There are no small, unimportant elements
in a significant event. Each step is critical to the success of that moment. Focus, for example, when landing an airplane. Don't get distracted. Each step in that landing is important to its success.

Dad regained his ability to speak at the hospital within a day or
two of the accident, as the effects of his concussion wore off. He told
us that he didn't know if he was going to recover swiftly or slowly, so
he gave only two instructions from the hospital room: go see Enoch
Nix at the National Bank of Bossier, which was financing a big land
purchase for us, and reassure Enoch that Mom and I could run Scopena in Dad's absence. I was not quite thirteen. He also told us to ask
him for advice when needed.

Mom and I went to see Mr. Nix early on the Monday morning
following the accident. We already knew from the doctors that Dad

would not operate the farm until planting the following spring, if then. It would just be me and Mom with help from the other kids and the labor force of Scopena. We would make the crop, we told Mr. Nix.

School was not going to be my focus for quite some time so we went to see the principal of Bossier High School. He understood. My mother's commitment to keep teaching me after school made it an easier choice. So for a while I would go to school only when I had completed my farm duties. As it turned out, for the better part of a year, I went to school only an average of three days a week.

Mr. Nix posed a different hurdle. He certainly knew Scopena. We often had hedging opportunities with a crop of about ten thousand bales of cotton, but it took large sums of money to hedge, and there was risk. The price can pivot in a day, fall 10 cents a pound or $50 a bale. Do the math: $50 a bale times 10,000 bales is $500,000 in one day that the bank must risk. The Bossier Bank and Mr. Nix provided that risk money to Scopena. If push came to shove, we produced the cotton that supported the risk of the hedges. Plus, Dad's record in hedging was quite good.

We made a lot of money hedging at 95 cents a pound when others had to take 80 cents on the open market, and we made that money thanks to the service and courage of Mr. Nix and the bank he represented.

Dad's accident raised the stakes. The bank had the land of Scopena as collateral against several crop loans. We had grown really big, really quickly on farm credit. Dad was in a hurry. Payback was slow and steady. The bank had the right in case of an accident to Dad to appoint a special farm manager. We argued, my mother and I, that we could run it better than a special farm manager; that we knew the land and all the cattle better than an outsider could ever know. Mr. Nix decided to let us make all the decisions on the farm. We would meet again before the start of next year to see how we were doing. It was a fair plan.

In truth, the experience made me want to become a banker

years later. I give credit to Mr. Nix for that. He was calm and steady, a middle-aged man who loved LSU football and had deep roots in the community. His wife was the typing teacher at Bossier High School. He had made a point to get to know Scopena and how it was run. He knew Mom and me personally from various transactions over the years.

Another banker might have required us to hire an outside farm manager or wanted to look at the weekly cash flow as the year progressed, but Mr. Nix did none of those things. He allowed Mom and me to run Scopena without interference.

The thing that I liked about Mr. Nix was the personal service that he gave to Mom and me. In his hands, a bank didn't just lend money, it provided service for Scopena. Without meddling, he came down to Scopena several times with his wife on a Saturday to see how we were getting along and to see if there were any questions about operations. He would check the cottonseed in the warehouse to make sure the collateral was in place to support the loan.

When I started banks years later, I used my experience with Mr. Nix as a template for the kind of bank I wanted to build. I did not want to have a consumer bank on every street corner. There were plenty of those. I didn't want to just have lines to a teller to make cash transactions. I wanted to provide service to small businesses on a professional basis—check all the details but don't harass. I wanted to have a written business plan for each customer. I wanted to be more than an ATM.

So we ran the farm in Dad's absence. Mom handled all the executive duties. I handled most of the field duties. Dad's absence made Mr. Boyd take his direction in the shop from me. He understood why Dad wasn't giving him day-to-day directions.

The other kids in the family were young so the accident didn't radically change their lives, although Punkin and Danny were old enough to be a big help. Christine continued to make breakfast, lunch, and supper. Dad's absence at the lunch table meant fewer and fewer people dropped in to eat with us, although we were too busy at the time to notice.

It's interesting that no one took Dad's place for the next six months at the head of the table. We just left it waiting for Dad's return, whenever that was to be.

Looking back, I'd have to say that Dad was a very fortunate man to have survived that airplane crash. There was a hole several feet deep in the hard dirt at the end of the runway. He had hit the turf going full speed. The instruments from the dashboard of the plane were embedded in his chest. For some reason I had pulled the altimeter from his shirt where it rested after the crash. I had done this while he was moaning in the plane and we were waiting on Mom to arrive at the site.

There were shouts of chaos from the men who had come with Mom, but she was calm and in charge during the whole scene. She didn't say a word to me, but I remember her squeezing my hand as she was getting the dressing around the wounds and stopping the bleeding.

As the car went racing off to the hospital, I remember that squeeze and I remember Mom being in charge, and I remember that every man there felt that Miss Adeline was going to make it alright. I, too, felt that way.

34

Gus

Dad's crash and his long recovery required Mom to spend more time in the field helping me with my responsibilities. She also continued to handle the functions of the office, like hedging the cotton crop and preselling the corn and soybean crops. She was really the substitute for Dad in and out of the office.

She was awesome in the execution of her duties, working with me on the field management at Scopena, while maintaining the office functions. Together, we gave the bankers a complete picture of Scopena.

She was not a figurehead in her role. It was ultimately up to her to decide what kind of crop we were going to plant in the winter to restore the land and whether we were going to hedge spring wheat.

She had help. Arthur England, the father of my pal Emmett, provided his skill and wisdom to Mom in the late fall when she spent a lot of time working on the gin. They met daily in the office at the beginning of the first shift, around 6:30 in the morning after the kids had departed for school. The cattle operation required daily coordination with my grandmother Mine, who could be temperamental. Mine would throw a fit if she didn't think things were being done her way. Mom managed to handle Mine diplomatically and prevent any major disruptions.

With my outside duties, I stayed out of Mom's glance much of the time. But I would attend the 6:30 meeting each morning when I didn't go to school to make sure I was keeping things coordinated: checking for bug infestations, mixing the proper insecticide for the crops, ensuring that the crop dusters did their job, sorting out problems with the payroll, and organizing the irrigation schedule and the cotton harvesting. We had a number of foremen who helped me.

Mr. Henderson was a tractor driver initially and had developed into a strong leader. He took care of all the harvesting equipment, both cotton and corn, and was a treasure to me. The men in his division could be temperamental. One of Mr. Henderson's specialties was to keep the men working, regardless of their imagined wrongs suffered in the course of a day's work under the grinding sun.

Mr. Henderson found the cotton machine drivers refusing to drive one morning because one of them had an upset stomach and the man blamed the iced water brought to each driver periodically. The other drivers refused to work in the harvest because of the "bad water." Mr. Henderson said that he would subsist on water only that day, taken from the same water bucket that had been labeled "bad." And he would take no lunch.

It didn't take long for the men to get the message and drift back to work, one by one. Mr. Henderson found out that the water wasn't the problem. The sick driver had spent the night drinking wine and was hung over. That's one example of how he resolved problems for the cotton harvesters.

Mr. Henderson was killed at Scopena in a tragic accident years later. He was operating a tractor in a faraway field by himself, when he became accidentally entangled with a disc, a machine designed to furrow ground as his tractor was pulling. He was run over multiple times by the disc and bled to death by the time he was discovered hours later lying on the ground.

The men all treated me as a member of management. We got along fine in Dad's absence. My summer work as moisture meter reader and as entomologist made it easier for the men to accept me. I did my duties as expected and also oversaw the supervisors. I took on items that required Dad's touch: disputes, major policy decisions, and broad outlines of responsibilities, for instance.

Nobody had a problem with that, it seemed, except for one man. For our purposes, I'll call him "Gus." He was younger than the other managers. He was in his early forties while the others were fifty-five and older. Gus had been at Scopena for about five years in the cotton and cattle operations. He acted like he was top man in those areas. His disagreements in the cattle operations with Mine, my grandmother, were notorious. She could be seen storming out of Gus's office several times during Dad's absence.

With me, Gus was tolerant but counted his opinion above all others. It seems he wanted to consult Mom if he had a problem with my instructions. We never had a direct conflict, but he would often quietly work around me to get his way on certain issues, like which cotton field to spray with insecticide after a late summer rain and which fields we had to check again.

These kinds of conflicts were to be expected. With Dad not being there to resolve them, we found solutions and limped forward. Then something happened in the Gus saga: He exhibited an unusual interest in Mom.

He began to stay after the early morning supervisors' meeting when all the other men left. The meetings were in the office, and for a time I didn't notice Gus remaining behind to visit with Mom.

Then, he invited himself to breakfast where he would eat bacon and eggs with us kids and Mom. Other men occasionally ate breakfast with the family at Scopena, but Mom seemed intimidated by Gus. She was quite a good looker and alone on that huge plantation at the age of thirty-one. Gus also began to stay later, coming into the office after 6:00 p.m., when work was over, and finding any excuse to visit with "Miss Adeline," as he called her. Sometimes it was nearly 8:00 at night before he left the office and returned to his home and family.

I noticed his extended hours and personal attention and mentioned it to Mom one day when she and I were alone. She said Gus missed Dad's direction and that he would be all right. She didn't say anything else.

Meanwhile, Dad was recuperating in the back of the house and doing daily physical therapy to be able to walk again. He wasn't scheduled to return to active leadership at Scopena for some months. He did not attend the supervisors' meetings in the early mornings and didn't witness Gus's after-work visits. He knew nothing of the full court press that Mom was receiving.

In the third month of Dad's recovery, Mom mentioned to him the time that Gus had been devoting to her, and she didn't know what to do about it. Dad knew exactly what to do. He came to the supervisors' meeting the next morning. It was not easy for him. He could hardly move on his damaged ankles except by crutches, but come to the supervisors' meeting he did.

He listened patiently while each of us gave him a full report. Mom was not at the meeting. As the meeting wound down, Dad asked if Gus could stay behind for a conversation.

Gus was substantially larger than Dad. At six feet and 225 pounds, Gus looked every inch the wild cowboy he used to be. But Dad fired him that morning and told me what he had done that day. He told Gus to get his belongings and not ever show up at Scopena again. Dad gave Gus one month to move out of his Scopena house. Afterward, Dad returned to his bed rest and rehab.

Mom was quite capable of handling the issue of Gus's advances on her own, but she decided to check with Dad to see if he had suggestions to avoid work-place trouble. He did and he handled it.

I remember feeling that something was right in the world after that day and that it was going to be right for a long, long time.

Gus moved out in two weeks, and he never did return to Scopena. I heard he went to work near Coushatta, thirty miles south of Scopena. Twenty years later, the newspaper reported that he was killed at the auction barn in Coushatta. During a payroll squabble on a Saturday afternoon, someone shot Gus to death.

Mom and I never discussed Dad's decision to fire Gus. Dad never told me what he said to Gus that morning, but he carried a pistol for years afterward. That was that.

35

LSU Football

We Roemers love LSU football. There are a lot of good teams in the country, but as far as we are concerned, there is only one "great" team: the fighting tigers of LSU. We loved LSU football not only because Dad graduated from the university, but because we went to the games—all the home games in Baton Rouge and any games played in Shreveport or Texas. We were passionate fans. We drove five hundred miles round trip on a two-lane highway—all in the same day—to see every game in Tiger Stadium.

I can remember my first game. It was a birthday present for my tenth birthday on October 4, 1953. I don't remember who we played. (I could look it up, but that would be cheating.) But I do remember going there. After we did the Saturday morning chores, Dad, Mom, Margaret, Danny, and I piled into our 1952 Studebaker at 8:30 a.m. Melinda and Melanie stayed behind at first because they were too young. Dad turned the car down Highway 71 South, headed to Coushatta, then to Natchitoches, Alexandria, and Lebeau. From there, we caught Highway 1 to Baton Rouge. The game would start at 2:00 p.m. LSU in those days alternated Saturday afternoon and Saturday night games. It was almost a five-hour drive, one way.

As it turned out, Dad had bought season tickets for us. So we were to replay this scenario, week after week. We followed the same relentless schedule. We did not stop for food. Sometimes Mom would pack sandwiches or cookies that Christine made. Dad stopped only for gas, and then begrudgingly for only about five minutes. This was no time for sightseeing, side trips, or rest stops. This was LSU football. We talked about LSU on the way down, and we either celebrated or lamented the outcome on the way back.

I remember one trip when, as we left Scopena, I started to talk about the value of the profit incentive to the economic health of the country. Nobody said anything in reply. Dad said nothing. Well, I liked the sound of my voice and rambled on about how valuable personal motivation was to individuals and to the economy. All the way to Coushatta and beyond, I talked. Silence in the car.

After we had been on the road for about thirty minutes with me talking, Dad finally spoke up. "Shut up," he told me. "Butch, this is an LSU football trip. While I admire your explanation of and reliance on the free enterprise system, this is an LSU football trip and until the game is played, we will live, eat, and talk LSU football. Do you have a problem with that?"

"No sir." And that was that.

If we left Scopena about 9:00 a.m., we could just make the game at 2:00 p.m. To be sure of arrival by kickoff, we'd try to leave Scopena at 8:30. The roads were two lanes all the way except the last few miles of highway 1 into Baton Rouge. On Saturdays, the traffic was fairly heavy.

If we arrived in Baton Rouge early enough, we would stop at Hopper's Drive-in. We got burgers and fries there, and Dad was so excited about the game that he let us pig out.

Once we got to the stadium, we parked as close as we could find a parking space. Only when I was governor years later did I ever have a reserved parking space. Dad didn't believe in paying for parking. So we usually walked a mile or more to the stadium.

We typically entered the stadium when the LSU band was on the field. Mom and my sisters loved the LSU band and the Tiger girls. We boys liked when the LSU players warmed up before the start of the game. Dad bought a single program for the game, and we boys tried to tie the numbers of the players to their pictures.

We sat through victories and defeats the same way: to the end, until all the time had run off the clock. We cut no corners. Afterward, we didn't socialize in Baton Rouge, visit friends, go out to eat, or have a few drinks with fans who sat around us during the game. We climbed into our car and began the five hour drive home. We immediately switched on the radio and listened to the postgame analysis. Each of us took turns interrupting the announcers to chime in with our own opinions. We listened to the analysis until either the show went off the air or we got out of range near Alexandria. Afterward, we continued our opinionated review of LSU's performance. If the game started at 2:00 p.m. and was over at 4:45 p.m., we were home at 10:00 that night. If the game started at 7:00 p.m. and was over by 10:00 p.m., we got home at about 3:00 on Sunday morning. We drove straight through to Scopena from the stadium whether it was afternoon or after midnight.

Usually in coming back from the games, we stopped for gasoline at a 24-hour station in Alexandria. I remember Dad used to let us buy a bag of fried pork rinds at the station. The one bag of rinds was for all five children. The two rinds that you got were so good. It wasn't that Dad was cheap in spending money on the kids. It's just that he had an expansive definition of how to waste money. Pork rinds were definitely a waste of money to Dad.

After getting home, we played for a minute with Shep and King, our two dogs. We soon fell fast asleep, as did the dogs. We were busy dreaming about our Tigers. The only compromise we made with the First Methodist Church in Shreveport was, rather than attend early service at 8:00 the next morning, we sometimes attended Sunday School at 9:30 a.m. And church at 11:00 a.m.

We would cap the day off by lunching at Morrison's cafeteria in Shreveport. I typically got some sort of steak for lunch with mixed vegetables, iced tea, and lemon meringue pie for dessert. We would drag ourselves home to nap or to ride horses in the afternoon. Later, toward the end of high school, we would fill Sunday afternoon with tennis matches in the front yard.

My two youngest sisters, Melinda and Melanie, began to join us in the car in the mid-1950s for the trip to Baton Rouge. That meant it was just like vacation, seven to a car.

We'd occasionally bring another person on the trip. I remember once we brought my girlfriend, Cookie, during my senior year in high school in 1959. It was a Halloween night for the LSU-Ole Miss game. She went into the stadium on my ticket, and I was going to buy a ticket from a scalper outside the stadium. Dad gave me one hundred dollars to buy the ticket, thinking that one hundred was more than enough. We had seen tickets scalped for less than ten dollars in past games and more than forty.

I saw a fifty dollar ticket for sale right before game time. But I decided that I could find a cheaper one after the game started, so I did not buy it. But fewer tickets were for sale outside Tiger Stadium than usual. After all, LSU was the top ranked team in the country while Ole Miss was number three. Everybody wanted to be inside. I saw seats being scalped for seventy-five and one hundred dollars. I waited. There had to be something cheaper.

The scene outside the stadium was unreal. Although I had been to many LSU football games, I had never been outside the stadium during game time. There was a whole community of LSU officials walking into and out of the stadium. Each seemed to be filled with official bluster and giving instructions to some nameless person. I was amazed.

There were people selling tickets. These scalpers seemed to be regulars at the game. Several of them knew the names of the LSU officials, and shouted greetings of familiarity to them. Other people were workers or volunteers in the concession booths and came outside to smoke a cigarette or take a break.

Then there were the police officers. There were Baton Rouge police officers, state police officers of various stripes, and sheriff's deputies from East and West Baton Rouge parishes and from Ascension and from Livingston parishes. They did nothing that I could tell but laugh and joke and look official. They were somehow disconnected with the football game going on inside the stadium. Maybe they provided crowd control. I don't know, but it seemed to me that they were totally nonessential and were everywhere. I was amazed.

At halftime, Danny was sent to find me. I described the problem. He nodded but didn't volunteer his seat, I noticed. After he went back inside, I bought a hot dog and a Coke. I still had $96 and change in my pocket to buy a ticket. But I still had no luck.

It was interesting "watching" the game from outside the stadium. The stadium noise let you know everything that we weren't seeing on the field. At one point in the fourth quarter, the roar of the crowd told us that LSU had done something magical. The word soon drifted down from the stands that the magic was Billy Cannon and that he had run a punt back all the way for a touchdown. LSU was now ahead, 7-3. The fifteen or twenty of us stuck without tickets on the underside of the stadium jumped for joy and were so excited, even though we hadn't seen a play or heard a radio description. I find myself sixty years later telling others that I was there at Tiger Stadium when Billy made his run. I was. I just didn't see the run.

With time winding down, I walked through an empty gate and saw a magnificent LSU goal-line stand against Ole Miss. LSU won, 7-3.

I didn't have a ticket, but I saw practically everything that I had wanted to see, except Billy's run. We talked Tigers all the way back to Scopena. Cookie was happy. Me? I was happy, too, but mainly because Dad let me keep the $96. That was a lot of money to me!

I carried my support for LSU to Boston. After Danny got there, he and I listened to the football games on a New Orleans radio station via shortwave. We would yell and shout and generally make a fool of ourselves at the Iroquois club. Sometimes Margaret would join us. We laughed about the memories of our drives to Baton Rouge to see the games.

Let me tell two more LSU stories. Our family started a computer software company in 1970. We called it IDS (Innovative Data Systems). By 1974, someone had developed software that was a mathematical matrix that recorded information and showed tendencies based on that information. It could be used in diagnosing many engineering problems. It could also be used to predict what plays a team would use in a certain situation (e.g., second down and three yards from a team's own thirty-seven yard line). Such knowledge could be very useful to a football coach.

I called Charlie McClendon, then LSU's head coach, and told him what we had developed. He said that he would like to see the tendencies of LSU and its opponents. Later in the week, I flew down to Baton Rouge and met with one of the assistant coaches. I showed him the tendencies of LSU and Mississippi State, its upcoming opponent, over the past year and for the previous week.

The coach was astounded and asked how they could get more. I left my findings and told him I would call the LSU computer squad and give them the program so they could generate their own findings. I believe that was the beginning of LSU football's fledgling contact with the power of the computer. I bet I wouldn't recognize what LSU does with computers today.

The second story of LSU football comes from my use of the box in Tiger Stadium reserved for the governor. I was astonished when I found out it existed. It sat about twelve people.

After my 1987 election, I proposed to take the whole family to the game, including Mom and Dad. The state police suggested that they fly me to the game by helicopter, land on the field, and walk me to my seats. I turned them down. So they suggested we land instead outside the stadium.

I said no again. I objected to riding to the game in the helicopter wherever it landed. I said I would ride to the game with my family by car from the governor's mansion. And so we did.

I used the box for all sorts of guests: family, friends, campaign workers, company executives of existing Louisiana companies, executives of companies looking to potentially relocate in Louisiana, and other people—big shots and common folk alike.

One memory stands out: I entertained Robert Fulghum, the famous author, by taking him to the LSU-Ole Miss game in 1990. He was stunned by the crowd's enthusiasm and the general uproar of the game in Tiger Stadium.

When we were driving back to the governor's mansion after the game, I asked him what stood out most about the game. He thought for just a split-second before answering, "it was the black Ole Miss cheerleader who raced up and down the sidelines carrying the rebel flag. He was oblivious to the world except Ole Miss football."

He had seen something unique with his writer's eye. The rebel flag, carried by a black man, had been transformed from a symbol of hate and slavery to a symbol of independence and spirit. I hadn't noticed that the rebel flag was carried by a black man.

LSU football—it's had a pretty good run in my family's life.

36

GIN ON FIRE

Another of the unique jobs on the farm was cotton ginning. We had one cotton gin at Scopena and another at Curtis, about five miles north of Scopena headquarters. Scopena gin ran two shifts normally, while Curtis gin ran only one normally. The first shift at Curtis gin ran from 6 a.m. to 6 p.m. The second shift, if necessary, would start at 6 p.m. and run until there was no more cotton to be ginned. Sometimes that was for three hours or longer.

Normally, Dad took the second shift at Curtis, but because of his accident, I had to step up and take his place. I was thirteen years old. It was not a big deal because cotton ginning only required four months during harvest (September through December, depending on the weather), and I had spent years becoming familiar with gin operations. I had six guys on the shift with me: a sucker pipe man to get the cotton into the gin; a trailer man to get the cotton trailers to the gin; a gin-stand man to keep the guts of the gin operating properly (there were three gin stands); two press men (to run the baling press); and a man to take the government cotton samples and roll the finished bales into the rail cars.

It wasn't easy managing a shift at the gin. There were many moving parts and many variables. It was noisy with the gin running at a high rate of speed and the sound of cotton racing through the gin pipes toward the gin saws. The flying lint and dust were constantly in the air. It could seem like chaos.

The gin was a building filled with industrial equipment: rotary saws, pipes, chutes, and a press to make the bale of cotton. It was the biggest building on the farm, wrapped in tin around a structure of cast iron pipes.

I maintained all of the many settings to make sure the gin ran efficiently. The gin's task was easy to describe—separate the seed from the lint and clean the cotton lint of as many sticks and as much dirt as possible—but hard to accomplish. The cotton delivered on each trailer had a different moisture level and had been harvested under different field conditions by different operators, so the gin had to be constantly adjusted. There was never a quiet moment. And when the shift was over, I would make the five-mile trip home by pickup truck, crawl into bed, and somehow be ready for school the next morning.

One of the dangers of running the gin was the gin-stand man getting his fingers caught in the spinning saws. The saws were spinning multiple times each second in order to comb the cotton for seeds and useless debris and to separate the seed from the lint. To keep the stands combing without interference, the gin-stand man had to run his fingers near the saws to remove sticks and knots of cotton.

Disaster struck when the man's hand would make contact with the circulating saws. There is not a gin-stand man alive in America who doesn't have scarred hands from the gin stands.

I know I do. My right hand came too close to the gin stand one night when I was removing a stick that was wedged in between the gin saws. I felt a quick jolt of pain and yanked my right hand out. It was spurting blood. About one-quarter inch of the tip of my right pinky had caught the gin stand saws. I didn't go to the hospital. In fact, I never left the gin. I was fine after pouring alcohol over the bloody wound to dress it, the usual treatment. But the little finger is still scarred sixty years later, and the wound still aches on some days after all these years.

Another danger in a cotton gin operation is fire. The gin was filled with cotton lint flying everywhere and coming to rest on exposed surfaces. This accumulation of lint was very combustible. There were thousands of shafts and pulleys turning in the gin, and tens of thousands of saw teeth in the gin stands. If left untended these saws and their friction cause most of the fires in a cotton gin. These turning shafts and spinning saws create heat that can turn into fire in a blink of an eye given all the lint flying around and accumulating. As a result, because of the air being so filled with combustible lint, smoking was prohibited in the gin. Fire danger was already great.

In fact, a fire would break out every week or so in the gin. The constant wear of the steel teeth rubbing against a stick caught in the saws was a frequent culprit. But fires could come from a cigarette on premise or a cigarette sucked into the gin from a cotton trailer outside.

The worst fires were small ones that flowed along the various windpipes in the gin to rest inside the lint of the cotton bale, leaving little trace of flame to the naked eye. Only the attention of the press crew observing smoke escaping from the bale or feeling a hot spot on it identified a possible source of fire. It was possible to load a bale onto the boxcar outside the gin without knowing that it contained a smoldering fire inside.

The danger of a fire within a bale is that it would slowly reach the surface, flare up, and cause a large fire in a railroad car or on a crowded platform filled with flammable cotton bales. Sometimes the smoldering fire would remain undetectable for days and then flare up and catch many bales on fire. The remedy was to set aside a suspect bale (one that was being ginned when a fire was discovered or suspected), not put it on the transport train, and watch it for a couple days as it sat alone on the platform. Usually there was no fire.

If a fire did break out within the gin, we would shut down the machinery to put it out. Once we thought we had extinguished the fire, we would operate the gin for fifteen to twenty minutes without cotton running through it to be sure. We would use this period to repair the source of the fire, if need be, and then we would resume gin operations. It was a lengthy process with no substitute for the elaborate attention to detail required. Fire was the fear of every ginner, and my memory was that it would usually strike when you were least prepared for it or least expected it.

One clear, cold November morning, fire struck Scopena gin. It occurred at 5:00 in the morning, on the day after Thanksgiving in 1955. We were never sure where the fire came from. Maybe it was from outside the gin and was sucked into it off one of the cotton trailers by the sucker pipe. Or maybe it was a friction fire from a stick wedged in the gin's saw teeth that rubbed against the relentless flow of cotton. Or maybe it came from somewhere else, such as a spark from the trash.

The gin started operating early that morning because we hadn't worked at all on Thanksgiving, but many farmers had and therefore the gin lot was filled with trailers loaded with cotton picked but unginned. The cotton gin usually started operating around 7:00, but that morning with the Thanksgiving lull we were in full operating mode by 5:00 a.m. The fire struck a few minutes after the gin started rolling.

Several factors worked against us, in retrospect. The gin yard was packed with cotton on trailers, the cotton harvest was at its peak, and every customer, including Scopena, had the mechanical harvesters running from before sun up that day. Usually there were six to eight cotton trailers in the yard when we started ginning, and the trailers came to the gin throughout the day as the cotton was harvested. But with the Thanksgiving day off, the cotton had stacked up in trailers all over the yard.

There were over sixty trailers stuffed with cotton on the yard at the crack of dawn that morning. At an average of 3.5 bales per trailer, over 210 bales of raw cotton were on the yard in trailers to be ginned that morning. Scopena could only gin about 10 bales per hour, or 200 bales per day at a realistic speed, when there were no fires and no mechanical problems.

So we were facing a full day of gin time before trailers already on the yard could be handled, plus the cotton that was being picked that day and brought to the gin. I remember saying in idle conversation that we had never seen the yard so crowded with cotton trailers.

Another factor that caused an unusual glut of cotton that day: the train that took our ginned cotton to Memphis every day had not run on Thanksgiving, so between three hundred and five hundred ginned bales were on the loading docks awaiting pick up. A ginned bale weighs about five hundred pounds and is worth $400 to $500 per bale. We had never had that many bales on hand prepared for delivery to Memphis, and we were adding ten bales an hour to the number of bales that we already had. Dad was to pay a price for deciding not to work on Thanksgiving and letting the cotton stack up the day after.

Yet another factor unusual for that day: the weather was ripe for fire. A front had passed through Thanksgiving morning, and a wind out of the north and west was screaming at thirty to fifty miles per hour. The humidity was exceedingly low for Louisiana. You clapped your hands, and it seemed like sparks flew. Static electricity was noticeably high. Low humidity meant a high risk of fire.

Scopena had eight mechanical harvesters running and more than five hundred cotton pickers bused in from the city that morning. We had raised the price for picking from its normal $3.50 per hundred-weight to $5 per hundred-weight. Gins were running full speed trying to stay abreast of the harvest or at least not to slow it up, and the cotton still stacked up.

The weather is such an over-riding factor because cotton is a dry weather plant and cannot be harvested in damp conditions. When you get a chance to harvest under the right weather conditions—no rain, no dew—you take it.

So there you are: the perfect storm—a yard filled with trailers, inventory filled with baled cotton (as many as five hundred bales, each weighing five hundred pounds), and weather ripe for harvest and fire (windy with unusually low humidity).

As I said, I don't know what caused it. But fire struck early. A trailer being emptied of cotton flamed up, and the fire was sucked into the gin where it spread to cover the lint throughout the gin, including the bale being ginned.

What was worse, the burning trailer was pulled away from the gin but was parked on the upwind side of the inventory platform, where up to five hundred bales awaited train pickup. I guess the workers weren't used to worrying about the wind, but it whipped the flames over the inventoried bales. They, too, began to burn. The gin crew, seeing this, moved the burning trailer from near the stored bales to the other side of the cotton yard. While moving the burning trailer, several others were caught on fire.

The crew realized that the trailers of cotton were at risk, so they began to pull the trailers away from the gin. By this time, the whole gin was on fire, and the trailers surrounding the gin began to burn, too. So did the baled cotton awaiting shipment. The brown grass around the gin also caught fire, as did the grass in the front yard at Scopena from trailers being wheeled, helter-skelter around the windy gin yard. Dad did his best to direct traffic amidst the chaos.

Scopena and its gin crew could not put the fire out. They had no experience with a fire in these wild conditions. They didn't have any firefighting equipment such as hoses or rakes. Their experience had been with small, interior gin fires, not wild conflagrations that were ablaze outside and inside the gin. It was a bonfire. It was overwhelming to the Scopena personnel.

So, Dad called the Bossier Fire Department at about 6:15 in the morning, something we had never done in the history of Scopena. But we had no alternative this day. While they were on the way, Dad stopped long enough to express the fear that the fire could threaten the whole headquarters. We heard the fire sirens screaming long before the trucks arrived, two in all. About nine firemen in uniform piled off. Dad met them in front of the gin and quickly described the situation.

The firemen concentrated on the fire in the gin building first. They used long rakes to pull the burning cotton off ledges around the interior of the gin building. The rakes had extra-long handles and they pulled burning lint from the top of the gin onto the floor where they soaked it with water from their hoses. They dumped the loose cotton on the concrete floor of the gin where it could burn freely and wouldn't enflame other parts of the gin. Dad supervised the process. Four firemen and Dad did this operation quickly and efficiently.

Otherwise, they worked as teams of three. Not a word was spoken. Flames burned brightly all around them. The team leader would give a hand signal, and the team would dash to another burning part of the building. They would immediately start raking the burning lint to the concrete floor where it would do no harm. It was amazing to watch them work. No wasted motion. No panic. All controlled action with a purpose.

Meanwhile, one of the Scopena men had pointed out the swimming pool to the fire department. There was no other water available close to the gin except a garden hose. So they dropped fire hoses into the swimming pool, and they pumped every drop of water out to combat the many blazes. They ran their hoses 150 to 200 feet from two pumping trucks to fight the blaze in the gin, the burning trailers, and the baled inventory.

After saving the gin building itself, they turned to the baled cotton stored on the concrete platform outside and divided the bales into three groups: those that were ablaze, those that we had to watch for fire, and those that hadn't been singed by fire. Dad directed the fire crew to identify which bales were in each group.

Dad took a group of Scopena men and separated the cotton trailers from each other so that the fire couldn't easily spread in the thirty-mile-per-hour wind from one trailer to another. They saved about ten of the sixty trailers that held three to five bales each.

It took the firemen about three hours to extinguish the fire in the gin building and another four to six hours to extinguish all the external fires: trailers, platform bales, the grass around the gin, and the grass around the Scopena yard and runway. They literally worked all day long.

In all, we lost more than six hundred bales of cotton, out of about ten thousand bales produced by Scopena annually. Nobody had gotten hurt, and we had saved the gin. One of the lessons imparted by Dad—"fast" action—had saved it. In fact, to add to the miracle, we tested the gin by running it without cotton for an hour later that day to determine if it had an internal fire. It didn't. We had the gin running by nightfall, and picking and production continued.

At dinner that night, we were so thankful that it wasn't worse. We were all wearing clothes blackened with soot. We were exhausted, particularly from the panic and hectic running around before the arrival of the Bossier Fire Department. Chaos can be tiring. Christine and her crew fed more than twenty-five of us that night at the Scopena table, including seven men from the fire department.

The gin was completely burned of the cotton that had been blown onto it by its operations, but the gin was constructed out of pipe and tin and therefore did not burn. The building and equipment ("the gin") remained functional.

Even then, our work was not done since we had to monitor five hundred bales we had moved to the concrete platform to make sure that they contained no fire inside. If a fire surfaced within a couple of days, we released the bale from its steel binders to put it out. This saved up to half of the bale. We put the saved cotton in a trailer and sucked it into the machinery to be reginned into another bale. For the bales free of fire after two days of waiting, we transported them by railcar to Memphis. The quick-thinking decision to separate the bales on the concrete platform saved about two hundred of the five hundred bales.

Several days later, once we had totally restored order, we sat down to take stock and try to determine how much our insurance covered. After lengthy negotiations with the insurance company that held the liability, we collected in full, and we paid all of our clients in full. This amounted to more than $100,000 in 1955 money. With inflation, it would be about $1,000,000 in today's cash. For us a lot of money!

The question in the insurance negotiations was whether Scopena's performance during the fire had been negligent and somehow responsible for the loss. The insurance adjuster ruled that Scopena had done everything expected or possible during the crises, but he recommended that Scopena train workers to fight fires and that we purchase equipment (hoses, rakes, pump) to douse a major conflagration. This annual training was to begin that summer, taught by members of the Bossier City Fire Department.

We did have a weapon that the adjuster said had turned the day in our favor: the swimming pool. One Bossier City firefighter had told me earlier when discussing the fire that the water from it had made a big difference in fighting the blazes. In fact, the fire expert in settling our insurance claim said that from now on, the swimming pool had to be full of water every time the gin cranked up.

Scopena gin still stands as the biggest building on Scopena more than six decades later. A building wrapped as always in tin with the name Scopena still painted on its roof, it operates no longer, as it costs too much to grow cotton commercially.

Curtis gin, which was located almost five miles closer to Bossier City, has been torn down to make room for a housing development for airmen from Barksdale Air Force Base.

37

SCHOOL ELECTIONS

Of course, there was an obvious political bent to life at Scope-na. I've told you that we read and discussed the latest news in the newspaper every day. Dad's volunteer work with the Bossier Rural Electrification Cooperative was part of that, as was his state-wide work with an REA generating plant, somewhat similar to the TVA. By the time I was twelve, I had begun to develop a keen interest in politics—in Louisiana and elsewhere.

Dad and Mom had shown an interest in national Democratic politics—the national REA and the farm programs in particular—but no member of the family was really interested in statewide campaigns for governor. The success of the farm did not depend on it. Scopena's success was dependent on federal farm policies, not state laws.

It's not that we were unfamiliar with state politics. Earl Long, Jimmy Davis—Louisiana governors—had been dropping by Sco-pena in search of campaign donations for many years. But plainly speaking, our financial interests lay in national, not state politics.

In 1956, President Eisenhower was running for reelection. As Democrats, we were interested to see who the Democrats would nominate at their national convention. We were especially interest-ed to follow the role of one of the key participants, a young senator from Massachusetts named John F. Kennedy.

We had heard about him because he had received a lot of publicity for over a year as a war hero who was now a rising political star. I wanted to watch and to learn. My grandparents, Granddaddy Ross and Mama, had gotten a television the previous year. I asked Dad if I could be excused from work for a day or two to watch the convention at GrandDad's. I promised that I would give a report on what I saw. He agreed, and I rode my horse down the levee seven miles to their home at McDade.

The floor debates, the committee hearings, the rules votes, the personality conflicts, the debate on where the party was headed, Kennedy's tussle with Senator Estes Kefauver for the vice-presidential nomination—it was all mesmerizing. I don't remember the issues in contention at the convention. I just remember the action and the excitement—and Kennedy: his ideas, his presentation, so youthful, so energetic, his voice so different in accent, so unique in cadence. His wife; she was gorgeous. Kefauver edged out Kennedy for the number two spot on the ticket, but I decided then and there what I wanted to do and be when I grew up. I wanted to be John Kennedy. I was twelve.

Since I literally couldn't be John Kennedy, I wanted to be as close to him as possible. I envisioned myself to be a politician already. I loved to talk and made a lot of friends at school and outside. I never met a stranger—that sort of thing.

Why politics? Maybe it was because it was new and exciting. Maybe it was a chance to be with people and not cotton plants? Maybe it was because I wanted a different challenge. Maybe it was feeling drained by those hot July and August days in the cotton fields. Maybe it was because I saw politics as a way to make a difference, a way to influence events and make the country a better place to live. Maybe it was because I wanted to marry a woman like Jackie Kennedy. Maybe it was all of those things. But for whatever reason, in the summer of 1956 I wanted to be John F. Kennedy.

In 1956, I started ninth grade at Bossier High School. By then, Dad was feeling better. Thanks to the operations on his ankles, he had begun to manage Scopena himself again. He was particularly concentrating on planting the new crop in 1957. As I began ninth grade, I was free to go back to school fulltime.

That fall I decided to run for president of the ninth grade. I don't remember how the decision was made, but I know that Jerry Payne was right in the middle of it. Jerry was the leader of a rock and roll band that played at all the high school dances and was very popular on campus. He and I were friends. He managed that first campaign—class president of ninth grade. He assured me that the position would not take too much of my time, so I could help manage Scopena. The election was held in the seventh week of the fall semester. Jerry had signs printed touting my candidacy (Roemer for President—Make Bossier proud!) and bought two thousand pieces of bubble gum wrapped in paper saying, "Buddy's the one." We passed the bubble gum out when people left the cafeteria.

There were five or six other candidates, and we had to give a five-minute speech before the entire student body at an assembly. I was nervous, but Jerry had it all scripted. The campaign ran like clockwork. He had me promise to host a schoolwide party in the summer if I won: "come to Scopena." The final result wasn't even close. I beat the five opponents on the first ballot without a runoff.

After I won, my duties were easy. Jerry was right. I was a member of the student council already and attended those meetings faithfully. But other than that, I was a pure figurehead. I thoroughly enjoyed meeting with the student leaders of other schools, but there was no heavy lifting. Years later, Jerry and I laughed out loud that it was the ideal kind of political job: all fluff and no substance.

We did have a party for all the students in the ninth grade at Scopena that spring. It was a huge success, with horse rides, tennis matches, swimming contests, and lots of chili dogs and chips.

The political victory and the party did set me up to run for another position two years later: student body president and head of the student council. Jerry and I planned this campaign in detail. He was tremendous as manager. He anticipated every move by the opposition and had an answer for them.

Our campaign platform was "Bold Leadership—Buddy Roemer Delivers." The only promise that we had made in the ninth grade president's race was a school party at Scopena, and we had delivered. So in the assembly before the election for student body president, we talked about the school party and said we would do it again. It worked. One of my opponents said that he was going to Scopena for the party, and, so as not to be hypocritical, he endorsed me for student body president.

Jerry and Cookie Demler, the head cheerleader and my high school sweetheart, small and beautiful, were my biggest helpers in the election campaign in high school. Cookie was a natural leader and was selected as head cheerleader when the school year started. She managed to put a "Buddy Roemer for President" sticker on her cheerleading uniform. I got free publicity before every student assembly and during every football game from Cookie jumping around, as cheerleaders do, with the "Buddy Roemer" sticker on her outfit.

Jerry was so talented that he turned campaign managing into a full time job when he was in his forties. He still runs campaigns for mayor and city council candidates in Bossier City and in Shreveport, and we're still close friends.

I was elected student body president for the 1959-1960 school year. It went by in a rush. We reorganized the student council and the association of student councils in northwest Louisiana. We put an image of the school mascot (a "bearkat"—sort of like a small bobcat) as part of an engraving in the ground floor of the school. And at Scopena, we had the biggest party in the history of Bossier High, as I fulfilled my election campaign promise.

We got permission from the school board to release Bossier High students that Friday at noon to have the party at a decent hour. It was a rousing success. Mom decorated the yard with bales of hay. About three hundred students showed up. We started at 1:30 in the afternoon with swimming and horseback riding. The horses were all on their best behavior. We also played baseball with a tennis ball. Others played tennis and used the shuffle board set by the swimming pool. There was music with a disc jockey for entertainment and hot dogs and hamburgers galore. I served as the host, made sure all the events ran smoothly, and refereed arguments that could have led to fisticuffs.

Fortunately, there were no fights or trouble of any kind. We shut down the party at about 12:00 in the morning by turning off the tennis court lights as a precaution. So some people literally said good night in the dark. As we said back in the 1950s: the party was a humongous success.

We had other parties over the years where members of the student body were featured guests, but this party topped them all for the enthusiasm and size of the crowd. At every high school reunion thereafter—the twentieth, twenty-fifth, thirtieth, fortieth, and fiftieth—the campaign party at Scopena was a big topic of conversation.

38

The Birth of a Politician

Each year, several boys are selected by the faculty of their high school and also the American Legion to attend a leadership conference in Baton Rouge before the start of their junior year in high school. This conference elected students to a legislature and other offices that mirror those in state government, including governor. The conference is called "Boys State," and is still held annually in Baton Rouge with about three hundred kids attending every year.

I was one of the two boys selected from Bossier High School in 1957. It would turn out to spur my dream of becoming a politician. A week-long program in late August, Boys State was like summer camp with a highly developed political edge. The schedule included a lot of civics lessons, with time to campaign. We met at venues scattered around Baton Rouge—the Prince Murat Inn, the LSU campus, the statehouse chamber, and the great hall of a hotel in Baton Rouge, among others.

Don't be misled: the real incentive for me to get into politics was not "Boys State," but rather the hot June, July, and August cotton fields of Scopena. Politics seemed easier than farming as I knew it. What I got out of Boys State was that I could be successful at doing something that required minimal effort from me. Boys State was a test run for me, nothing more.

I decided to run for governor as soon as I hit town. I had no preconceived notion of what was going to take place at Boys State. I had not talked to anyone who had been to prior Boys State conventions, but all the talk by the camp counselors at the original Boys State assembly was about the office of governor. I decided that's the job I wanted to hold. That's where I would test my skills at politics.

I didn't really know what a governor was. I just knew he was the head man. I wasn't the biggest or the most well connected there, and I hadn't talked with any delegate beforehand. But I was used to being the head man in my mind, so I decided to run for governor.

The first day we were organized into two political parties and began to run for local offices below that of governor, such as state legislator, mayor, and judge. I was elected as a state senator. It took all night long to win the election, with a runoff thrown in. I was exhausted, and pressed for time, because I immediately turned to the governor's race.

The trick was to win the party's nomination for governor against a tough field of candidates. It wasn't the Democratic or Republican Party but some invented name peculiar to Boys State. Ballot after ballot was cast in the primary, and I couldn't believe it. I won each round. My ability to rev the audience to high levels of enthusiasm was helping me win. I had practiced in the summers, walking in the cotton fields behind the hoe hands and while walking in the fields as an entomologist. I pretended that I was addressing the Democratic convention in some great city, and I would thunder some address. Boys State was a natural for me, because speaking before a live audience was the key for success. I was skilled before we ever got to camp. I had practiced speaking for dozens of hours. It was an unfair advantage.

· I hadn't thought of this before, but the hoe hands at Scopena must have thought that I was a lunatic, speaking to the empty cotton fields for hours at a time. I would be walking and gesturing as if I had an audience. I was completely wrapped up in the performance. If the cotton plants could talk, what a tale they could tell. I was "bouncing" again, except my dreams of glory were actual practice that I would employ on the campaign trail for Congress and for governor or for president.

The candidates spoke before each ballot, and I emphasized that I would, if elected, make Louisiana a force in the national organization for the first time in its history. I won my party's nomination for governor at about 5:30 in the morning. It had been two nights consecutive with just brief snatches of sleep.

I immediately began to organize our state ticket for Boys State: governor, secretary of state, attorney general, commission of elections, commissioner of insurance, commissioner of agriculture, etc. It took hours. I didn't have a Jerry Payne around for support or to organize a campaign. I did it all without him.

Exhausted, I tried to catch a nap, but everybody needed something and wanted to see me right then. The election was going to be held that night. (A nice guy from Shreveport, Brown was his last name, was the nominee of the other party.) The two nominees were supposed to give speeches. The two parties had the same number of delegates, but the delegates were free to vote for their favorite. I liked my chances because speechmaking was my forté. There was no way I was going to be beat at giving a speech.

But as nightfall approached, I started feeling tense, most unusual for me. I was feeling the pressure of the moment. We drew straws that night to determine the speaking order. I won and chose to go second. I figured I might learn something from my opponent's speech if he preceded me.

We spoke in the statehouse chamber in the capitol, and it was packed with delegates. I had not prepared any remarks but had made an outline of points that I wanted to make and felt ready. My opponent went first, and in his five minutes he did a good job. I remained confident when it was my turn. I got up to speak, but no words came out. I looked down for a split second, wondering if the microphone was working. I could hear it hum. I looked back up and saw the mass of delegates in the room waiting on me. Still no words came out. I couldn't talk.

The crowd was chanting and yelling. My delegates knew I was a good speaker since they had heard me several times already. But the opposing party's delegates didn't know, and I could see them waiting, wondering, listening closely.

Then, the chamber began to grow quiet. Both friend and foe—and those not sure—grew quiet. The room was filled with silent people. I stood before them, alone and quiet, unable to make a sound. Mute.

I tried every trick I knew. I tried to say a few words off the mike, but nothing came out. I turned my back on the audience to clear my throat, but it didn't help. I finally got down off the podium, but no words had come. I guess I had frozen up. Maybe the pressure was too much for me. I didn't know what the problem was. It never happened to me, before or since.

So I got back on the podium and waved like some entertainer. I stepped down from the podium and went to my guys on the edge of the chamber. I was whipped, stunned. The vote was held shortly thereafter. I lost. The Boys State show rolled on without me. The party was over. I can't remember the details of what anybody said after the vote. I just know there was a lot of hugging and some crying.

We had another day before we went home. It passed like a blur. People were very nice to me, very understanding. I was selected the most outstanding delegate at Boys State that year. I guess they were feeling a little sorry for the delegate from Bossier. Either way, I felt so alone, so isolated from events. I rode the bus back home in a seat by myself. The bus, with Shreveport and Bossier delegates, let me out on the side of Highway 71 at Scopena.

When I thought about Boys State years later, I felt it had been a huge success for me. I mean I had lost for governor, but I had won everything else. This was easy. I just needed to improve my performance under pressure, and without sleep, and I was going to be fine. I was going to be governor someday.

I told Dad and Mom what had happened at Boys State. I was down. They told me that I was a great public speaker and a great story teller and that I shouldn't lose that gift. Dad argued for one thing: speak publicly again as soon as possible. He felt speaking was like riding a bucking horse. Once thrown, the sooner you got back on, the better success you would have because the horse would respect your determination. You couldn't be beat, so the horse better stop bucking and start obeying.

Maybe it was just the person regaining his confidence, and it had nothing to do with the horse, but I agreed with Dad's point, so I called my Sunday School teacher that night and asked if I could give a special report on John Newton, the Englishman who wrote the Methodist hymn, "Amazing Grace." I had just read a book about Newton, and I was ready. I told him of my failure at Boys State and that I needed to climb back on the horse. He said there was room for me on the program in two weeks, and I could have fifteen minutes. I had read about Newton's life and thought it was an appropriate story for the Sunday School class.

The night before I spoke to the class, I wondered if I would hesitate or choke. The next morning, I stood before the class and talked of how Newton had been a sea captain and described his great sins (debauchery, swearing, and captaining a slaving ship). Facing death, he turned his life around and wrote "Amazing Grace," the most widely sung song in the world according to some experts. I didn't pause at all and felt very satisfied with the effort. Once again I spoke from an outline. No written speech. Dad had been right. Getting back on the horse was the place for me to be.

Dad and I discussed the lessons I could learn from what happened at Boys State. Besides getting back on the horse, he also talked about the importance of getting my rest before a high-tension endeavor. I followed that advice in the future whenever I had a major speech to give. In Congress, I would nap in the office before a big speech whenever I could. As governor, my days were always hectic, but I tried not to be too tired before a major speech.

In the years after the debacle at Boys State, I would run across someone who had been there that night in Baton Rouge. They would always say something quietly like, "I was a delegate to Boys State when you were a candidate for governor. Sorry you didn't win, but you were terrific." I would smile and remember the hundreds of speeches I've given since then, and would feel so thankful that I got back up on the horse with John Newton.

Boys State was a valuable testing ground for me. Because of it I knew before I was fourteen years of age that I was going to be governor of the great state of Louisiana. It was just a question of picking the right moment to run—and getting plenty of sleep beforehand.

I was to win the race for governor in 1987 when I was forty-four. I received the endorsement of the New Orleans *Times-Picayune*, the Shreveport newspapers, the Monroe paper, the Alexandria paper, and the Baton Rouge newspapers late in the race and won going away. I was in last place at 6 percent before the endorsements with no chance of victory. I had won four successive campaigns for Congress, but looked like a north-Louisiana only candidate for governor.

By the way, my nephew, Jude Melville, was elected governor of Boys State years later. When I was governor, I went to the capitol to celebrate his victory and to say hello to folks. While there, that feeling of helplessness from decades earlier came rushing back to me.

39

HARVARD OR BUST

As I said, following the 1956 Democratic National Convention, I wanted to be John F. Kennedy. An obvious place to start doing that would be to attend his alma mater. So in 1956 I knew that I wanted to go to Harvard College, even though I was not scheduled to graduate from high school until June of 1960.

I figured that the only way to get to Harvard was to graduate near the top of my class. Ninth grade was the test case in my mind. I either would show my ability then or I would end up going to LSU, my back-up school.

It turned out that I was a very good student. I got straight A's in ninth grade. Math and the other subjects were easy for me because of the home schooling with my mother.

We decided to take our summer vacation between the ninth grade and the tenth grades to Boston and the East Coast. Dad had recovered well enough to travel, and we wanted to visit Harvard and let them know I wanted to attend there. Of course, Harvard had never heard of me, but we were able to get an interview with the admissions staff after we sent them my ninth grade records and other documents like SAT results, etc.

As usual, we drove up, and we stopped in Gettysburg, Philadelphia, and New York City. Gettysburg was interesting because the battlefield was preserved just like it happened, and I had heard about

Buddy in the tenth grade at Bossier High School

it all my life. But in real time, it looked smaller than I had imagined from reading about it in the history books.

We saw the usual sights in Philly (the Liberty Bell and Freedom Hall) and in New York City (the Empire State Building, the Bronx Zoo, and Yankee Stadium). New York City was big, but after a day that's all it was: just big. The memorable part of the trip for us was

Boston, Cambridge and Harvard.

Boston is a special town given the American history centered there: Faneuil Hall, North Church, the Freedom Trail, even Fenway Park, if you're a baseball fan. We saw them all, as well as all the universities located there: Tufts, Boston University, Boston College, Simmons, Wellesley, Suffolk, MIT, Harvard, Emerson, and more.

MIT and Wellesley were awesome, but we fell in love with Simmons and Harvard. Simmons was an unexpected treat. It was an all-girls school located near Fenway Park. It's not nearly as beautiful as Wellesley, but it was much closer to downtown Boston and known for its high academic standards. We met with the administration of the school and got a warm reception. My oldest sister Margaret would take a strong interest in Simmons, and they reciprocated, taking her in the class that graduated in 1966. Years later, my youngest son, Dakota, would attend, graduate—and captain the soccer team—at Suffolk University, which was located in downtown Boston.

I loved Harvard. We saw all the sights on campus. It looked like what I had envisioned while at Scopena, 1,600 miles away. Clean and prim. It looked like every blade of grass was in its place, manicured and well-kept. The history of Harvard was breathtaking. I was overwhelmed. Harvard was the place for me. I didn't even think about visiting or applying to any other college.

Dad, Mom, and I met with several administrators in the admissions office while the other kids toured Lamont and Widener libraries. The officials were very efficient. They knew a lot about me after talking with Bossier High School principal Frank Lampkin. They knew about my grades, my perfect 800 score on the SAT test, and my leadership potential as the ninth grade class president.

When we entered the meeting, they saw Dad walking with his labored gait on his steel ankles. That led to a conversation about the accident and the role I had played as a teenager helping run the farm. From there, Mom and Dad described my background and my study habits. Mom described her home schooling efforts for each of the kids. They were amazed when Mom told them that I read and reported on the Harvard classics years ago.

As I was listening to Mom and Dad, I wasn't nervous. The administrators put you at ease. I was wearing a pressed shirt and slacks, so they asked me if I attended school in that attire. I told them that there was no uniform at Bossier High, that I usually wore a t-shirt and blue jeans. They also asked me about my activities outside of school. I said I played varsity tennis, and that I loved baseball, duck hunting, and horseback riding. I added that my fall job was cotton ginning and that my summer job was hoeing instructor, moisture meter reader, and entomologist. I got the sense that they liked all of my answers. I must admit that I sat there without a doubt that I was going to Harvard in a couple of years. I didn't mean to be cocky. I just knew that was the school for me. Nothing had changed my mind.

At the end of the two-hour meeting, I guess they had enough information to make a determination of Harvard's interest on the spot. The events of the past year showed the kind of maturity they were looking for in a young student. They gave me a writing test with a limit of five hundred words. Then, late that afternoon, they met with Mom, Dad, and me and said "yes," they wanted me and would take me early. They would take me at the end of my sophomore year or at the end of my junior year. It was up to me.

We asked for time to mull it over. They were asking me to give up two years of my high school eligibility. It was a big decision. We talked about the Harvard offer all the way back to Scopena, which took two days.

My brother and sisters thought that I should go right then. Why waste time at good ole Bossier High School? Get ahead of the world and build on the lead, they said. I hesitated. I could go to Harvard in a year or I could go back to Bossier High School for three years. I decided to give my vote to Mom and Dad. I felt comfortable that they knew what was best for me.

My parents believed that I should graduate from high school and enter Harvard as a regular freshman. Mom was particularly adamant. She noted that I was already a year younger than my classmates. She thought high school was special and that, unless I planned to live permanently in the northeast of the United States, I should develop a relationship with people in Bossier and graduate from Bossier High School. She also noted that life consisted of more than books and knowledge. By spending more time at Bossier High School, I could establish lifelong friendships with classmates and gain an even deeper knowledge of Bossier Parish and Louisiana. Harvard could come later.

It was the right choice for me. Years later, when I ran for Congress and, later, for governor of Louisiana, I was so thankful to have graduated from Bossier High School. The friends that I had made at Bossier and the sense of community were invaluable.

We called Harvard's head of admissions. He accepted our decision with understanding. When I asked if I was assured of a spot at Harvard in two years, when I would apply during my senior year, he said it would depend on my worthiness then. There were no guarantees. Harvard wanted me now. They might not want me then. Whether they did would depend on my grades and special achievements over the next two years. In other words, I would not be guaranteed admittance. I'd have to take my chances with the advantage of my acceptance earlier. I did apply again to Harvard at the beginning of my senior year. I applied to no other university. I was stupid or headstrong, I guess. But I was being honest. I only wanted to go to one school.

Months later, when I received Harvard's reply to my application, I was in Coach Murray's class on government. The principal, Mr. Lampkin, brought the letter from Harvard addressed to me. He was aware of my application and knew I was awaiting a response. He said that he had never had a Harvard applicant in one of his schools before. He stopped the class and came down the aisle with the letter.

I hadn't been nervous at all anticipating the letter, but being in front of everybody in the class and the fact that I had recently read an article reporting that Harvard was awfully selective suddenly made me anxious. What if they turned me down? Seeing Mr. Lampkin walk down the aisle provoked a stab of fear.

My hands were trembling as I opened the letter. There was no way to tell from the unopened envelope. There were no happy face markings or big, bold banners blaring "you have been accepted." But they took me. The U.S. Postal service has never been better to the boy from Scopena. The letter was short and sweet, a single sheet. But it would change my life and allow me to pursue my dreams. Mr. Lampkin started clapping as I read the letter out loud. He was very proud and pleased. He knew it meant the world to me. The rest of Mr. Murray's class joined him in applause. I was to begin in August of 1960 as a freshman and spend my freshman year in a dorm named Matthews South in the Harvard Yard.

Mr. Lampkin announced the news to the student body that afternoon over the school intercom. When I got on the school bus at 3:15, Mr. Madden, the bus driver, was all smiles and congratulations. Punkin and Danny met me on the school bus, and they were all excited. In fact, Mom and Dad met the bus at the Scopena stop and led a celebration at the office.

I didn't have much to say at school or home. I hadn't sensed what a big deal getting into Harvard was for everybody else. Later that year, I was selected valedictorian of Bossier High School for 1960 after a record of straight A's. I thought that was a neat accomplishment, but it didn't create near the uproar as getting in to Harvard did. I got to give the graduating speech because of my valedictory achievement, but among me and my classmates, the Harvard selection ranked first.

The next big deal on my agenda was going to the senior prom with Cookie, my high school sweetheart. We had been going together for three years. Cookie and I only had one major falling out during our time as sweethearts at Bossier High School and that was when I made a B on my first six-weeks report in Miss Jaynes's tenth-grade speech class. I wasn't used to getting B's, and it could be raised to an A by mid-semester if I worked hard, so a day or so later I told Cookie that we had to breakup: my studies came first and our relationship was taking too much time. Cookie exploded, saying that I hadn't studied and that all I needed to do was crack open a book and concentrate in class to get an A. I thought about it for thirty minutes and agreed with her, and we were back together. I made A's for the rest of the year.

Now, for the senior prom, I was trying especially hard to impress her. I knew that this was a big night for her. I planned the prom date for weeks. I knew Cookie was going to be the prettiest girl at the prom. How was I going to measure up as a date? I wanted to impress her especially since I was going off to Harvard at the end of summer and was going to be away from her for long periods. She was quite a girl, very level-headed and practical. She was in fact the person who I relied on to keep me in touch with the "city" world, my last three years on Scopena.

I made my preparations. Dad lent me his Buick. It was a decided improvement over my own International Harvester pickup truck that I used around Scopena. I got a beautiful corsage from the florist. Next, I made reservations at a restaurant that Cookie liked called "The Piccadilly Pizza House." It served delicious Italian food. Finally, I got a tuxedo tailored to fit—a first for me.

The night was beautiful. I remember it like it was yesterday. I actually looked good all decked out. I was so proud. I had washed and waxed the car two times to be sure that it shined.

When I went by the florist that afternoon, she had the corsage prepared to perfection. Cookie already had my high school ring around her neck, so I couldn't do anything more there, but I bought a special box of chocolates to remember the occasion.

I got so busy with the preparations and making sure that everything was perfect that I lost track of time. I arrived nearly an hour late to Cookie's house to pick her up. She broke down in tears. We were late for the prom. But we ended up having a great time. It was a special evening, and I'm glad I stayed in high school to enjoy it. I just wish I hadn't danced like a klutz. And little did I know that Cookie and I were to get married at the end of my junior year in college, and she was to work for the president of Harvard College my two years at the Harvard Business School.

40

MY FIRST PLANE RIDE

During the first week of August 1960 on a hot, bright Tuesday morning, I left Scopena for the Shreveport airport to fly to Boston and Harvard. I was sixteen years old. I had been up in our crop dusting planes at Scopena, but I had never been in a commercial airplane that carried passengers. My parents and family took me to the Shreveport airport. Cookie met us there. There were many tears. Mom and Cookie led the crying parade, but Margaret, Melinda, and Melanie weren't far behind. Dad and Danny were excited.

I, too, was excited. I was going to Boston. I was saddened to be leaving my family, Cookie, and Scopena, but youth is not wise enough to have regrets, and I'd be home for Christmas. It's funny: the girls of the family, Mom, Cookie, Punkin, Melinda, and Melanie were saddened by my leaving even though they knew I would be coming back in a few months. The boys, Dad and Danny, were excited about the adventure and the thought that I'd only be gone for what seemed like a few days. Danny and Dad were very talkative, the girls less so.

Dad had given me a brand new Accutron watch for the occasion and for graduation. From something I had read, I knew the watch had cost Dad more than one hundred dollars. I had never owned anything so expensive, and it was my first watch. I wore it like a badge of honor, like a job well done.

It was a propeller plane all the way to Boston, with stops in Monroe, Jackson, Birmingham, Atlanta, and Newark. I was flying on Delta Airlines; that's why we stopped in Monroe. It seems that one of Delta's founders was from Monroe. There weren't many passengers on the leg to Monroe and only a few joined to Atlanta from Jackson. But, man, in Atlanta things picked up, and the trip to Newark was packed. When I got off in Newark, I had more than a one-hour layover before the flight to Boston. I decided to get something to eat.

I wandered in the lobby of the terminal and found a good place called Stouffer's kitchen. Afterward, I went to the men's room. The airport was packed with people, and the men's room was no different. But I had plenty of time and patience. I found my way to a men's stall, did my business and went to wash my hands. I was very careful with my new watch, taking it off my left arm and resting it on the side of the sink as I washed my hands.

Just then I spotted Moose Skowron, the all-star first baseman of the New York Yankees. Moose was washing his hands as well. I introduced myself and told him what a big fan I was and how excited I was to see him. He smiled, thanked me and asked how long I had been a Yankees fan. Forever, I told him and said it must have been rewarding to be on a team with Yogi Berra and Mickey Mantle. He said it was and said it had been nice to meet me. The whole encounter took three minutes.

I turned back to my wash bowl to get my watch. It was gone. I checked the other bowls, thinking that I had gotten confused about where I had left it. I still couldn't find it. I checked around the crowded room. It wasn't there either. I raced into the outside corridor. I didn't see anybody wearing my watch. I ran down to the lost and found station and left my name and address in case they found it.

My watch was gone. My gift of a lifetime. My graduation gift. My going off to Harvard present. My first watch, gone—and gone due to my neglect and inattention. How stupid and foolish could one person be? It was a big city lesson for me. People will steal.

I made my flight to Boston with no problems. Upon arrival at

Logan airport, I stuffed my luggage into an airport taxi and told the driver to take me to the Harvard Square, Harvard Yard. I was still upset by the loss of the Accutron watch. But I couldn't help but feel awe during the trip down Memorial Drive in that taxi! My nerves were strung tighter than a tennis racquet. To arrive at Harvard Square and to drag my luggage into Harvard Yard was an experience unlike any I've ever had.

I had made it. I was an entire world away from how I had grown up. I was on my own. As my favorite speaker, Dr. Martin Luther King Jr., would say, I was free at last. Thank God almighty I was free at last.

A cop stopped me when I first entered the Yard—I guess for cluttering up the campus with my bags. When I identified myself as an incoming freshman, he took one of my bags and led me the 150 feet to #1 Matthews South. He then showed me the residence building where my room key was housed.

The yard was immaculate and green with fescue a half a foot high. The flower gardens were in bloom around the outside rim of the yard. People were playing Frisbee at the far end. It was August so the temperature seemed perfect at 80 degrees. There was a big, lit digital thermometer at the entrance to the Yard. It had showered that afternoon so rain puddles remained on the blacktopped walkways that cut through the yard. This was to be my home for the next year.

I called Scopena that night from the pay phone near Harvard Square. I had trepidation about Dad's reaction to my losing the watch with less than ten hours of use, but he said he understood my mistake and said that I had so many things going on at once, it was a wonder that I managed to get myself to Boston in one piece. I felt better afterward. I must admit, however, some of the sting of the loss of the watch remains after all these years.

In fact, of all the memories of my first week—the first visit to the Harvard Bookstore, my first meal at the freshman mess, the first class with other students—the thing that I remember the most was the theft of my watch from Newark's airport men's room on the trip up to Boston.

41

COMING HOME FOR CHRISTMAS

The days ahead were filled with exams, placement tests, scheduled classes, and unscheduled movies. Pretty soon I realized that it was approaching Thanksgiving, and I had been gone from Scopena since the first week of August. The longest I had been away from Scopena and my family prior to this was a few days here and there over the course of a few tennis tournaments, family vacations, and Boys State. But this was to be quite a journey through Thanksgiving and on to Christmas.

During this time, I realized that I was going to make it at Harvard just fine. The work there wasn't too hard, but I had worried when I discovered that many freshmen had gone to some fancy Massachusetts, Connecticut, or New Hampshire prep school. I thought they might have some advantage, some special preparation, over a public school boy like me, but they didn't, as it turned out. They started fast, but I just worked longer and harder and came out fine. I was far from top of the class, but I could pass any course. My usual grade was a B or C, and I flunked German Conversation my sophomore year, but I memorized the Latin book my senior year and managed to pass the language requirement. When I made an A or B, it was because a course interested me enough to study. I often didn't go to class. I was wonderfully lazy as I wasn't expected to be valedictorian, and I would take some days off and go visit a museum in Boston or go to the Red Sox or Bruins game. I enjoyed myself. "Anything but class" was my philosophy for a while.

But homesickness was a deeply felt problem, and the university did nothing to combat the feeling. You were left to your own devices. The freshmen were all stuck together in Harvard Yard so we would talk and mix with each other. But that's it. There were no activities for those of us who were desperately lonely. Maybe the homesickness came from me being so young. Anyway no one else seemed to be concerned.

Scopena was such a different life—a different world—compared to Harvard. It was like I was from a different country—a foreigner in a strange land. It was like living on Scopena but seeing the world in the eyes of a black worker. Harvard couldn't understand me, and I just couldn't understand the black worker, looking back.

The girls in the surrounding college—Radcliffe—were unacceptable to me. First of all, I think I was the youngest student in school and most of the female students were aiming higher than a pimply-faced sixteen-year-old. Cookie and I had decided to go out with other people at college. This was difficult for me at Harvard because it was all boys. There were schools with girls around Harvard—Radcliffe, Wellesley, Boston University, and Simmons, for example—but it was a project to get off campus. Radcliffe was the girls' portion of Harvard. However, I found them to be more competitive than friendly, more intimidating and smart than desirable.

A second and more important factor besides my being underage was my southern-ness: skinny, strong accent, country appearance. I hate to say years later, but maybe it was me?

For all these reasons and more, that first year was generally girl free. I kept my mind off my loneliness by going to the movies by myself and reading books. Boston was filled with film festivals of various stripes, and I attended many. Meanwhile, the Widener Library was the largest university library in the world, and I buried myself deep in its stacks. The library had some unusual items in its inner vaults. For example, it had every copy of the weekly magazine, *Sports Illustrated*, ever published. I proceeded to read them all. I had received every copy of *Sports Illustrated* at Scopena beginning with its first publication in the 1950s, but to read them all again was like a journey down memory lane for me.

Thanksgiving was hard for me. My roommates—Brian Silver, Joe Minnoti, and Bill Davis—all went home, but I stayed on campus. Boy was I homesick!

I did call home for Thanksgiving, from the pay phone at the corner of Harvard Square and Massachusetts Avenue. I reversed the charges and talked a blue streak. Among other things, I told them about my airplane ticket that had me arriving on the 23rd of December at 6:30 in the evening. I couldn't wait. In barely four weeks, I would be home for Christmas.

I felt better after we spoke. I went to the dining hall that night for Thanksgiving dinner. There were only about one hundred people in a room with a capacity for maybe five hundred. I was so thankful to have a place to go. They even served dressing with the turkey. And we had ice cream with a big "H" on it. As a rule, I never ate the ice cream, but this lonely Thanksgiving it hit the spot.

It was the first time in my life that I had no member of my family around me for Thanksgiving. The memories of Scopena and my family kept me going.

✳ ✳ ✳

It's funny how slow December dragged by. I had a number of school projects and papers that I had to finish during the final three weeks. One project was due on December 22. My faculty advisor agreed to allow me to deliver it a day early so I could go home a day earlier. I changed my airplane ticket and arranged with Cookie to have her pick me up at the airport in Shreveport. Cookie lived in Bossier City and was already home from Louisiana Tech, a fine college an hour away from Bossier City in Ruston. We were still very close, although we both felt the strain from the long distance.

I didn't let my parents or any members of my family know that I had changed my plans. I wanted to surprise them.

I got to Boston's Logan airport early on the 22nd and found that the flight to Atlanta had been delayed for three hours. There was nothing to do but wait. So I walked around and tried to relax. I had worked overtime in order to finish my schoolwork quickly so I could surprise my family with my early arrival. I was tired but excited. I visited the coffee shop. I still had two hours and forty minutes before the plane departed for Atlanta.

I spotted an empty bench and decided to lie down. Surely there would be plenty of notice before the delayed flight's departure. I stretched out on the wooden bench and proceeded to fall into a deep slumber—something that I hadn't done in weeks.

I jumped up with a start sometime later. "Final call. Flight to Atlanta. Final call." I rushed to the gate. No one was there. They had changed the departure gate while I was sleeping. I raced to the new gate. All the passengers had boarded. The attendants had closed the gate and were gathering their paperwork to move on.

I begged to be let on the plane. I showed them my ticket and said that I had fallen asleep on a bench. I said I was going home for Christmas and couldn't miss my plane. I will never forget what the gate attendant did. She whirled, opened the departure door and went running down the ramp, screaming, trying to stop the plane from leaving the gate.

She succeeded. The gate opened, and I made my way to my seat. I was the last person on the plane. The gate attendant smiled and smiled. I would never forget her name: Sarah. It was on her Delta name tag.

Cookie was at the Shreveport airport to pick me up. We hugged and kissed. I was excited to see her.

We caught up on much of the gossip of what high school class-mates were doing while we drove the thirty minutes to Scopena. At the same time, it was so exciting to drive through Bossier City and view the old high school and everything else. I had been gone since

August. It seemed longer.

When we got to Scopena, it looked just like I'd left it. The corn fields were harvested, but it had been wet that fall so many of the cotton fields hadn't been picked yet. That always meant crop loss, but a farmer couldn't do much about wetness. We could fight dryness with irrigation, but wetness meant a delay in harvest, which often meant disaster for the pocketbook. It was one of the reasons that I wasn't going to be a farmer. I had already decided; I was long tired of playing roulette with the rain in Louisiana.

As soon as we pulled up, we went in the office. Mom wasn't there. She had gone to town to get supplies, and the other kids weren't home from school yet. The radio operator said that Dad was at the corral, working cattle. That was just over the levee behind the shop about a mile away from the Scopena office.

It was a brisk December afternoon with a bright blue sky. Scopena was calling to me from the birds in the shop building to the cattle bellowing across the levee. I decided to run to the corral cut.

Along the dirt road, workers in the implement shed and those sitting on home verandas waved greetings. I saw them all. Somebody was cooking cornbread for supper in one of the houses. I still remember that smell. Truthfully, most of what I remember was the memory of Dad.

It went like this.

I ran up the levee to the corral that was built on top of a levee-annex on the other side of the main one. There were cattle in the corral. I saw Dad's Jeep with King sitting on the front seat, waiting on him as usual. I went to the Jeep and gave King a swipe in the way of telling him hello. I did not immediately see Dad. All I could see were a dozen or more black cowboys all over the corral. I also saw my grandmother, Mine, who was examining the cows in the holding pen. Before I could shout at her, one of the head cowboys, Robert, hollered "Mr. Butch," and climbed down off the corral fence to greet me. But Dad moved first.

As we approached each other, I didn't know whether to shake

his hand like the grownup I thought I had become, or to hug him like father and son. "I'm early," I said, as we stood for a moment face to face.

"I missed you, son. Welcome home," he replied, and we hugged. Mine joined us in a threesome of wrapped hugs. It was a feeling like I've seldom had—to be at Scopena after all that time; to be home after all that change and challenge. I felt safe again. Just like that day when I came home from Peters' Grocery after running away on my first day of school.

I remember wondering if any of my roommates had the kind of homecoming that I had. My guess is that they hadn't.

It's been fifty-six years since I arrived at Scopena a day early and met my Dad and grandmother on the levee near the corral. Yet it is like time has stood still. I still remember the cowboys sitting on the top of the corral railing; the horses looking to see what all the non-cattle fuss was about; King sitting in the Jeep waiting on Dad; Mine wearing khakis and with a bridle in her hands; the sounds of the several hundred cattle calling and mooing over the pain of being branded; the cold, crisp day of afternoon sun at Scopena; and Dad walking down the levee with his arms outstretched to greet me home.

EPILOGUE

Scopena Shrinks

Well, that's the end of the stories of Scopena in the years 1950-1960. I left out many tales of family meetings and tennis matches and horseback rides and card games and school bus conversations. I left out the hours on the lawnmower or on school projects or with a wooden baseball bat hitting gravel rocks over the trees on the east side of the front yard. In other words, this is not a revisit of my daily schedule.

This does not tell the story of Scopena in the years after graduation from college, nor does it describe my life while I was at Harvard. Rather this is a series of events that happened between the time I was five years of age until I was sixteen and returned to Scopena every summer and Christmas while I was an undergraduate in college. Most of my life, including the people found in my life, are not in these tales. They came later.

One person who is in these tales and who played a significant role in what I was to become after Scopena was Dad. He guided me into my vocation (Executive at IDS, farming at Scopena) and my avocation (campaigns and politics), and so had the most profound effect of my life. I can truthfully say that he was the most complex person I ever knew, and when it came to my life, the most loving—except for my mother.

When I graduated in 1964, I came back to run the farm for one year, but Scopena wasn't really on my mind, long-term. I spent time investigating new crops (potatoes, for example), but I was interested in graduate school to pursue a profession somewhere off the farm. I didn't want to be a farmer. My heart just was not into it. I wanted to be a politician. How can you divine the whims of youth? I didn't put down farming, but I wanted something different.

People laugh sometimes when I say that I wanted something easier than farming, but I did. It's hard to walk those hot cotton fields to check insects; to chop cotton in 110 degree weather; to stay up all night to irrigate fields of cotton and corn; to run the gin for long hours after school; to get the labor sorted out at 6:30 every morning; to keep the detasselers on task through the scalding hot sun in July and August; and to do all of this and have it not rain a drop in the period of June through September, have your crops burn up, and then have it rain all of October and November when you try to harvest.

I wanted something easier. I admit it. I've got an idle streak in me, where I want my time to be spent discussing life and working on solutions of the world's problems. I didn't see those opportunities on the farm. Wherever I meet a farmer—China, Louisiana, France, Texas—I know the hard work and courage it takes and my full admiration goes to the person. I tried to represent the heartbreak and courage of every farmer when I was a U. S. Congressman.

Back at Scopena after I graduated from college, I struggled for much of that year with whether to enter law school or business school. I chose business. Most politicians study law; I wanted to study business to be different. I believed it to be relevant to the issues facing Louisiana and the United States: budget stabilization and economic growth. I still think it was the influence of my father that switched me from law, where everyone thought I was going, to business.

From the time that I first remember, Dad had a reservation against lawyers. He liked their education and erudition, but he thought their job slightly dishonorable: to keep actions legal, not necessarily right. Business, on the other hand, was competition in raw form; may the best or luckiest man win. There was no double standard in business.

You were judged by actions in business. If you won, you won. No legal hanky-panky. "Legal" was word games; "business" was performance.

From my study of economics, I figured that a business education would give me the most variety and opportunity in the years ahead, and I thought that the study of business would give me an advantage in politics. Among a bunch of lawyers, I thought my business training in matters like the budget and economic development would serve me well.

I didn't see the problem that would later become apparent to me in Washington, D.C.: the system is bought, purchased by wealthy individuals and corporations for their personal interests. Washington has become home to the elite who love the arrangement of you scratch my back and I'll scratch yours. It's a system that has no room for the average Joe. That's why there is no change. Nothing ever gets done. The system is not designed for change or progress. It's designed to be immobile.

When I was in the system, I didn't see the inertia, the self-dealing, the falseness of it. Thanks to my father I figured out some of the traps that make caricatures of real people—for example, I didn't take PAC money as a member of Congress or as a candidate for governor. But I took unlimited individual contributions in my campaign for governor—$5,000 or $10,000 and thinking back that can cause problems. If Trump or the people who succeed him can stop business as usual in Washington, D.C., they will have changed America.

In the years that followed my graduation from Harvard Business School, I returned to Scopena to farm only one or two years. When I was at Scopena, I spent a lot of time working for a new company that we started at Dad's suggestion. Danny and I had been pushing him to buy computer stock in the late 1960s, to get our feet wet in what we realized was a new, coming industry. Dad, as usual, did us one better. He suggested we start a computer service company of our own. So we did in 1969 and called it Innovative Data Systems (IDS)

IDS assisted firms that wanted the power of a computer, but didn't know anything about computer software. Among other things, we created a computer room with a gigantic mainframe at Scopena. We had several computer programmers at IDS, plus Margaret, and Melinda and Melanie (between children). I spent most of my time on the road selling computer services for IDS throughout Texas, Arkansas, and Louisiana, and soon became its president.

Dad began to change the direction of his life in the early 1970s. As Margaret, Danny, and I became active in managing IDS and Scopena, he had more time on his hands. He signed on to manage Congressman Edwin Edwards's campaign for governor of Louisiana—fulltime. We didn't really talk about it much as a family. It started innocently enough.

For years we had been meeting as a family to interview candidates for local (mayor, sheriff), state (governor, commissioner of agricultural), and federal offices (congressman, U.S. Senator), when there was an upcoming election. We would meet with the candidates as a family unit at the dining room table and we would have, at times, a heated discussion about the candidates' beliefs, the strategy for the campaign, the organization, what actions would be taken while in office, funds required to be successful, and chances of victory. There was an almost endless variety of campaign chores that the family members could provide to the candidate for a fee, but the family had to decide whether the candidate in question would be a good officeholder. Most candidates never hired IDS to do any service for them, but regardless they had to pass the upfront test: would they be the best officeholder running for that office in this election?

Put another way: We wouldn't do service for a candidate in Louisiana, Texas, Mississippi, Alabama, Tennessee, Oklahoma, or Missouri that we didn't endorse.

It must have been an exhausting session for the candidates. All the Roemers were prepared and there seemed an endless round of questions. The family didn't just listen to the candidate's opening statement; they tore the statement apart. Each family member was capable of analysis; and they questioned the candidates extensively from Mom to Melanie.

It could be brutal, but it was never personal. In the end, the family might pass, and we would let them know. Sometimes there would be only one candidate for a position that the family was interested in. Sometimes there would be multiple candidates for one job and the family would have multiple interviews before reaching a decision.

The family would then meet as a group to discuss the candidates interviewed and make a decision. When we had decided on a candidate, we would talk about how to assist the candidate. Sometimes it was money they needed and we would give a contribution and phone other potential contributors to make a donation. Although there were differences of opinion at times, I can never remember an instance where we failed to arrive at a unanimous course of action on a candidate, even if that course was no endorsement in the race.

Some campaigns needed management. The campaign run thus far was not indicative of the type of woman or man that we knew the person to be. So we would take on the task of managing the overall campaign.

Some of the help we provided was polling and mailing addresses that could be invaluable to the candidate. We ran the poll every couple of weeks and the results we would share with our candidates. This information could be of vital importance to the candidate, telling him he was trailing and needed to change his campaign, or when an issue was looming large, or when he was in good shape and needed to keep doing more of the same.

My sister Margaret and I ran the polling operation. We had worked out a methodology that allowed us to take randomly generated telephone numbers and get a statistically accurate sample with only 324 completed calls. The old number had been 580 calls, or nearly two days extra in polling. Two days could be a long time in the middle of a hotly contested campaign. Now, we wouldn't get regional subsets accurately with that few numbers (New Orleans, or north Louisiana, for example), but for statewide results, or comparison with a previous poll, the numbers were valid for campaign management. We were faster than anyone else and just as accurate.

We eventually hired a young assistant, Elliot Stonecipher, who had a gift for numbers and questions, and took the operation to the status of one of the finest polling firms in the South.

Besides polling, we performed a "mailing" function for our candidates. Mailing was not something that most candidates used, but we had developed a unique "telegram" mail out that could be found nowhere else in Louisiana campaigns. It looked like a telegram, and its strength, unlike most direct mail, was that it was read. The reader found it irresistible. With the right message, which we composed using the findings of our latest poll, the reach to the constituency was strong and purposeful. Many a campaign was successful, because of the success of the "telegrammed" message sent the last few days of a campaign.

At times of need, we provided management of local campaigns, but normally our support for these local campaigns was limited to a personal donation, calling for financial support for friends or business associates, and "telegram" mail outs.

We hired Jerry Payne at IDS and he joined with Margaret and me to manage local campaigns in the early 1970s. The one campaign that Dad became directly responsible for was the gubernatorial race of 1971-72, which featured a strong competition for governor with, among others, Edwin Edwards, a congressman from southwestern Louisiana, and J. Bennett Johnston, a state senator from our backyard in Shreveport, Louisiana.

There were many people running for governor in 1972, but early in 1971 we as a family decided on which candidates we wanted to interview in the gubernatorial race. Only three interested us, and so we decided to bring in those three: Gillis Long, Edwin Edwards, and Bennett Johnston. Gillis was a congressman from a district close to Scopena and had dropped by on more than one occasion to say hello and was well liked by the family. He had a strong civil rights record in Congress and the family liked that; Bennett Johnston was another obvious on our list of three. He was a relatively young state senator from Shreveport who had made a splash in the *Shreveport Times* newspaper as a reformer, and he already enjoyed the support of many of our associates and neighbors. Bennett would have been an easy choice for governor, but there was a lingering suspicion among family members that Bennett was not a new breeze in Louisiana politics, that he was a Shreveport blue-blood interested only in the status quo, with keeping Shreveport over Bossier City, and whites over blacks. The family desired some explanation of these feeling.

Finally, there was Congressman Edwin Edwards, from Crowley, a rice community between Lafayette and Lake Charles. He was attractive and was younger than Gillis, and he had a great civil rights record. Edwards had always supported Dad on his agriculture issues like supporting REA and opposing farm subsidies. Dad liked Edwards and told the family, but early on he wasn't ready to endorse Edwards over a family friend like Gillis Long, or a hometown boy like Bennett Johnston if they were favored by the family.

These were not the three candidates running first in the polls, nor were they the favorites to win the race, but they were the three that we felt we could support.

Dad proposed that we listen to all three, choose the best man, and go from there. So we did. Many good people were running for governor—Taddy Aycock, Louisiana's lieutenant governor, for instance, who ran first in the polls for a long time and then faded—but we had made our picks and called the candidates' headquarters to arrange a trip to Scopena more than a year before the race. As it happened, Johnston was first to be scheduled, Edwards second, and Long last. All candidates were interviewed within two weeks of each other. So no candidate had an advantage over the other. We told them the schedule of the other two candidates, and said that we would endorse a candidate before thirty days after the last candidate's appearance. They wouldn't have a long delay. They would know where they stood.

The whole Roemer family was in attendance when Bennett Johnston appeared. He gave about thirty minutes in opening remarks. He promised to place north Louisiana first in his appointments and in his projects priorities, unlike other governors, who seemed always to place north Louisiana last. He then answered questions from the family. In addition to the Roemer kids—all now in their twenties—black State Representative Alphonse Jackson and family friend Laurence Guidry were in attendance.

Bennett made a point of dismissing the black vote beyond the desire of getting that vote where he was known. He said he would not pay for blacks to be hauled to vote, and would win with white and blacks with enough pride not to be bought. Bennett was grilled about what he was going to do about opening Louisiana up to people from other states, like Texas. The Roemer family felt that Louisiana was not the land of opportunity for its citizens. Texas seemed more attractive in certain ways than Louisiana—taxes, education, small business growth, regulation. There were many ideas of how to attract new enterprise and jobs to Louisiana, like expanding horseracing outside New Orleans to include Lake Charles and Shreveport. Bennett was doubtful about this idea as he didn't support gambling.

He thought what we needed instead was to make Louisiana a "right to work" state. That change alone would attract new industry and make our people more attractive as employees. We liked it. Bennett further thought that Louisiana needed to break away from the politics of the old, and elect a new generation of leadership, cleaning up the role of government for everybody—whites and blacks, in north and south Louisiana.

Bennett didn't seem to have much passion for government's role in achieving racial equality, although he did feel that new jobs (created as a result of right to work) would help all workers—white and black. Bennett made a very favorable impression on the group. He was friendly, warm, and outgoing. He answered questions directly, and some questions, when he didn't know the answers or hadn't made up his mind yet, he said he would consult with us at some future date to get our input before a decision was made. Bennett left the room in good shape, a local boy who looked like a winner.

The Edwards interview was only two days later, on Saturday. He was not known by any of the family members or the invited quests (Alphonse or Guidry), except for Dad. He was a handsome man with carefully combed graying hair and a thick Cajun accent. He was a lawyer, like all the candidates we had selected to interview, but he didn't talk like a lawyer. He spoke of the problems of agriculture and the farmers, who were just hanging on to their farms because of the tough times for farmers across America. He didn't look or sound like a farmer, but after a few minutes of his presentation we were convinced that he knew the issues of agriculture and how important they were for our state. He said that agriculture was the number one industry in the state, and he would treat it that way. We liked that.

He told us further that Louisiana missed adding value to the raw crops of state by not processing these crops to a higher value. He used pine trees as an example. He said in north Louisiana we grow some of the finest pine timber in the world, yet our timber gets sent to Mississippi and North Carolina to make furniture. He said he would approve tax incentives to allow the furniture-making industry to grow in Louisiana.

One idea that he had to get done, he said, was a constitutional convention to shorten and make more modern the Louisiana Constitution. This idea really intrigued the group, as we felt the constitutional convention was the proper forum for Louisiana to start over. As a matter of fact, Alphonse Jackson and I were two of the 105 delegates elected to the Louisiana Constitutional Convention in 1972.

Congressman Gillis Long was scheduled to present the next Monday, but Edwards was the talk of the group for the next few days. He not only stood out in his knowledge of agriculture, but his idea of a constitutional convention as a way to start over, along with his civil rights boldness, was appealing. No other candidate mentioned civil rights and the black vote as forthrightly as did Edwards, making affirmative action as a part of his planned strategy, and vowing to reverse Louisiana's 175 years of segregationist history. He vowed to campaign for the black vote expressly.

We liked that as a family. We not only liked that he pledged to end segregation where he could with his own appointments, but he also pledged to actively appeal to the black vote as part of his campaign. He didn't hide his need to turn out the black vote and to get a large percentage of that vote for himself.

Gillis Long, when he came two days later, seemed less aggressive on relevant issues, i.e. civil rights and economic development, than the other candidates. Gillis did his best and he was in better shape in the early polls than his opponents, but his ideas were not as far reaching as the others, and he seemed more bogged down in the details of the campaign than either Edwin or Bennett. He was a fine candidate, but he and his ideas didn't hit it off with the group. He reminded them of an old style candidate. It was like Gillis for campaign manager rather than for candidate. Gillis was obviously the third choice among the candidates.

The family debate between the supporters of Johnston and those of Edwards was waged for a couple of days after the interviews. But, by the time the following Saturday rolled around and we met to decide, the decision was clear: Edwards was the unanimous choice, including Alphonse Jackson and Laurence Guidry. Our job now was to make him a winner.

Note: this was very ironic for the family to choose Edwards as a candidate for governor, for this was the man whom I would beat for governor in 1987 when Edwards was seeking his third term, and who, then, beat me for reelection in 1991.

When Edwards was informed by Dad of the family's endorsement he was ecstatic and wanted to come see the family again and thank them. Before his arrival midweek, we began to plan the campaign in north Louisiana. Edwards fooled us. He hadn't merely wanted a meeting to thank us, and he hadn't desired just a north Louisiana strategy. Instead of these important regional and personal interests, Edwards asked Dad and the family if Dad could become his statewide campaign chairman and move to Baton Rouge to run his campaign.

He and Dad talked about the role of campaign manager and

Dad asked that the campaign be run legally and said he wanted Edwards's word on that. Dad then asked him if certain legal actions (vote hauling, black endorsements) would be denied him in the campaign. Edwards said, "of course not. I want to win and I expect to win." It seemed a "business" approach to us, from a lawyer.

Dad seemed pleased and told Edwards he was satisfied and would give him an answer in a few days.

When the family met the next day to consider the developments of the week, they were excited. They felt that Dad would do a great job as campaign manager and that Edwin needed someone strong like Dad to run the campaign. Dad liked that he would have a free hand to do what had to be done to win. Edwards would win the campaign, and we would be better off as a state. We decided to take him up on his offer. Margaret, Danny (who had just completed the Harvard Business School), and I assumed the duties at Scopena and IDS, while Mom and Dad planned to move to the Prince Murat in Baton Rouge to run the campaign.

The first thing that Dad did was have IDS run a baseline poll of 1,600 sample size (with two hundred samples from each of the eight congressional districts to see where Edwards stood by congressional district in the state), and then do a smaller 350 sample size every two weeks thereafter to see how we were doing. It was agreed that I would report to Dad every two weeks. Dad would report to Edwards or the press when he would want them to see something.

In addition, IDS began to garner a revised list of registered voters for use in our "telegrammed" mailings. This kind of mailing had never been done for a statewide campaign in Louisiana, and it was the kind of cutting edge technology for campaigns orchestrated by Dad. The use of a New York cinematographer for the television ads was first instituted for the campaign by Dad.

It was an exciting and hard-fought campaign, and the final victory margin reflected Edwards's political skill, the black get-out-the-votes payments, the polling data that had never been available to a campaign before, the massive "telegram" mailings, and the decisive campaign managerial style of Budgie Roemer. What was the ultimate winning factor? Maybe all were. It was so close. Out of more than two million votes cast, the margin of victory had been less than 4,500 votes, or one vote per electoral box. My polling was off a little saying that Edwards would lose by about half a point depending on voter turnout. The results showed that Edwards's turnout was good, and as a result, the election swung his way in a squeaker.

Dad's tough management and innovative procedures had made the difference in a very tight campaign according to many political experts. Edwards immediately rewarded Dad by asking him to be commissioner of administration for the state of Louisiana, running state government from operations to budget. Edwards knew what he was getting: a tough, no nonsense administrator.

It was quite an honor to be able to run state government and, although Mom and Dad would have to remain in Baton Rouge for a majority of the time, we children thought we could run Scopena and IDS. As a family, we decided to give it a try for a few months and see what happened. After just a few months, we thought it was working.

The campaign had been a route to use Dad's talents for a bigger stage. He could always come back, and his family would always be protected there, but he could be free of the entanglements and obligations of Scopena. He went from campaign advisor, to campaign manager, to commissioner of administration, to consultant in Baton Rouge without a break. Maybe Dad took this new vocation because it was a space that didn't compete with Margaret and Danny and me.

When Dad left Scopena, Margaret ran the operations of IDS. She worked with all the programmers and was quite successful as a computer executive. I became the salesmen for IDS and traveled throughout Louisiana, Arkansas, Oklahoma, Texas, Mississippi, and Tennessee gaining customers for Margaret to process. Danny took care of Scopena, both the farming and the cattle. All things worked wonderfully on the Scopena front.

Meanwhile, Dad loved his job in government. He ran the government and Edwards ran the political issues. They fit together like a hand in the proverbial glove. Edwards rarely interfered with Dad's operations of the state, because he had minimal interest in the processes of state government; Dad had no political interests that superseded Edwards's ambitions, and derived his satisfaction from the state performing well.

This few months' trial as commissioner of administration became "permanent" for Budgie. He lasted all of Edward's first four years, and all four years of the second term as well. Dad did eight consecutive years as commissioner of administration; eight years as the head man of state government, virtually free of active supervision of the governor; eight years building a reputation as a man of integrity and honesty; eight years of performance; and eight years gone from Scopena and the family embedded there.

Edwards didn't have to be concerned about state government; Roemer didn't have to be much involved in the dirty reality of state politics. They seemed a good team. Conveniently blind in one eye each.

Edwards had various scandals in Louisiana politics. Some seemed petty; some not so petty. There were accusations of highway contracts going to a favored contractor; of Edwin's then wife (Elaine) receiving a gratuity from a Korean middleman; of favoritism for certificates of operations in the department of hospitals. Yet nothing stuck, and all fingers pointed to the politics of Edwin Edwards at the heart of the scandals. The good reputation of Budgie Roemer remained unsullied.

Budgie gloried in the job, spending an ever increasing amount of his time in Baton Rouge. He became known as the operational brains behind the Edwards machine. His trips to Scopena became more infrequent, with his absences stretching for weeks at a time. Adeline, on the contrary, spent longer and longer away from the Pentagon Apartments, which was Dad's home in Baton Rouge, and back at Scopena. Mom began to absent herself from Dad's Baton Rouge activities. By the end of Edwards's eight-year run, Scopena was the center of her activities, not Baton Rouge. She spent more and more of her time helping Danny at Scopena.

When Edwards finished his two terms, Dad didn't come home to Scopena. He got a house with Mom's help and continued his work in Baton Rouge, lobbying for certain organizations and pursuing other business interests. He came to Scopena every couple of weeks, tops.

The end of the 1970s and the beginning of the 1980s were tough on Dad: the Edwards terms were over; he no longer had his position of power as commissioner of administration; I had been elected to Congress and had left Louisiana; Mom had returned to Scopena; and Scopena and IDS were running fine without him, with Margaret and Danny and Mom taking leading roles. And then he found himself indicted by a federal grand jury on a charge of accepting bribes from a state contractor.

The federal prosecutor was investigating the relationship between Edwards and Carlos Marcello, a federally targeted alleged crime boss in New Orleans. The Feds were in the midst of a plot to destroy Governor Edwards somehow. What they purported to find instead was a link between Budgie Roemer and a state contract to Carlos Marcello for maintenance on state property in New Orleans. What the Feds used to indict Dad were letters sent by his office to Marcello's in the course of normal business. By a stretch, the federal prosecutor used the racketeering statutes of the federal government to ensnare Dad.

As the Edwards administration wound down, Dad said he was guilty of nothing and would stand trial. The federal grand jury and the federal prosecutor supposedly offered him a deal: if he would reveal certain information about Governor Edwards, he would be cleared. They wanted to find the governor guilty under the law, not the commissioner of administration. Once again, Dad said that he and Governor Edwards were guilty of nothing, that the government had misused the racketeering statutes, and that he was ready to stand trial if required.

He stood trial in New Orleans. It was hotly contested, expensive, and in the end, Dad was found guilty of accepting a bribe from Carlos Marcello. He was sentenced to more than three years in a federal prison in Fort Worth, Texas.

The trial had been exhausting physically, emotionally, and monetarily for Dad. He never recovered from the shock of it all. He had protested his innocence before, during, and after the trial. He said that the national government wasn't concerned about the "truth." That they were only concerned with getting Edwin Edwards whatever the costs or facts. He was dismayed by the tactics of the federal government, and felt they had run over his rights on a number of occasions—all to get Edwards. He furthermore said that the Feds use of the racketeering statutes was unconstitutional and would not stand up to appeal. He was right. The Court of Appeals overturned the conviction months later.

Dad never committed a crime. He said he was innocent—and he was—but the information that he passed to Marcello was a matter of public record, available to anybody, and Dad knew it. Marcello didn't know it. The Feds didn't know it. And Dad laughed all the way to prison, and later was set free—not telling the FBI a thing. Dad was his usual anti-social, smart-alecky self, and he got burned by his own government. The government was willing to hurt Dad to catch Edwards, but it didn't work. It makes you see the government for what it sometimes is: fraudulently wrong.

I asked Dad how it happened, when we were alone one day before his trial, and he said he would tell me more about this later. He never did. All he said was the Feds were interested only in horse trading, not in solving a crime. Maybe he was protecting me somehow? Dad was always protecting me from Louisiana politics, even though I was a Louisiana politician. Maybe by putting me off, he was protecting me.

Dad's stint in prison was cut short by the Court of Appeals, but he said that his time in prison was the most boring and frustrating time of his life, except for time he spent in the Army Air Corps during World War II. I've spent some time here analyzing Dad's fall. I will just say that injustice and Dad's name became synonymous.

While Dad was in prison and after a lengthy review, the court of appeals ruled that the racketeering laws could not be used to entrap people as they had in Dad's case. Just like Dad said he was. Dad was cleared immediately and his record expunged, and he was released from prison. He was free and clear. He was never paid a penny by the federal government, although he had spent millions to fight these personal charges, and he never recovered from the time and embarrassment he wasted in jail.

It seemed a very strange episode in the life of Charles E. "Budgie" Roemer II. It seems to me a clear misuse of the federal government's power against a private citizen/public official. That misuse of power should give every citizen pause and a shudder.

Released from federal prison, Dad spent time in Baton Rouge and at Scopena, but never quite settled in either. Although he maintained a home in Baton Rouge, he spent more time at Scopena than during his Edwards years, raising commercial tomatoes for a Shreveport grocery chain. He never talked about his time in prison—it was like he wanted to forget it—and Scopena became a place of comfort for Dad as it had been for each of us at times during our young lives.

I was elected congressman from the fourth district of Louisiana after the time Dad was found guilty, and when I ran for governor in 1986-1987, he was out of prison. My campaign managers and I were afraid of Dad becoming an issue in that campaign if he attended meetings. So, for the first time in my life, Dad was kept isolated from my campaign affairs and, thanks to my decision for separation, enjoyed none of the direct pleasures of my successful run for governor.

He would occasionally come to the governor's mansion in Baton Rouge and we would visit, but he was not a key advisor in my four years as governor. This was my loss, and I missed his guidance and wisdom. I say that this was my loss from a personal point of view because I always enjoyed Dad's company, but also from a political point of view because I lost the reelection race for governor. The absence of Dad's wise political counsel was sorely missed. I had no substitute for his political genius.

In truth, missing his advice was worse than anyone knew. His advice was not about policy, but politics. I really regret that I didn't figure out a way to keep Dad connected to my political thinking while isolating him from my policy actions. I was so afraid that Dad was policy-damaged that I failed to use his political skills. I wanted to be my own man. Well, I managed to lose the reelection by myself.

Mine, Dad's mother, succumbed to cancer in 1979, and her pet cattle were sold several years later. Dad suffered the onset of Alzheimer's after the turn of the century. He eventually could not remember anybody's name or where he was. He was about eighty and was in good physical condition, but his mind had departed. Mom took care of him with help from Melinda, Melanie, and Margaret. Margaret and Mom were the members of the family that were able to give him the most comfort.

Dad passed away on the night of July 7, 2013, in the same bed that he had slept in since his mother, Mine, had passed at Scopena years before. Mom was asleep beside him. He was eighty-eight.

Dad's funeral was at First Methodist Church in Shreveport, and it was attended by hundreds of his Bossier and Shreveport acquaintances, state troopers from around the state, farmers from all across Louisiana, Texas, and Arkansas, state workers from New Orleans, Baton Rouge, Monroe, Lake Charles, and Alexandria, and dozens and dozens of Scopena workers—past and present.

It was quite a show. Edwin Edwards did not attend.

✳ ✳ ✳

I started my own political career in 1972 by running for Edwards's called constitutional convention and was elected as one of 105 elected delegates. We rewrote an over one-thousand page document to under fifty pages and the citizens passed it overwhelmingly in 1974. I then ran for Congress in 1978, after Joe Waggoneer retired after an eighteen-year career representing the fourth congressional district. The decisive factor in that race for me came when I called the Red River navigation project a "boondoggle" supported by people who cared more for their politics than they did the country. The politicians all blasted me for caring about the country rather caring about the local need, but I had made my point. After an immediate sharp drop, my numbers turned around, and I took off rising in the polls. Although I ran out of time and fell short, I finished a close third out of fifteen in the race.

I wanted to run again in 1980, but I hemmed and hawed, afraid I would lose. Finally, I made up my mind on the last day of qualifying.

My decision to finally make the race was the belief from Scopena that "focus" would win for me, and that I needed to get back on the horse as soon as possible. The House seat was mine, and I needed to act like it. I had been helped by the losing effort in 1978.

This time I finished second in the first primary to first-term incumbent Claude "Buddy" Leach, and I therefore made the runoff, where I captured the votes of the other candidates who had opposed Leach in the primary. Consequently, I won the vote in the runoff by a wide margin.

I won the seat three more times without opposition in the 1980s and turned my sights to the governor's race of 1987-1988. Due to skillful debate tactics and the endorsement of almost every newspaper in the state, I led the first primary for governor with more than 33 percent of the vote. With no candidates for governor supporting him in the second primary, the man who finished second to me—Edwin Edwards (29 percent)—dropped out, and I won the race for governor. I officially assumed office on March 15, 1988.

In the meantime, life had moved on at Scopena. In the 1980s while Dad served time in a federal prison and I served as congressman in Washington, D.C., I visited him in prison on several occasions. Once I flew to Fort Worth with Governor Edwin Edwards, who I was to beat in the next gubernatorial campaign and who was to beat me for reelection, and twice by car with Mom and family members. Dad was chipper at all times, saying that his appeals would set him free, and that he was innocent. He said it was boring beyond belief.

One of the nice things that happened to us is that over Christmas that year, the family met Dad at Edwards's ranch in Texas for a two-day vacation from prison. It was good to have time away from prison, even if only for forty-eight hours. Dad actually laughed a few times. Why Dad got out for the Christmas break, I don't know. I guess it was his good behavior and no risk of flight.

I remember the laughter, because I can tell you that the shock of his conviction can still be felt by family members. Bribery was contrary to everything we and he stood for. He had developed the reputation as a smart, effective, and honest broker in all matters—a man of honor—in and out of the family.

My experience at being a congressman and governor and first child gives me no wisdom here, and Dad wouldn't talk about it except to say that he wasn't guilty and that's all we needed to know. It wasn't money, or Edwards, or power. It was Scopena he missed. It was his anti-social attitude and the absence of Mom and Scopena that caused him to get caught in a web of his own design. It was the state trooper with the pulled gun during the front yard pumping over the highway incident where Mom saved further confrontation; it was Dad arguing with the neighbor over using water in a commonly-owned lake; it was Dad trying to prove himself in a social setting without Mom to guide him.

Dad's problems caused Scopena to gradually shrink. Dad sold significant parts of Scopena for years to pay his enormous legal expenses and debts. The large farming operation became a thing of the past. We sold the large timber holdings to a corporation. We sold the cattle and then sold the pasture land that was used to maintain them. We sold some of the crop land to surrounding farmers.

We turned over the farm operations at Scopena to a hired supervisor and then to a nephew, Drew Lefler, my sister Margaret's oldest. Drew did a wonderful job of maintaining the farming operation. The girls worked on the computer company (IDS), which, located on Scopena, successfully executed doctors' billing and REA cooperative billing and medical billing for public schools.

When Dad's battle with Alzheimer's began in 2005, Mom watched over him at Scopena. He died there July 7, 2013.

In later years, I went back to Scopena every week or two to see Mom and Dad. After Dad's death, Mom declined naturally. She was ninety-two. Passing through Baton Rouge going to the funeral of Dad's sister (Peggy) in New Orleans, she stopped over at Scarlett's and my house. She tripped over my small dog at my house and broke her hip. After weeks in the hospital nursing home in Baton Rouge, she was transported to Scopena and spent her final days tended to by Margaret and visited by all others. She passed away on January 29, 2016. With her death Mom closed the chapter of Scopena history that she and Dad had started nearly seventy years ago.

On my visits before Mom died, I walked down the halls of the old farm house and passed the shelves of books that we read to expand our knowledge of the world. They were still there, untouched for some time now, growing old from neglect.

But so much was missing: the voices of Mom and Dad were quiet. By then, there was less than a thousand acres of land, some corn and cotton but no cattle. No hybrid seed corn was grown anymore with the geese and the Curtis gin gone. Money's truck garden was long gone. Less than fifteen people work on the farm now under Drew's direction, down from up to three hundred during the 1950s. The office is mostly quiet, with three people there, not nine. The Shetland ponies were given away; the tennis courts are almost never used any more. The shop is still there but no longer served as the center of the universe. The treehouse and the cypress trees that held it are gone.

I honor them all with my memories and this small book, dedicated to Mom and Dad.

It has been said that everybody on earth wants the same thing—to be heard. That was always the friendly part of Scopena. You could find somebody to listen to you. A needy family would get temporary housing. A guy needing a job would get employment. A child who had run away from school would find safety. Somebody who wanted to talk politics would find an engaged audience. A drunk would find a sober opinion. Someone down on his luck would find a shoulder to cry on.

I am so thankful to have grown up at Scopena. It was the central part of my childhood, it made me what I am today, and it's something that I'll never lose. It centered on a unique set of circumstances and values. My three sisters and brother feel the same way. It was honest, and raw, and warm, close, fair and loving.

A large part of those core values were enforced by Dad. He did many great things as commissioner of administration: a strong budget with education priorities, bringing quality people into state government, and so much more, but Dad was to be remembered by those who worked around him as a man with strong core values—honesty and warmth, to name a couple. Dad needed a person to complete and connect him to the world outside his mind, and that person was Mom.

There are people in the world who need another person or persons to keep them on an even keel. Dad needed Mom. This point might be a small thing to most people, but to Dad maybe not. Just like in his human conflicts that he let Mom resolve for him on Scopena, maybe his core values required an outer screen like Mom—to keep him renewed and strong—always. It always worked when they stood together.

Interestingly, a gift of Scopena to me was the gift of hard work. No matter where I went (as congressman, as governor, or as founder and CEO of a good-sized bank during the banking crisis of 2008), Scopena worked me the longest hours and in some of the most difficult circumstances I faced—all at a very young age.

It was so hot, and the physical intensity was draining. Working in a hoe field in the broiling July sun caused blisters to form on the exposed parts of my body, including on my exposed chest from the v of my t-shirt. A pipe blowout at 2:00 in the morning in the irrigation field required working in water flowing like it was rushing from the hose of a fire hydrant. Every job afterward seemed easy.

I met Robert Frost, the great poet, when I was a young student at Harvard. He wrote a poem about life's journey and life's choices entitled, "The Road Not Taken." It begins, "Two roads diverged in a yellow wood," and deep within the poem he writes, "yet knowing how way leads on to way, I doubted if I should ever come back."

After all these years, that's the way I feel about Scopena: I doubt if I should ever come back. I'm old and am afflicted with the effects of a lifetime of Type I diabetes. I walk like an old man maybe ten years older than my real age. Dad and Mom have passed away, Mr. Boyd and the noon lunch table are gone, as are Christine, Emmett, the gin crew, and so many others.

My brother and sisters still survive and in visiting with them, I find they hold Scopena sacred, as do I. Dad, Mom, and Scopena— they were the best.

Farming is still the toughest job in the world. So hang in there, Drew, we're all with you.